Greenhill Books

MILITARY
LESSONS
OF THE
GULF
WAR

MILITARY LESSONS OF THE GULF WAR

Authors and Senior Analysts

Rod Alonso, Defense Intelligence Agency
B.L. Cyr, Jr., U.S. Army Intelligence Threat and Analysis Center
Bruce George, M.P., House of Commons
Gerald Hopple, George Mason University
David C. Isby, Independent Author and Consultant
Tim Lister, British Broadcasting Corporation
Raimondo Luraghi, University of Genoa
Joel Nadel, U.S. Army Intelligence Threat and Analysis Center
James Piriou, House of Commons Staff
Joe Sanderson, House of Commons Staff
Peter Tsouras, U.S. Army Intelligence Threat and Analysis Center
Bruce W. Watson, Defense Intelligence College
Bruce W. Watson, Jr., Virginia Polytechnic Institute
Elmo C. Wright, Jr., U.S. Army Intelligence Threat and Analysis Center

Research Associates

(all are affiliated with George Mason University, Fairfax, Virginia)

- Richard DeJong
- David Dunphy
- Brian Gagne
- Jane Helwig
- Michael Kirsch
- Rhonda Lotzbire
- Daniel O'Hara

- Yong Pak
- Georgia Sakell
- Patricia Smith
- Cheryl Stears
- Wendy Taylor
- Scott Vitiello
- Brian Wood

MILITARY LESSONS
OF THE
GULF
WAR

Bruce W. Watson • Bruce George, MP
Peter Tsouras • B.L. Cyr
and the
International Analysis Group
on the Gulf War

Edited by Bruce W. Watson

•

GREENHILL BOOKS, LONDON
PRESIDIO PRESS, CALIFORNIA

Military Lessons of the Gulf War first published 1991
by Greenhill Books, Lionel Leventhal Limited,
Park House, 1 Russell Gardens, London NW11 9NN

and

Presidio Press, P.O. Box 1764, Novato, Ca.94948, U.S.A.

CONTENTS

ILLUSTRATIONS

Photographs

Maps

Figures

This book is gratefully dedicated
to those who gave their lives in
THE GULF WAR
in the cause of liberty and freedom
and to
GERALD W. HOPPLE
June 20, 1949 – June 28, 1991
whose final analytical effort appears in this book.
A scholar, educator, author, and most of all, a friend,
he will be missed.

PREFACE

Given the one and a half million people in uniform who took an active part in the Gulf War it was, when compared with other conflicts of the same or greater size, relatively short in duration and, for the victors at least, surprisingly inexpensive in casualties. However, the significance of the war is not in its size or casualties, but in the tremendous political, scientific-technical, and military effects it will have on us all. Written after the relevant facts were available, this book makes the following unique contributions:

First, it is the collective effort of people from four nations (ten, if one includes the many military attachés at embassies who provided information about their military forces and diplomacy). This book provides a complete overview of the conflict's international dimensions. Virtually every chapter, whether it deals with diplomacy, military operations, or a more specific subject, weaves the actions and roles of all major participants into a narrative that fully explains the war's dynamics.

Second, in most cases, it has been written by people who observed the conflict in an official capacity. Hence, the book speaks with considerable authority.

Third, this book has the relevant statistical data on the war's air, ground, and naval forces, orders of battle, dimensions of combat operations, combat losses, and related facts.

Fourth, the book goes beyond providing a military account of the war to explain why the conflict's military aspects were important, and how the war affected many other aspects of our lives, such as freedom of the press, the danger of terrorism, and the morality of war. This bridging of the military and civilian aspects of national life is, we feel, a unique contribution that will be of value to many readers.

Fifth, the book is based on corroborated, researched fact. During the course of the war, and subsequently, many stories appeared in the press which have been uncorroborated, subject to hype, and when examined, have a paucity of information. One story for example dealt with the production of U.S. bombs-to-order in a matter of hours, and there have been a plethora of stories on British and American special forces which are full of glory. The subsequent release of information may prove some such to be true, but if they could not be corroborated, they were omitted from this book.

Finally, the book does not consider the war in isolation, but sees it as a highly significant event in a dynamic, rapidly changing international situation. It is difficult to exaggerate the war's importance to today's international affairs, and the book attempts to convey the impact of the war on them.

While the efforts of an editor are important, a work's value ultimately rests with the abilities and effort of its authors, and I was fortunate to have the very best. Having edited many books on defense issues, I have never had a team of writers who has been as competent or has worked as industriously as those who have written the following pages. Collectively, this book represents thousands of hours of work by the best people in the business. Bruce George, MP, supervised a team of Parliamentary researchers who provided much of the material on Great Britain, France, and Europe. Raimondo Luraghi graciously supported our efforts from Turin and Rome. Rod Alonso, Pete Tsouras, Elmo Wright, Larry Cyr, and Joel Nadel went far beyond the usual duties of authors to actively participate in the project. The researchers at George Mason University in Fairfax, Virginia, were marvelous, and their work reflects most favorably on the University's Public Affairs Department.

Augmenting this wealth of talent has been a most exceptional publisher. Lionel Leventhal is unique in the publishing trade in that he takes an active interest in the quality of the books he publishes. He and the rest of his team spent many hours providing additional materials and offering comments on materials submitted. Their efforts were extraordinary, and increased the book's quality significantly. To them, I convey my deepest gratitude.

I would like to express my deep appreciation to Charles Messenger, British military historian and defence analyst, who provided so much information and advice. The book benefitted significantly from his efforts.

I would also like to thank the hundreds of people in the British Ministry of Defence and U.S. Defense Department, who provided me with the most accurate, complete information available. A great deal of this book's accuracy is due to their kindness.

I am also grateful to Will and Lisa Engler and Portia Redfield, who supported me during my research trips to New York.

On a more personal note, I would like to thank my family. In terms of the book's wide scope and number of contributors, this has been a book that has required intense concentration and application, and when deadlines became critical, I enlisted their assistance as part of the "U.S. team." I begin by thanking my wife for her active support here and for 25 years of encouragement. My son, Bruce, was very productive, and his work appears in the following pages. Daughters Susan and Jennifer spent hours in the library retrieving documents and reinterpreting rough materials for the charts that appear in the book. Ella provided information on Egypt and copious amounts of coffee. To all of them, my heartiest thanks and a promise that I will emerge from my study when all this is over.

Bruce W. Watson
August 1991

The information in this book is based upon the research and experiences of the authors and does not represent the positions or policies of any agency or department of the United States Government, British Government, or any other Government. The information was derived from unclassified publications and sources and is intended to neither confirm nor deny, officially or unofficially, the views of those Governments.

KEY DATES

1990

Aug. 2 – Iraqi forces invade Kuwait at 0200 (local); U.N. Resolution 660 condemns invasion.

Aug. 6 – U.N. Resolution 661 establishes embargo.

Aug. 7 – President Bush orders U.S. forces to Saudi Arabia.

Aug. 8 – Iraq annexes Kuwait; first U.S forces deployed.

Aug. 9 – U.N. Resolution 662 declares annexation of Kuwait null and void.

Aug. 10 – Cairo Summit condemns Saddam.

Aug. 11 – first British air power arrives.

Aug. 15 – Iraq begins peace overtures to Iran.

Aug. 17 – Western navies begin blockade of Iraq.

Aug. 26 – U.N. authorizes nations to enforce embargo.

Nov. 29 – U.N. Resolution 678 authorizes force to expel Iraq after January 15, 1991.

1991

Jan. 17 – 0300 (local), Coalition air campaign commences.

Jan. 18 – First Iraqi Scud attack injures 7 in Haifa and Tel Aviv.

Jan. 19 – U.S. deploys Patriot missiles, with crews, to Israel.

Jan. 23 – Iraq begins pouring oil into Persian Gulf.

Jan. 28 – Iraqi aircraft relocating to Iran.

Jan. 30 – Iraq launches ground assault at Khafji.

Jan. 30/Feb. 1 – Iraqis forced out of Khafji.

Feb. 12 – U.S. bombs Amiriya bunker, killing Iraqi civilians.

Feb. 24 – 0300 (local), Coalition ground assault begins.

Feb. 25 – Iraqi Scud near Dhahran kills 27 Americans.

Feb. 27 – Kuwait City liberated. Cease fire declared.

March 3 – Cease-fire talks held.

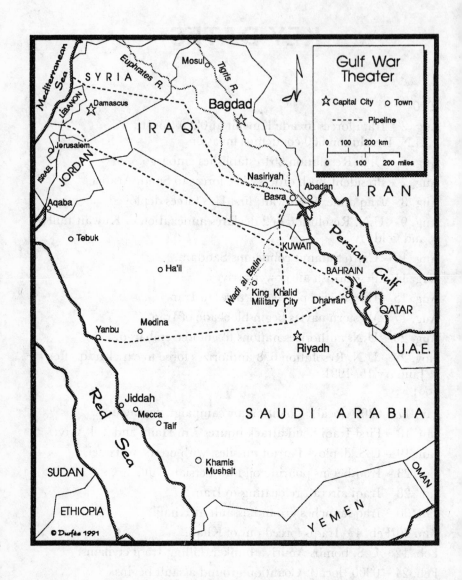

Gulf War Theater

☆ Capital City   ○ Town

- - - Pipeline

| 0 | 100 | 200 km |

| 0 | 100 | 200 miles |

Mediterranean Sea

Euphrates R.

Tigris R.

Mosul

SYRIA

Damascus ☆

Bagdad ☆

IRAQ

Jerusalem ○

JORDAN

Aqaba ○

Nasiriyah ○

Basra ○

Abadan ○

IRAN

Tebuk ○

Ha'il ○

KUWAIT

Persian Gulf

BAHRAIN

Wadi al Batin

King Khalid Military City

Dhahran ○

QATAR

Yanbu ○

Medina ○

Riyadh ☆

U.A.E.

Red Sea

Jiddah ○

Mecca ○

Taif ○

SAUDI ARABIA

Khamis Mushait ○

SUDAN

OMAN

© Durfee 1991

ETHIOPIA

YEMEN

PART I
THE PRELUDE

1: The Iraqi Invasion of Kuwait
by
Bruce W. Watson
and Bruce W. Watson, Jr.

At about 2 a.m. (Baghdad time) on August 2, 1990, three Iraqi Republican Guard divisions invaded Kuwait. One proceeded down a coastal road to Kuwait City, a second seized the inland oil fields, and the third proceeded to the Saudi Arabian border. Kuwaiti A-4 aircraft and Chieftan tanks fought for three days until their fuel and ammunition were exhausted. The small Kuwaiti Navy also made a valiant showing, with the last two fast attack craft escaping while firing at pursuing Iraqi tanks.

Iraqi forces quickly captured Kuwait City and the Emir's palace, while the Kuwaiti ruler, Sheik Jaber al-Ahmed al-Sabah, fled to Saudi Arabia and established a government in exile. On August 3rd, the remainder of Kuwait was captured and by the 4th, Iraqi forces were amassed along the Kuwaiti-Saudi border for a possible invasion of Saudi Arabia. If Iraq occupied Saudi Arabia, it would not only establish itself as the secular leader of the Arab world, but also would control 45% of world's oil.

The reasons for the invasion dated back to the creation of present-day Kuwait. In 1899, Great Britain and Kuwait signed a treaty in which Britain assumed control of Kuwait's foreign affairs. This was done in order to thwart German imperialist designs in the region, and after World War I began, London established a protectorate over Kuwait. World War I also led to the collapse of the Ottoman Empire and the creation by the European powers of Iraq and a number of other countries. These events and decisions, reflections of the European balance of power that did not consider the region's culture or politics, still reverberate, and the finding of oil and later, in the 1970s, its greatly enhanced value, aggravated troubled, at times tribal, situations. Kuwait was an artificial creation imposed by the West, and it both denied Iraq a considerable amount of oil and restricted its access to the seas. This arrangement was never accepted, and when Kuwait received its independence on June 19, 1961, Baghdad almost immediately claimed it, basing this on the facts that Kuwait had been a part of the Ottoman Empire, that it was an artificial British creation, and it threatened Iraq's access to the sea. Threatened by invasion, Kuwait appealed to the British, whose military reaction in July 1961 was enough to thwart Iraq. Kuwait was admitted to the United Nations and the Arab League, but Iraq did not renounce its claim, would often resurrect it, and would cite it to justify the August invasion.

THE IRAN–IRAQ WAR

There were other reasons arising from events in the 1970s and 1980s that would prompt the invasion, and one of the most significant was the Iran-Iraq War. The cause of Iraq's invasion of Iran on September 22, 1980 was that the new Irani Shiite state was messianic and wished to expand its influence throughout the Islamic world. In doing so, it began to interfere significantly in Iraqi affairs, attempting to influence Iraq's sizeable Shiite faction. (About 55 percent of Iraq's population is Shiite, an additional 20 percent is Kurdish, and the ruling Sunni minority accounts for about 25 percent.)

Iraq failed to defeat Iran decisively, and after a year, Irani forces went on the offensive, regained almost all of their lost territory, and approached Basra. Here the offensive failed, and the war became a stationary battle of attrition. Meanwhile, Iraq began to develop nuclear and chemical warfare capabilities that would profoundly influence subsequent events. The nuclear capability was seen as such a danger to the Israelis that they conducted a preemptive air attack and destroyed Iraq's primary nuclear facility. The chemical warfare capability was also significant, and Baghdad used it against Irani forces in 1984, 1985, and 1986, and on its own rebellious Kurdish population.

These capabilities alarmed the West. The United States developed a policy that was intended to halt both the Iran-Iraq War and the development of the Iraqi chemical and nuclear warfare capabilities. The military aspects of this policy provided the United States with considerable resources. In January 1983, a new unified command, Central Command (CENTCOM), was established and assigned responsibility for a huge geographic area, including the Persian Gulf. It was given over 800 people, and the forces assigned to the Rapid Deployment Force also were increased. As a result, CENTCOM was given seven Air Force tactical fighter wings, two strategic bomber squadrons, five Army divisions, a Marine Corps Expeditionary Force, three carrier battle groups, a surface action group, and five maritime patrol squadrons. U.S. military positions throughout the Middle East were also expanded to handle the deployment of large numbers of U.S. troops. $523 million was spent to build an airfield in southeastern Egypt, while supplies were prepositioned in Oman and Diego Garcia.[1]

THE MOTIVES BEHIND IRAQ'S INVASION OF KUWAIT

There were five reasons for Iraq's decision to invade Kuwait 23 months later. Iraq could not repay about $80 billion that had been borrowed to finance the Iran-Iraq War. It could argue that the war was in Kuwaiti and Saudi interests since the enemy was Iranian messianic Shiite fundamentalism, which potentially threatened them. Kuwait's decision to not forgive Iraq's $65 billion debt provided economic and emotional justification for the Iraqi invasion.[2] Second, the Kuwaitis were incredibly rich and had huge investments abroad. Access to this wealth could resolve Iraq's financial problems. The third reason was alleged Kuwaiti oil drilling in the Rumaila oil field, which lay in disputed border territory, and the fourth was Kuwaiti overproduction of oil. Gulf revenues were depressed as a result of an oil glut on the spot market in the late-1980s, and on July 17, 1990, Saddam threatened to use force as retribution for Kuwaiti overproduction and underpricing. He claimed that Kuwait and the United Arab Emirates had cost Iraq $14 billion in oil revenue. When Saddam suggested peace talks, the Emir of Kuwait provided the final justification for the invasion when he failed to consent to face-to-face peace talks, preferring Arab League mediation instead.

Thus, as Baghdad prepared to assault Kuwait militarily, Saddam concealed these preparations by lying to the United States and by agreeing to allow the Egyptians and Saudis to mediate an end to the quarrel. President Bush sent the U.S. Ambassador to Iraq,

April Glaspie, to meet with Saddam, who told her to convey to Bush that he had peaceful intentions and was not seeking a U.S.–Iraqi confrontation.[3] Meanwhile, on July 31, 1990, Iraqi and Kuwaiti spokesmen met in Jidda, Saudi Arabia for negotiations concerning oil and territorial disputes, but the Iraqis walked out of the meetings on August 1st.[4] Many nations of the world, with the United States and Great Britain in the forefront, could not accept the annexation of what had been a peaceful nation, and a countdown to war commenced.

NOTES

1. Caspar W. Weinberger, *Annual Report to Congress: Fiscal Year 1988* (Washington, DC: Department of Defense, 1987), as cited by George S. Witt in *Point Paper: During the Iran-Iraq War, How Did the United States Use Its Forces in Pursuit of Strategic Goals and How Successful Was This Use?* (Washington, DC: Defense Intelligence College, 1990); and James A. Russell, "U.S. Lays Groundwork in the Persian Gulf," *Defense Week* (22 September 86): 8–9.
2. Carlyle Murphy, "Iraq Accuses Kuwait of Plot to Steal Oil, Depress Prices," *The Washington Post* (July 19, 1990): p. A25.
3. This July 25, 1990 meeting was Ambassador Glaspie's first with Saddam since her arrival in Iraq in 1988.
4. Carlyle Murphy, "Mubarak Says Iraq, Kuwait Will Begin Talks this Weekend," *The Washington Post*, July 26, 1990, p. A34.

PART II
DIPLOMACY

2: Coalition Diplomacy
by
Bruce George, MP, Raimondo Luraghi,
Bruce W. Watson, Tim Lister,
Bruce W. Watson, Jr., Jane Helwig,
Georgia Sakell, and Patricia Smith

Great Britain and the United States led the effort to create a
Coalition to force Iraq to leave Kuwait. Political factors and intense
diplomacy delayed the Coalition's military operations as the United
Nations first tried sanctions and then resorted to military operations
when it saw that the sanctions were not working.[1]

All the Coalition's members were crucial to its success, and each
came to it with its own problems and perspectives. America had
strengths and weaknesses. One weakness was the spectre of its great
defeat in Vietnam. Second, there existed a Presidential-Con-
gressional dispute as to which branch of government controlled
U.S. foreign policy. Congress had set limits on the time a President
could deploy troops without its approval, and this could play in
any lengthy troop deployment to Saudi Arabia. Third, an overriding U.S.-Soviet rivalry had been resolved. Now America was the
only superpower, and while others might look to it for protection, it
might not be willing to assume the role of world's policeman. On
the plus side, after several difficult years, America had regained its
confidence under President Reagan and this was continued under
President Bush. Bush also had more foreign policy and national
defense experience than any previous President. He had served as
UN Ambassador, Ambassador to China, CIA Director, and Vice
President, and his intellect and this experience were strong assets.
These factors were present when the Iraqi invasion occurred and
would influence U.S. policy in the Gulf War.

Great Britain was naturally disposed to rescue Kuwait by its long association with the Gulf. Even after withdrawing from east of Suez in 1971, she maintained an informal security relationship with some of the Emirates and Oman. In 1990, she had a large officer contingent attached to the Omani armed forces, many important military liaison teams in the region, civilians working in Kuwait, and the Armilla Patrol in the Gulf. Her response to the invasion reflected Mrs. Thatcher's belief that aggression must be reversed and international law vigorously upheld. She felt that these principles ran in tandem with U.S. decisiveness and against the cautious indecision of her European allies, and chided other NATO members, saying, "It is sad that at this critical time, Europe has not fully measured up to expectations." (Appendix A lists financial and other support that nations provided).

Although at the outbreak of the Gulf War French public and political opinion would be firmly behind the French contingent-Operation *Daguet*, the political decision to join the Coalition created problems. France's ties with the Arab world and a large Muslim-Arab population were concerns, although during the war opinion polls of Arab immigrants were surprising; 24% were pro-Saddam, 24% were against, and 52% had no opinion (SOFRES). This quelled French fears of internal problems, and opinion polls taken during the war showed that 70% of the public favored France's participation. Parliamentary support was strong, with only the communists and the National Front opposing. Because most of the Italian public supported the Andreotti government, Italy joined the Coalition without any insurmountable political difficulties and maintained her pro-UN position during the war.

It is difficult to discuss a pan-European response, given its diverse political, social, and cultural themes. While the European public was outraged with the Iraqi invasion (84 percent of British and Dutch, 70 percent of French, 66 percent of German, and 62 percent of Belgian voters supported the war's aims in February 1991), Europe's erratic diplomatic reaction posed its governments against each other, giving rise to name-calling. Britain's Minister of State for Defence Procurement Alan Clarke accused the allies of running for their cellars at the first sign of trouble, and the British press accused Europeans of cowardice, selfishness, and appeasement. The strain of the crisis made the fault lines running through Europe embarrassingly clear.

Although Saudi Arabia enjoyed warm relationships with

America and Great Britain, allowing the deployment of thousands of troops was tantamount to a cultural invasion. In this conservative Islamic nation that was the home of some of Islam's holiest sites, this was a significant act, and was approved only after great deliberation. Conversely, Riyadh had no alternative, since to not accept such aid would leave it defenseless against an Iraqi invasion. Egypt had a different agenda. President Hosni Mubarak had been embarrassed greatly by Saddam, who let him believe that he had been instrumental in resolving Iraqi-Kuwaiti differences, while Saddam intended to invade Kuwait all along. Saddam and Mubarak were also competing for leadership of a progressive Islamic national block, and Iraq's chemical, nuclear, and biological warfare programs threatened Middle East peace, and with it, Egyptian security. Syria must have had apprehensions when it entered the Coalition in that its extreme anti-Israeli stance and its state sponsorship of terrorism had often placed it against Great Britain and America. However, President Assad's great hatred for Saddam and fear of growing Iraqi power were sufficient to convince him to join the Coalition.

FORMING THE COALITION

The United States

Bush froze Iraqi assets in the United States soon after the invasion occurred, and Secretary Baker and Soviet Foreign Minister Shevardnadze issued a statement condemning the invasion from Moscow.[2] This was important because it set an initial U.S.-Soviet position on the invasion, and at a minimum, meant that there would probably not be a U.S.-Soviet confrontation.

Bush then met Thatcher in Aspen, Colorado. At the time, he did not believe that Iraq would invade Saudi Arabia and was leaning against a military response. However, Thatcher argued that Iraq would invade and that the only option was to send troops to the region. This established an Anglo-American cooperation that would be the core of the Coalition. Given their reticence concerning the presence of foreign troops in Saudi Arabia, the Saudis were approached cautiously. Cheney and Powell discussed a Coalition force with the Saudi Ambassador, and when Bush learned that the Saudis were not going to permit the deployments, he let them see satellite photographs of Iraqi forces amassing for an invasion along their border. The King reversed his stand and accepted the troop deployments.[3] Support was solicited from other Arab nations, and the Soviets agreed to honor the sanctions against Baghdad and to halt further arms sales. Japan, and China agreed to boycott Iraqi and Kuwaiti oil. Turkey, given its proximity to Iraq, faced a difficult situation, but with firm assurances, it joined the Coalition and closed the oil pipeline to Iraq on August 7th.[4]

In January, the United States still had not resolved the issue of whether the President or Congress controlled foreign policy. Bush had sent U.S. forces to Saudi Arabia and had committed the nation to support UN actions if Iraq did not withdraw, and there was great public approval for his policy. Thus Congress was faced with either supporting Bush, thereby conceding considerable power, or of opposing his commitment. The latter option was so unpalatable that Congress delayed taking action, and then approved Bush's actions just days before the war.

Great Britain

From August until the war's end, the ruling Conservative party did not waiver in its determination to defeat Saddam, despite the trauma of a change of leadership from Margaret Thatcher to John Major and low ratings in opinion polls due to the disastrous introduction of the new and unpopular poll tax. Having learned, from its lukewarm support for the Falklands War, that less than wholeheartedly supporting British troops was costly in elections, the opposition Labour Party was firm in its support for Operation Granby and two senior official opposition spokesmen who were at odds with the deployment were relieved of their portfolios. However, Labour stressed that British and U.S. actions should be clearly sanctioned by the United Nations and that they not be seen as an Anglo-American action at King Fahd's behest. Opposition to the use of force was slight if vocal, involving some 30 MPs on Labour's left out of a total of 650 MPs. Innate anti-Americanism was combined with the belief that "Desert Shield" was for the benefit of U.S. oil companies and that the sudden U.S. reverence for international law and the United Nations was hypocritical considering U.S. actions in Grenada and Panama. A final exception to the broad consensus was former Conservative Prime Minister Edward Heath, who went to Iraq in an effort to secure the release of British hostages. He warned that a conflict would result if U.S.

and European troops occupied a hostile and devastated nation and urged a negotiated solution under which Iraqi forces would withdraw and the Arab League would provide a buffer force between Kuwait and Iraq.

France

France was criticized at home for its ambiguous stance. Political wavering, the Defense Minister's resignation, and last ditch attempts at peace did not make her popular with her allies. In this respect, France pursued an independent policy in her long held wish not to be under America's shadow. Alternatively, since she did not want to give her Arab friends the impression that she had abandoned them, she pursued every possibility for peace. After a week of what the British Press called "dithering," France supported removing Saddam from Kuwait. While it took six weeks and the violation of the French Embassy in Kuwait before she began Operation *Daguet*, her historic and economic ties with the Middle East were not ones that she wished to lose. Thus, while she was under severe criticism from the beginning of the conflict, she played, fully, every role and function asked of her by the United Nations and the Western European Union (WEU).

Italy

In Italy, there was relevant political opposition to the Coalition despite overwhelming popular support. This was not spawned by the "Democratic Party of the Left," a coalition of communists and a multifarious array of small leftist parties, but from a right-wing "catholic" front that claimed to be inspired by the Pope's pronouncement against war. Despite the fact that the Pope later made a distinction between peace with justice that was to be sought, and peace at any price that was not, fundamentalist catholic groups, represented primarily by the right-wing group "Communion and Liberation" and the reactionary weekly *Il Sabato*, spoke out with a vengeance against both the United States and any Italian part in the Coalition. Some even proclaimed that Italian soldiers should desert. The communists, ignoring their atheistic tradition, immediately allied themselves with these reactionary groups. Although they refused to declare their solidarity with Italian troops deploying to the Gulf, there were some responsible politicians, such as Sr.

Napolitano in the "Democratic Party of the Left", who refused to take such absurd positions.

The major problem was not from this alliance's mass rallies and propaganda, but unprecedented opposition from *inside* the Christian Democratic Party. While this was not supported by the Pope, it appeared to be supported by some Vatican figures, such as the editor of the *Observatore Romano*, the Holy See paper.[5] The Christian Democrats in the government held firm, although they may have had some misgivings. Solid support from Socialist Party ministers, especially Foreign Secretary de Michelis, who adamantly supported the intervention, and from other minor lay parties, Liberals, Republicans, and Social-Democrats, helped the Christian-Democrats to persevere, and the government majority was compact, firm, and never wavered. The "declaration" from an undersecretary that approved a Soviet peace plan was a personal one, and met with an immediate rebuttal from the government.

The Italian military could offer only a limited response because it was under reorganization from a large conscript army into a smaller, professional one. In the interim, a conscript's service obligation was reduced to ten months. This was simply not enough time to prepare for desert warfare, and the training he did receive prepared him for emergencies on Italian borders that were topographically very different from the sands of Kuwait.[6] Nonetheless, since Italy was very vulnerable to international terrorism, the Army had to be mobilized to provide protection against anticipated terrorist attacks.[7] Since there were about 1,500 targets to be protected, the Army was almost completely mobilized and 96% of the trained personnel, totalling 90,000 men, served in two groups of 45,000 troops.[8] Italy was also a main U.S. supply route and the U.S. Air Force established a major logistical facility for large tanker aircraft at Milan's Malpensa International Airport to refuel B-52 bombers flying from British bases to Iraqi targets. She also sent several Stinger missile batteries to help protect Turkey, and two Italian first-rate brigades of paratroops and naval infantry (marines) were placed on alert, ready to respond to a NATO defense of Turkey, should it be attacked by Iraq.

The European Community and NATO

Twelve European states froze Iraqi and Kuwaiti assets and embargoed Iraqi oil, while the EC supported the UN resolutions, vowing to maintain its embassies in Kuwait for as long as possible. However, even the EC's greatest supporters had to admit that in terms of a military commitment, the crisis had deflated the Community's image as a forceful actor on the world stage. The West European Union (WEU) could coordinate a European military response because the obstacles to a NATO role "out-of-area" did not apply to it. Established to strengthen the European defense identity, it acted as the linchpin of a European minehunting operation in the Gulf during the Iran-Iraq War, when WEU naval forces protected their own nations' maritime traffic and acted jointly against the mine threat. However, the members' command and control, foreign policies, and rules of engagement differed greatly and the idea of a unified command was seen as unrealistic. Six WEU nations – Great Britain, Italy, France, Belgium, the Netherlands, and Spain – agreed on August 21st to send naval ships to the Gulf in a co-ordinated operation, but these were under national control because their nations had different views on the crisis and on the WEU's role as the executor of EC's security policy.

A concern was the Iraqi threat to Turkey. On September 10th, the United States requested that the operations of NATO's ACE (Allied Command Europe) Mobile Force and Naval On-Call Force for the Mediterranean (NAVOCFORMED) be extended eastward to show support for Turkey and fill the gaps left by U.S. ships deploying to the Gulf. By January 10th, 42 fighter aircraft (18 Belgian Mirage-5s, 6 Italian F-104s, and 18 German Alpha ground attack aircraft) and German and Dutch Patriot, Roland, and Hawk air defense missiles from NATO's Allied Mobile Force Air had been sent to Turkey as a deterrent against Iraqi missile attacks.

The Arab Members

Arab coalition members were essential components of the Coalition, but due to the massive deployment of Western power, numerically they were only a small portion of the total force. Their importance was not as front line troops, but as support in freeing the Western nations for action, and they were of course essential politically. Different languages and procedures and incompatibility of communications systems, as well as the Arab members' religious and political sensitivities, made coordination a very real problem. This was overcome through liaison officers, who were attached to formation headquarters. They were able to keep their parent formations informed of the situation and brief the formation to which they were attached. When U.S. close air and artillery support was given to Arab formations, U.S. forward air controllers and artillery observation teams were attached. Several U.S. ships also had Kuwaiti naval officers aboard. Even so, there were not enough British and U.S. officers available for liaison duties, indicating that CENTCOM had not given this sufficient attention during its contingency planning. In order to make good the shortfall the British went so far as to call for volunteers from among English speaking Kuwaiti exiles in Great Britain. These were given temporary Army commissions and flown to the Gulf. At the highest command level in the Gulf, however, General Schwarzkopf was able to draw on General de la Billiere's, considerable military experience of the region and its peoples.

MAINTAINING THE COALITION

Having been created, it remained for the Coalition to act effectively against Iraq. The activities of its military forces were guided by the United Nations, which passed twelve relevant resolutions between August 2nd and November 29th (see Appendix B). Britain led the way in devising resolutions for restoring peace and security in the Gulf and introducing punitive sanctions enforced by a naval embargo. Both she and America convinced the United Nations to delegate the conduct of military operations to them and both resisted Soviet efforts to revive the UN Security Council Military Staff Committee. In Saudi Arabia, there also was close cooperation. Britain subordinated her forces to CENTCOM, but made it clear that if problems developed they could be referred to the commander of British forces, the Defence Secretary, and the "War Cabinet." The overall British commander, Air Chief Marshall Sir Patrick Hine, was based at Headquarters Royal Air Force Strike Command at High Wycombe outside London. As a result of these efforts, Resolution 660, demanding that Iraq withdraw from Kuwait, passed unanimously on August 2nd, followed on the 6th by Resolution 661, which imposed the embargo.

Two factors, that the embargo be complete and that the issue of

Iraqi aggression remain divorced from the traditional Arab-Israeli issue, created problems. The embargo placed tremendous pressure on Jordan, which did not completely seal off Aqaba and its borders to Iraqi commerce (see chapter 13). Likewise, Israel's killing Palestinians during the October 8th Jerusalem riots (see chapter 13), gave Iraq a chance to link the Occupied Territories issue to its invasion. The Coalition weathered both of these problems, but a third was more enduring: the embargo was not immediately effective. Sanctions and blockades have poor records of success, and as the embargo's effects were assessed, it was concluded that it if it were to succeed (and this was a question in itself), then it would take a long time, certainly at least a year, to force Iraq to withdraw. Atrocities by Iraqi troops in Kuwait; the fact that a months-long military presence would be costly and would mean a lengthy disruption in oil production with serious economic effects; Saudi concern over a Western presence in their country during the pilgrimage season; the possibility that the war would be fought in the summer's brutal heat; intense pressure on King Hussein; and the chance of another incident in the Occupied Territories were all factors that weighed against such a delay when success was so uncertain. Also, London and Washington believed that war was necessary, because if Saddam withdrew, then they would have to commit to a costly long-term peace-keeping force, and Saddam would be free to continue his nuclear, chemical, and biological warfare programs. Thus, while the sanctions kept the military pressure on, by November it was obvious that they were not enough to force a withdrawal from Kuwait, and Washington and London began actively advocating the use of force. France, China, and the USSR all opposed this, but British and U.S. efforts culminated in Resolution 678, which approved the use of force to expel Iraq if the latter did not leave Kuwait by January 15th.[9] The threat of war prompted many initiatives to prevent it. Working to sustain the Coalition's resolve, America and Great Britain responded to these proposals, while continuing to demand an unconditional withdrawal from Kuwait. At times, London took the lead in sustaining the pose; on one occasion Thatcher was rumored to have advised Bush that "now is not the time to become wobbly, George."

While there was agreement within the European Community on political and economic measures against Iraq, Britain was dis-

appointed that the WEU did not act more decisively. The WEU
agreed to coordinate naval affairs through a working group of
military commanders, but they did not consider a unified military
command or uniform rules of engagement. Thatcher had already
asserted that NATO should be ready to act beyond its historical
area, and after the invasion, she called for a revision of the NATO
treaty to allow "out-of-area" interventions.

France

The events at the United Nations had repercussions in Paris. While
the decision to use force lies with the President, he was criticized
for his handling of the conflict. No real debate on the use of force
took place at the Assemblee Nationale and it was not until January
14th, hours before the outbreak of war, that Deputies were given a
chance to vote, which left little time for serious discussion. France
was also often criticized for working for a negotiated settlement,
but much of this criticism was due to her independent stance and
refusal to accept decisions being made for her. A third issue was
her insistence on not being seen as under the U.S. shadow. French
forces deployed to the Gulf were kept isolated from other Coalition
forces, with the Division *Daguet* located in a remote desert camp
that did little for French troop morale. A fourth issue was Defense
Minister Jean-Pierre Chevenement's resignation two weeks into the
air campaign, after his decision that French air strikes would be
limited to Kuwaiti targets was overruled by Mitterrand. His departure was overdue and he was chastised for not having done so earlier
as he was against Mitterrand's "reasoning in terms of war," which
affected France's relations with her allies. Another embarrassment
was the broadcast of an uncensored interview with French soldiers
in Saudi Arabia shortly after the war began. They said they did
not know why they were there, and only became aware that hostilities had begun when they heard on the radio that Coalition
aircraft had begun operations. These and incidents such as Mitterrand's failure to mention his last minute peace plan to Prime
Minister Major in a meeting only hours before he unveiled it, left
France in a familiar position with her allies–integrated and yet
alone.

LESSONS LEARNED

One lesson of the Coalition experience was that America benefitted because in its leadership role, it showed great consideration for foreign sensitivities. Bush's personal approach was very successful, and America emerged from the war with greater prestige, which could be valuable as he worked for the new world order. Whether this could be sustained in the postwar period was problematic, but at war's end, guarded optimism was warranted. Finally, the White House had regained control of U.S. foreign policy, and this might figure prominently in future U.S. commitments overseas.

For Great Britain, the crisis showed that her longstanding "special relationship" with the United States was still there, and it was Mrs. Thatcher who initially seemed to lead the way, notwithstanding those who said Britain's future role lay wholly within the European Community. The leadership changed with her departure, but there was no change in substance and the British collaboration with the United States was unwavering. The wide ranging and indecisive European response served to support those who have argued that the nation should delay a greater European Community commitment; others argued that the crisis occurred too soon in what may be a lengthy process to create a political and militarily united European unit, and London should have been, and now be, fully committed and involved.

For France, while the Coalition improved Franco-American relations, France had pursued an independent course, reflecting considerable disparity between her views and those of others. For Italy, the war was a success. Despite political tumult, she faced her duties and successfully projected her power into the Gulf, in this, her first combat endeavor in over 40 years. For Turkey, the war meant a decision between NATO and the Arab world, and Ankara opted for NATO. It also showed that NATO would honor its commitment to that nation, and Ankara should have felt more confident concerning her security at war's end. For the Saudis, the Coalition meant security from Iraq, for Egypt, it meant a greater regional leadership role, and for Syria, it offered the chance of better future relations with London and Washington. For the European Community, the Coalition showed that it was far from united, and that there was a lot of work to do before unity is achieved. At a minimum, the Community must address how to establish a coherent military defense of its political, economic, and strategic interests.

NOTES

1. Some observers have said incorrectly that a lack of military power delayed Coalition military operations. While it took time to amass forces for the invasion, in August the Coalition had enough naval power in the area to defend Saudi Arabia, and Iraqi forces were overextended from the Kuwaiti invasion and needed time to establish the logistical lines in order to advance into Saudi Arabia.

2. Margaret G. Warner, "The Moscow Connection," *Newsweek* (September 17, 1990): 24.

3. Michael Kramer, "Read My Ships," *Time* (August 20, 1990): 21, 25.

4. Russell Watson, "Baghdad's Bully," *Newsweek* (August 13, 1990): 17–21.

5. See, for example, the rabid anti-American article from the Editor Biagio Agnes the day of the beginning of the Desert Storm offensive.

6. See the problem on the transformation of the Italian Army into a professional one: *Constituzione della Difesa e Stati di Crisi per la Difesa Nazione*, edited by Giuseppe de Vergottini (Rome: Rivista Militare, 1991).

7. On the Italian struggle against international terrorism, see Raimondo Luraghi, "The Mediterranean," in *NATO After Forty Years*, edited by L.S. Kaplan, S.V. Papacosma, M.R. Rubin, and R.V. Young (Wilmington, Delaware: SR, 1990), pp. 115 ff.

8. All of these data, as the following, come from the relation of the Italian Chiefs of Staff to the Parliamentary Defence Commission, March 13, 1991, unless otherwise specified.

9. Gerald F. Seib, "Bush Dodges Bid to Convene Congress on Gulf Issue; Baker to Lobby 3 Nations," *The Wall Street Journal*, November 7, 1990, p. A16; Abraham D. Sofaer, "Asking the U.N. Is Asking for Trouble," *The Wall Street Journal*, November 5, 1990, p. A14; "What's News – World-Wide," *The Wall Street Journal*, November 27, 1990; and November 30, 1990, p. A1; and Robert S. Greenberger, "U.N. Security Council Clears Use of Force to Oust Iraq from Kuwait after January 15," *The Wall Street Journal*, November 30, 1990.

3: Iraqi Diplomacy in the Gulf War
by
Bruce W. Watson,
Bruce W. Watson, Jr.,
Cheryl Stears, and Scott Vitiello

Iraq's diplomacy was hallmarked by failure. It failed to: prevent U.N. resolutions and embargoes; halt the deployment of Coalition forces to Saudi Arabia; secure an active commitment from any nation to support it against the Coalition; link its occupation of Kuwait to Israel's occupation of the West Bank and Gaza; convince the Arab world that the Coalition deployments were an intrusion of infidels into the Islamic world; and prevent the war. Having said this, we must also note that there was some imaginative creativity in Saddam's policy and that it caused problems for the Coalition.

FAILURE TO JUSTIFY THE INVASION

Iraq invaded Kuwait to retaliate for what it saw as Kuwaiti injustices and because it could not pay its huge Iran-Iraq War debt. When Kuwait would not renegotiate Iraq's debt it gave Iraq economic cause for invading, since its undefended wealth offered an easy solution to Saddam's financial worries. Kuwait's drilling in the disputed Rumaila oil field and its overproduction of oil that depressed oil prices were additional provocations.

The fact that other nations might not accept these reasons as legitimate grounds for the invasion under international law meant that they might oppose Saddam's aggression, and duplicity in his policy assured it. Before the war, Saddam told the U.S. Ambassador to Iraq that he did not want a U.S.-Iraqi dispute, and he led Egyptian President Hosni Mubarak to believe that he would not invade Kuwait. Mubarak was furious at being deceived by Saddam. He had set up the mediation conference in July, and immediately stated in public that war had been averted. These moves and Iraq's bullying of delegates at Arab meetings caused many to question

Iraq's integrity. This was crucial, because the Saudis later said they asked for U.S. aid because they felt that the Iraqis tried to deceive them during discussions after the Kuwaiti invasion, leading them to conclude that Iraq was about to invade them. It should also have led everyone to conclude that, if Iraq invaded Saudi Arabia, then an invasion of the United Arab Emirates would soon follow. If these moves were successful, then Saddam would have a major influence over the world's oil.

POLICY THEMES

Hostages as Human Shields

When Saddam announced on August 9, 1990, that he intended to detain the hostages, he elicited world criticism, which became condemnation when one of the hostages, James Worthington, died of a heart attack. This became a major and prolonged issue (see chapter 12) and while parties were often successful when they went to Baghdad to ask for the release of hostages, Saddam never seemed to realize that most of these people, Edward Heath, Willy Brandt, Jesse Jackson, and others, did not represent their governments. In sum, Saddam was never able to use this issue to dissolve the Coalition, and he finally announced that all of the hostages would be released on December 5th.

The Overture to Iran

Saddam also attempted a reconciliation with Iran. On August 15th, he said he would release all Iranian prisoners of war and return virtually all the territory taken during the Iran-Iraq War (1980–1988). This totalled some 164 square miles in the Ilam region, including the strategic Shatt al Arab waterway. This theme was pursued further on September 9th, when Foreign Minister Tariq Aziz met Iranian Foreign Minister Ali Akbar Valyati to convince Iran to break the blockade. Although the two nations restored diplomatic relations, Iraq never convinced Iran to take any military action against the Coalition. While Teheran did provide small-scale aid by allowing humanitarian truck convoys to proceed to Iraq, it remained neutral in the war. In the end, while some Iranian extremist fundamentalist groups supported Saddam, the government was not prepared to do so for several reasons, including the costly Iran-Iraq War, traditional enmity toward Iraq, Sad-

1: This B-52 "Stratofortress" bomber is seen taking off on an Air Campaign mission on January 29, 1991. The B-52 bombers showed that in spite of their age, they can deliver high conventional munitions tonnage over long distances on very short notice. Those flying from Great Britain were refueled from tankers staging from France or from a major logistical facility established at Milan's Malpensa International Airport. The B-52s flew a total of 1,624 sorties during the war, and delivered 25,700 tons of munitions, or a total of 72,000 different munitions. Among the tactical weapons the B-52s delivered were Combined Effects Munitions. Each contained 202 three-pound BLU-97/Bs, each of which could penetrate 118 millimeters of armor. The B-52s had a combat mission capable rate of 81%, and they delivered 29% of all U.S. bombs, and 38% of all U.S. Air Force bombs.

2: These F-4G Wild Weasel aircraft, deployed from George Air Force Base, California, are seen flying in formation over Saudi Arabia. Armed with AGM-88A/B/C HARM passive radar-guided high speed anti-radiation SAM killers, the 48 F-4Gs deployed for the war conducted a total of 2,500 combat sorties and sustained an 87% combat mission capable rate.

3: An F-15E Strike Eagle aircraft is seen moving in to refuel from a KC-135 Stratotanker. Two of the 48 F-15Es deployed were lost during the 2,200 sorties that the Strike Eagles flew during the war. The F-15Es maintained a remarkable 95.2% combat mission capable rate during the war. F-15Es can carry AGM-65D/G Maverick imaging infrared radar-guided armor killing missiles and GBU-24 bombs which were used against Iraqi chemical, biological, and nuclear targets, bridges, and aircraft shelters.

The 256 Stratotankers that were deployed flew 4,967 sorties and a total of 19,089 hours. Collectively with the 46 K-10 Extenders that were deployed, they refuelled 14,588 aircraft and delivered 68.2 million gallons of jet fuel.

4: The USS *Saratoga* is seen underway in the Red Sea while launching air strikes on Iraqi targets on February 15, 1991. *Saratoga* and her escorts were deployed from their home port of Mayport, Florida, shortly after Iraq's invasion of Kuwait, proceeded to the Mediterranean, and transited southbound through the Suez Canal on August 22, 1990. She, *Kennedy*, *America*, and *Roosevelt* were all on station in the Red Sea, and *Midway* and *Ranger* were on patrol in the Persian Gulf when the air campaign began and all supported intensive naval air strikes throughout the campaign. *America* then voyaged from the Red Sea to the Persian Gulf and was the only aircraft carrier to launch air strikes from both the Red Sea and the Persian Gulf during the war.

5: Two crewmen are seen standing near F-14 aircraft on USS *John F. Kennedy*. *Kennedy* was deployed to the Mediterranean and transited the Suez Canal, so that she was on patrol in the Red Sea when the air campaign began. The carriers launched a total of 11,461 combat and support sorties during the war.

6: President George Bush is seen greeting U.S. military forces after speaking to them on November 25, 1991. American leaders were determined that the mistake of Vietnam-forgetting U.S. combat forces-would not be repeated. The President and Mrs. Bush had dinner with deployed troops on American Thanksgiving Day, and a continuous train of dignitaries, including Secretary of Defense Dick Cheney, Chairman of the Joint Chiefs of Staff General Colin Powell and other U.S. military and civilian leaders, visited the troops. Yellow ribbons abounded in America, leading recording artists produced "Voices Who Care", and grammar and high school students wrote to their "pen-pals", troops in the Middle East, creating a bond between the home front and the battlefield that has not existed in America since World War II.

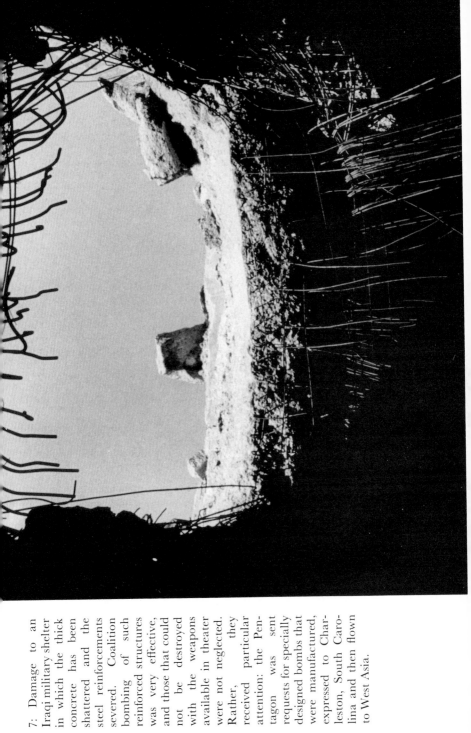

7: Damage to an Iraqi military shelter in which the thick concrete has been shattered and the steel reinforcements severed. Coalition bombing of such reinforced structures was very effective, and those that could not be destroyed with the weapons available in theater were not neglected. Rather, they received particular attention: the Pentagon was sent requests for specially designed bombs that were manufactured, expressed to Charleston, South Carolina and then flown to West Asia.

8: Two military personnel inspect the damage done to a warehouse in Dhahran following an Iraqi SCUD missile attack on February 25, 1991. The structure, which housed the 475th Quartermaster Group (Provisional) was completely destroyed, 27 U.S. military personnel were killed, and 98 others were injured in the biggest single loss of Coalition life in the war. The Scud had not been intercepted by Patriots and after the war, there were rumors that a Patriot had malfunctioned and shut itself down, thereby allowing the missile to strike the barracks.

9: U.S. military personnel inspect the remains of a Scud missile recovered by an Explosive Ordnance Disposal Team from the 4409th Combat Support Group. Scud's inaccuracy precluded its use as a viable military weapon, and Iraq's use of the weapon on civilian centers in Israel and Saudi Arabia initiated a new type of terrorism. Iraq launched a total of 86 Scuds, 40 against Israel and 46 against Saudi Arabia. Many were intercepted by Patriot missiles and others fell in isolated areas, but enough fell in population centers to make their use a significant aspect of the war. By the end of the war, the 40 Scuds that fell in Israel claimed four lives, injured at least 185 people, left 4,000 homeless, and created a major disruption to public life. In the end, however, Iraq's aim of drawing Israel into the war and breaking the Coalition did not work, and the Scuds against Israel stand as a new dimension in malicious terrorism.

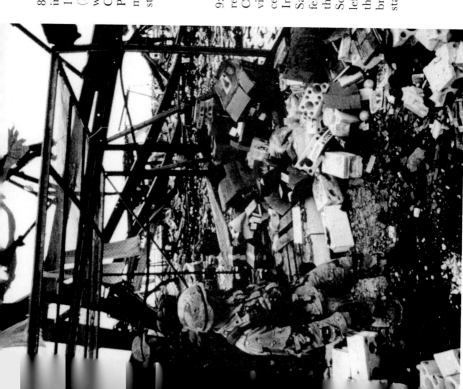

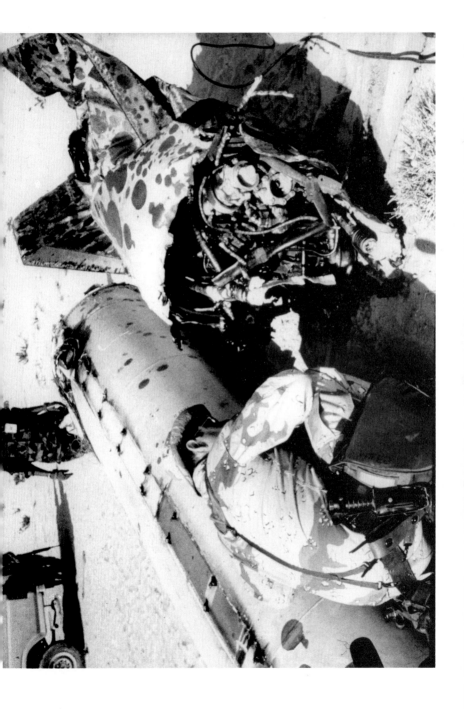

10: The wreckage of a Soviet-made Iraqi MiG-25 Foxbat aircraft. The Iraqi Air Force was estimated at 1,000 aircraft, including 750 combat aircraft, making it the world's sixth largest air force at the start of the war, but the actual strength may have been higher. Composed of Soviet-made MiG-21 Fishbeds, MiG-29 Fulcrums, Su-24 Fencers, Chinese-made MiG-21s, French-built Mirage F-1s, and other combat aircraft, as well as about 250 support aircraft, Iraq's Air Force suffered heavily during the war: 35 aircraft were lost in air-to-air engagements, 55 in air-to-ground engagements, 31 were destroyed by Coalition ground forces, and 6 crashed while fleeing to Iran. Another 141 were estimated to have been destroyed in shelters that were struck, and 148 were flown to Iran, where they landed safely. This amounts to 416 aircraft, or 41% of the entire Air Force, but actual loses may be significantly higher, as the Coalition's method of estimating aircraft destroyed in hardened aircraft shelters was very conservative.

11: The hopeless mass of destroyed and abandoned vehicles shown in this photo, taken on February 26, 1991, gives an insight into the chaos that reigned as Iraqi forces fled northward from Kuwait in the closing days of the war. The Iraqi military became an undisciplined rabble who gathered the loot they had stolen from Kuwaitis and fled in whatever transportation they could find. However, once on the highway, they created a massive traffic jam as they tried to drive northward. Subsequent Coalition air strikes created a nightmare, and the route was renamed the "highway to hell".

12: This Iraqi T-55 tank became stranded as it attempted to pass over an abutment. The bulk of Iraqi tanks in Kuwait were obsolete models, and only the elite Republican Guard had the T-72. Before the war, Iraq fielded the world's fourth largest Army. Battle-hardened in its eight-year war with Iran, the Army had some of the world's most modern weapon systems and a biological and chemical warfare capability. Its ground order-of-battle was impressive, it had about 5,500 tanks, about 10,000 armored vehicles, about 3,500 artillery pieces, and about 200 multiple rocket launchers.

13: Former prisoner of war Major Rhonda Lee Cornum is seen disembarking from an International Red Cross aircraft on March 4, 1991. A flight surgeon assigned to the 2/229th Aviation Brigade, Major Cornum was one of many Coalition POWs. Early in the Coalition's air campaign, Saddam Hussein threatened to use the POWs as human shields at Iraqi military installations. The British and American response was to consider such an action as a war crime, which may have deterred Iraq. Iraq released a total of 45 Coalition POWs after the war (21 American, 12 British, 9 Saudi, 2 Italians, and 1 Kuwaiti), and most said that, given the circumstances, they had been fairly well treated.

14: Fires roared furiously from Kuwaiti oil fields on March 2, 1991. All 950 Kuwaiti oil wells were set afire by Iraqi force in the closing days of the war, in a spiteful, malicious ecoterrorist action that created major ecological damage. To make matters worse, the Iraqis mined the approaches to many of the wells, thereby further impeding firefighting efforts. British and American oil firefighting teams were called in to put out the fires that consumed an estimated five million barrels of oil daily, but it would take them a long time to complete this task.

15: This Hardened Aircraft Shelter (HAS) was destroyed during Coalition strikes that also destroyed planes, buildings, and tanks at an Iraqi military installation. By the end of the war, the Coalition's Air Force had conducted 109,876 sorties in just 43 days. U.S. air and naval forces alone expended 88,500 tons of munitions, including 6,520 tons of precision munitions.

16: General Norman H. Schwarzkopf, Commander-in-Chief, U.S. Central Command (CENTCOM), and Saudi Arabian Lieutenant General Sabin Abdel-Aziz al Douri are seen speaking to Iraqi Lieutenant Generals Mohammed Abdez Rahman al-Dagitistani and Sabin Abdel-Aziz al Douri during negotiations on March 3, 1991 that ended the Gulf War.

dam's duplicity, the strength of Coalition forces to which Iran was very inferior militarily, and the economic need to improve relations with the West.

The Holy War – Scott Vitiello

Saddam also tried to discredit the Coalition by depicting it as an infidel intrusion into the Islamic world, and on August 10th, he called for a jihad, or holy war, to expel Coalition forces. In doing so, he posed as a devout disciple of Islam, a role that he had assumed on prior occasions.

In previous years in the contrasting traditional and progressive cultures of the Islamic world, Saddam's actions characterized him as a progressive, but as the Iran-Iraq War dragged on he tried to align himself with Islam to appeal to Islam's traditionalists by showing that he was not a secularist. A report was published that traced his heritage back to Fatima and Ali, Mohammed's daughter and son-in-law, who are loved by Shiite Muslims. Saddam, in Muslim attire, was seen on television on pilgrimages to Mecca, and posters of him praying were posted. This was not completely successful because it did not accord with the Ba'ath Party's essentially secular nature.

A jihad is a holy war. Only leaders who are caliphs or successors of Mohammad can call jihads, and no successor has been proclaimed since 1924.[1] Saddam hoped to establish himself as a caliph through his connection to Ali, Mohammed's son-in-law, but his call for a jihad failed to convince the majority of Moslems. The most significant response was from the Palestinians, many of whom signed up to fight the Coalition. However, they were probably more interested in Saddam's support for their cause than in a jihad, per se. At any rate, none ever reached the front lines and their protest was limited to influencing King Hussein of Jordan. Elsewhere, there was some popular support for Iraq, but this failed to influence national policies.

Contrasting these modest and politically insignificant gains were major defeats. On August 10th, members of the Arab League in Cairo voted to send troops to Saudi Arabia and demanded that Iraq withdraw from Kuwait. Also, when 400 leading Islamic figures met in Mecca on September 13th, they not only refused to support Saddam's jihad, but also authorized Kuwait to proclaim a holy war against Iraq. Thus, Saddam's attempt to mobilize the Islamic world failed because he attempted to stretch reality too far, and his credibility suffered accordingly.[2]

Free Oil – Cheryl Stears

As the embargo began to affect Iraq, Saddam tried to combat it. The price of oil had risen by 50 percent because of Iraq's invasion, reaching $30.00 a barrel in September. Saddam used this to attempt to break the embargo by offering free oil to Third World nations on September 10th. While stating that this was meant to help those nations that were suffering because of the embargo, he cast the situation in anti-imperialist rhetoric. He said he was prepared to supply Third World nations with oil free of charge because in this time of oil shortage, the United States, Israel, and the "procolonist" nations would ensure that they had the oil that they needed and that other nations would get only that which remained. The offer was open to all nations regardless of their positions in the ongoing crisis, but the nations had to arrange for their own transportation. Thus, Saddam was inviting them to test the embargo.

The ploy failed for several reasons. First, it was met with disbelief and mockery, because it appeared transparent in light of Iraq's unwarranted seizure of Kuwait, its brutal treatment of Kuwaitis during the occupation, and its threat to use foreigners, including Third World citizens, as human shields. Second, the Coalition had greater credibility since it took measures to help those nations hurt most by the embargo. Finally, the Coalition said that even if the oil were free it violated the embargo, and ships would not be allowed into Iraqi ports to collect it.

Involving Israel

A major weakness in the Coalition's cohesion was Israel. A traditional ally of the United States, it relied on U.S. support whenever its anti-Palestinian policies alienated Arab nations or evoked UN condemnation. Saddam attempted to link his seizure of Kuwait with the Israeli Occupied Territories. On August 12th, he said that he was prepared to resolve the crisis if Israel withdrew from the Occupied Territories. Reacting to the slaying of Palestinians by Israeli police on October 8th, Saddam said that he would attack Israel if it continued to occupy Arab lands. This bid to link the Iraqi invasion to the Occupied Territories was a continuation of a diplomatic theme he had begun earlier, but skillful Coalition diplomacy kept the two themes apart and considerable pressure on Israel to temper its treatment of the Palestinians defeated his tactic.

Iraq's Diplomatic Dialogue with Coalition Partners

A major issue in the Iraqi-Coalition diplomatic dialogue was the embassies in Kuwait. Iraq demanded that they close as Kuwait was now the 19th Province of Iraq, whereas the Coalition defined Kuwait's seizure as illegal and kept them open. On August 22nd, Bush said that he would defy Iraqi orders to close the U.S. embassy by August 24th, and Saddam quickly labelled this as an act of aggression. Iraq turned off the water to embassies on the 26th, and on September 14th, Iraqi troops entered the Canadian, Dutch, and Belgian embassies, as well as the French ambassador's residence, where they removed four French citizens, who were later released. This pressure backfired, since an enraged Mitterrand responded by ordering several thousand French soldiers and dozens of planes and tanks to Saudi Arabia in response for this illegal intrusion. The embassies gradually were closed, with the U.S. and British embassies closing on December 13th and 16th, respectively, after all the British and U.S. hostages in Iraq had been freed and those in hiding had left Kuwait.

An uncompromising Iraqi diplomatic stance scuttled many opportunities for a peaceful solution to the crisis. When talks with Jordan and UN Secretary General Perez de Cuellar in August both failed, Iraq proposed that he and Bush publicly address each other's nations. Their taped broadcasts had no effect on the impasse. King Hussein's October peace initiative failed, and in November, the United States worked to convince the United Nations to authorize military action. To win such approval and possibly out of a desire to exhaust all peaceful options before resorting to war, Bush insisted that Iraq fully understand the Coalition's resolve. On November 30th, he invited Iraqi Foreign Minister Tariq Aziz to Washington and said he wished to send Secretary Baker to Iraq. While Iraq accepted this offer, it believed if it delayed the talks, then Bush would delay combat action beyond the January 15th deadline. Thus, Iraq wasted the time it had left. On December 9th, Saddam said that his schedule prevented him from meeting Baker before January 12th, and Bush promptly accused him of stalling. Both agreed to an Aziz meeting in Washington on December 17th, but could not agree on a date for Baker's visit to Baghdad. When Bush

threatened to suspend the talks unless Saddam agreed to see Baker
no later than January 3rd, Iraq suspended them. After Algerian
and European attempts at peace failed, U.S.-Iraqi talks were
resumed on December 26th in Baghdad. Bush finally directed Baker
to meet Aziz in Geneva and, if these went well, to proceed to
Baghdad for meetings with Saddam. When criticized for independent diplomacy after the United Nations had approved a deadline, Bush said that the Baker mission was merely to ensure that
Iraq understood the Coalition's resolve to act after January 15th.
The Baker-Aziz meeting failed to move Iraq. Subsequently, in a
last minute attempt to avert war, Secretary General Perez de
Cuellar met Saddam. He also failed to move Saddam. Believing
that it had exhausted all other options, the Coalition began its air
campaign on the 17th. Iraq believed that it could retain at least
part of Kuwait through talks and could avert war through stalling.
Both beliefs grossly miscalculated the Coalition's resolve, with dire
consequences.

The Scud Missile Attacks
After the war began, Iraq launched 40 Scud missiles at Israeli cities
(see chapter 12 and Appendix C) in hopes of bringing Israel into
the war, thereby forcing some Coalition Arab members to leave,
and possibly bringing other Arab nations into the war on Iraq's
side. This tactic failed because Washington and London convinced
Israel to remain neutral, and provided protection through Patriot
missile deployments.

The Soviet Gambit, February 1991
On February 11, 1991, Soviet envoy Yevgeny Primakov went to
Baghdad to pursue a Soviet initiative that might have saved Iraq
from further destruction (see chapter 4). This created a problem
for Bush in that the Soviets were hopeful about a settlement and
the possibility that the Soviet Union would support Iraq might
have thwarted the Coalition's military operations. From a rational
perspective, given the existing military situation, Saddam should
have accepted the Soviet proposal immediately and without res-
ervation. However, he tentatively agreed, and then kept retracting
certain stipulations and adding more of his own. The final result
was an offer that the Soviets passed to the Coalition but one they
could not actively support.

LESSONS LEARNED

Some lessons to be gleaned from Iraqi diplomacy are old ones. First, military power is linked to political power, and nations should rarely undertake political actions unless they have enough military power to defend them. Second, military action, such as Iraq's invasion, must be politically credible – it must be viewed as justified by others. Iraq convinced almost no one of its right to invade Kuwait. Third, when attempting to break an enemy alliance, as Saddam tried to break the Coalition, one must determine and then focus one's efforts on the pact's weakest point (Clausewitz called this the center of gravity). Saddam's attack against the Coalition correctly identified the U.S.-Israeli relationship as the weakness, but rather than focus his efforts here, he diffused his effort by assailing many aspects of the Coalition. This detracted from the alliance's greatest weakness and diminished Saddam's credibility when some of his efforts were clearly ill-founded.

Other lessons reflect the recent change in regional power relationships. The Soviet-American rapprochement and critical Soviet domestic problems were not completely understood by Saddam. Thus, when the Coalition acted against Iraq, a Soviet military response was not forthcoming, and the Coalition was free to pursue its goals without fear of a superpower confrontation.

Saddam never seemed to realize this. There were chances to resolve the crisis, and in each he chose the most assertive, least compromising option. At several junctures in the Autumn of 1990, he could as a concession probably have withdrawn from Kuwait City but retained significant benefit from his invasion by staying in the Bubiyan and Warba Islands and the Rumaila oil fields. Had he done so, it is doubtful that the Coalition would have held together. In the end, his inability to compromise brought all negotiations to unsuccessful ends, and Iraq not only lost all it had seized, but also suffered great destruction.

NOTES

1. Richard N. Ostling, "Islam's Idea of 'Holy War,'" *Time* (February 11, 1991): 51.
2. Kim Murphy, "400 Islamic Scholars Back U.S. Role and Authorize Holy War Against Iraq," *The Los Angeles Times*, September 14, 1990, p. A18.

4: The Soviet Role

Bruce W. Watson,
Jane Helwig,
Daniel J. O'Hara, and Brian P. Wood, Jr.

Any discussion of contemporary Soviet foreign policy must consider the ongoing Soviet reconciliation with the West. Does it reflect a real abandoning of Marxism-Leninism and a forsaking of the USSR's global aspirations? The economic disaster that Soviet Marxism-Leninism has created, recent military reductions, the abandonment of Eastern Europe, a political liberalization and governmental reforms, all relevant Soviet leadership statements, and other factors indicate that this is the case. Conversely, is the current Soviet posture merely a tactical ploy that is meant to gain Western aid, only to use this to pose a greater threat in the future? The USSR and Russia before it, have faced economic and technological dilemmas in the past, and each time have come to the West to drink from the technological well. Peter the Great drank, and Catherine the Great, and Tsars Alexander II and Nicholas II drank very heavily. Later, U.S. industry provided substantial aid in the 1920s, and Stalin received Lend-Lease aid that allowed him to continue the war on the eastern front. And in all cases, economic and technological weakness was not allowed to interfere with the state, which was a system of total power.

This chapter assumes that there has been a genuine forsaking of Marxism-Leninism and that Gorbachev's goals are to: preserve the integrity of as much of the USSR as possible; to transform the economy; to gain technological help from the West; to recast the military into one that offers strategic defense and a strong regional capability; to insure that newly united Germany is so integrated into Europe that it does not again pose a military threat to Russia; to associate, even ally itself with the new European political-economic structure; and to play a significant role in that structure. In this context, the current situation is transitional, one in which Soviet foreign policy is evolving from a world view to one that focuses on regional events and interests. Soviet actions in the war reflected this transition, combining diplomatic neutrality that reflects the new policy with limited military assistance to Iraq, a trapping of the old.

Gorbachev's foreign policy of national self-determination is a renunciation of Moscow's earlier policy of actively influencing the world to advance communism. Implicit in this repudiation is the understanding that old allies, old radical regimes, would no longer be assisted. However, since immediately setting these allies adrift would impact critically on Moscow's credibility, there is a transition period in which Moscow is providing less support before it ceases all help. This period may end at the end of the current five year plan, and in the interim, Soviet involvement is being curtailed and the clients are expected to take measures to insure their future self-reliance.

From this vantage point, one can understand what appeared to be conflicting Soviet actions in the Gulf War. Iraq had been an important Soviet client, one that offered a balance to Iranian theocratic messianism. In September 1990, many observers said Moscow was at a crossroads, having to choose between its old confrontational policy and its new cooperative posture. In reality, there was no choice. The recent changes in the USSR had so weakened the military's power that, short of a strategic confrontation, Moscow could not have stopped the Coalition. Thus, while it is plausible that the Soviet Union knew of the invasion before August 2nd, it is also likely that Moscow warned against such a course of action. Thenceforth, its diplomacy was to convince Saddam to withdraw from Kuwait while it continued to provide low-level assistance to him.

SOVIET DIPLOMACY

Soviet-American diplomatic cooperation was evident at the start of the crisis. Secretary of State James Baker and Soviet Foreign Minister Eduard Shevardnadze, in the midst of talks when the invasion occurred, issued a joint statement condemning the "brutal and illegal invasion" of Kuwait, and the Soviets stated that they would immediately suspend Iraqi arms deliveries. Having said this, it remained for the Soviet Union to define precisely its role in the crisis. Baker urged it to play an active role in the Coalition, but Moscow opted to not be involved militarily. Admitting that there were Soviet military advisors in Iraq, it said later that it would withdraw all of them except those who remained voluntarily or those with valid "contracts" with Iraq. Soviet policy was to provide minor aid to both the Coalition and Iraq. During Secretary Dick Cheney's October visit to Moscow, he was told of Iraq's military posture, the types of Soviet weapons that they had, and about Iraq's chemical warfare capability. Thenceforth, the Soviets tried to convince Iraq to withdraw from Kuwait, while U.S. policy was to gain Soviet support, or at least its neutrality in the crisis. It appears that the USSR was willing to acquiesce because this cooperation not only coincided with Gorbachev's policy, but also could be traded for substantial aid. Still, Soviet policy remained independent. Gorbachev said that while the USSR and the United States were partners, "we are prepared to cooperate, but we will not be led."[1]

While the Soviet response reflected Gorbachev's foreign policy, it was also to Soviet economic advantage in that there were so many economic and diplomatic concessions made to Moscow in this period that it appears that it was trading its support for aid. During a late-October diplomatic trip, Gorbachev signed several trade agreements with Spain and France, and just before the vote on the U.N. resolution to authorize force against Iraq, Saudi Arabia agreed to lend the Soviet Union $1 billion. Other loans included $1 billion from France, $1.5 billion from Spain, $6.3 billion from Italy, over $10 billion from Germany, possibly $1 billion from Kuwait, and $5 billion from other Gulf states. On the diplomatic front, several nations, including Saudi Arabia, Iran, Japan, and Israel re-established relations with Moscow.

Soviet policy changed after December. After Shevardnadze resigned in protest when Moscow repressed dissent in the Baltics and the USSR, Soviet policy was far less clear, creating problems for the Coalition. On February 11, 1991, Soviet envoy Yevgeny Primakov went to Baghdad to persuade Saddam to withdraw his forces from Kuwait. Saddam agreed to cooperate in "finding a peaceful, political, equitable and honorable solution to the region's central issues, including the situation in the gulf."[2] This was far from an unconditional withdrawal from Kuwait.

The Coalition continued the dialogue with Moscow but made no concessions concerning its demand that Iraqi forces withdraw from Kuwait. However, the Soviets continued their diplomacy as the Coalition made final preparations for the ground war. Bush had serious concerns, but agreed with Gorbachev that it might be possible to end the war. The Soviets negotiated intensely but Iraq still demanded several concessions, saying that it would free all POWs immediately after a cease-fire, would begin withdrawing from Kuwait under UN supervision 24 hours after hostilities ceased, and would complete its pull out in a fixed time, if a cancellation of all sanctions against it were tied to its withdrawal, and if there were guarantees that debate would be held on the Palestinian issue. Bush called this initial Iraqi acceptance and then the long list of demands a "cruel hoax."[3]

Several reasons account for these Soviet diplomatic efforts. After Shevardnadze's departure Soviet policy was much less purposeful, reflecting the great influence he had exerted. Another reason for Moscow's actions was the Baltic repression itself. It was as serious as the Hungarian Revolution of 1956 and the Czechoslovakian action of 1968 in terms of political repression and physical brutality, and while it never approached the slaughter of 1956, it certainly was bloodier than Prague in 1968. Had the Gulf War not occurred, it would have been a major incident adversely affecting Soviet-Western relations. However, by working to keep the West pre-occupied with Iraq, Moscow probably hoped to minimize the reaction to the Baltics. The third reason pertained to the Soviet military relationship with Iraq. The huge destruction of the Soviet equipped and trained Iraqi Army could not have been pleasing, and the Kremlin may have been desperately seeking a way to avert Iraq's total defeat in a ground war, even if this meant pursuing a policy that was not completely to Washington's liking. Finally, Soviet prestige also influenced their actions. While Gorbachev's foreign policy indicated that the USSR might play a more regional role in world affairs, recognizing that one's world influence is declining is a difficult truth for a nation to accept.[4] Although Great Britain did this gracefully when she granted India and other Commonwealth countries their independence, there are a host of other powers in history that could not accept a new reality and acted accordingly. Soviet statements reflect that this was the case.

The Military Role

While Soviet foreign policy reflected neutrality, its military policy was one of low-level assistance to Baghdad. The evidence indicates that the Soviet Union indicated early on that there would be no major military posturing in Iraq's defense. Rather, Moscow recommended withdrawal, but if Iraq did not withdraw, then it would provide limited assistance to its former client. Many rumors, most emanating in the early weeks of the crisis and some based in fact, persisted concerning Soviet involvement in Iraq during the war. Moscow was said to have foreknowledge of the invasion of Kuwait and quite possibly planned the major details of the assault. Soviet General Albert Makashov went to Baghdad on July 17th, two weeks before the invasion, and remained there until August 13th. He reportedly assured the Iraqis of Soviet military support in their endeavors. Unsubstantiated reports said that the Soviet Union continued its arms shipments until the air war began. Some were airlifted, and most came overland through Jordan. In late October, there were unconfirmed reports that Soviet Spetsnaz troops were guarding Saddam against coup attempts or assassination. In mid-January, 1991, the CIA purportedly identified as many as 400 Soviet trucks believed to contain munitions moving from the USSR through Iran to Iraq. This assistance purportedly was continued into the war. Soviet military advisors were initially kept in Iraq pending completion of their contracts, and some allegedly helped the Iraqis aim and target Scud missiles. The Soviets launched four strategic imaging reconnaissance satellites to monitor the region. Iraq was said to have access to "real time" satellite images and was informed by the Soviets of U.S. satellite overflight schedules so that the secret Scud launching locations would not be revealed. Soviet advisors allegedly participated in military operations against Coalition forces in the Kuwaiti and Iraqi theaters of war, manning antiaircraft batteries and servicing intelligence needs. U.S. intelligence was said to have heard Russian on Iraq's army tactical radio network, and the transmissions were traced to Iraqi tank battalions and regiments. One intelligence source was to have concluded that the tank units were being commanded by Soviets.[5]

While most of the above assertions remain unsubstantiated and some will prove to be incorrect, we can reasonably conclude that there was some Soviet assistance to Iraq. Additionally, while the

Soviet military is restructuring and there are continued good relations with the West, it is prudent for the Soviet military to continue assessing Western military power. The War provided such an ideal opportunity for intelligence collection that Soviet surveillance, by satellites and other means, should and was expected. In sum, Soviet military involvement reflected a policy in transition from one that had supported Saddam to another that stopped such support. During the war, Moscow's most significant action was to not block Coalition efforts either diplomatically or militarily. In this context, the relatively little assistance provided to Iraq, while it cannot be quantified exactly, nonetheless was inconsequential to the extent that it did not impede substantially Coalition diplomatic or military activities.

LESSONS LEARNED

Soviet policy during the war reflected Moscow's independence and an accurate view of the existing international situation. In desperate need of aid from the West, it successfully traded moderation for assistance. Militarily, it provided some help to Iraq, but this was so limited that Moscow was not directly implicated. Gone was the intense Soviet-American standoff and horrendous escalation that had characterized so many crises in the past. Now Moscow declined a massive military response, while pursuing an independent policy that sought to limit the war's dimensions. Of greatest significance was the fact that now wars were again possible, as one of the two powers that had kept peace was no longer willing to play that role.

NOTES

1. *Tass*, December 18, 1990; and Michael Parks, "Soviets Want to Be Partners but Not 'Yes Men' to West," *The Los Angeles Times*, November 20, 1990, p. A6.
2. "Don't Save This Face," *The Economist* (January 12, 1991): 11; and "The Desperate Last Throw of a Cornered Gangster," *The Daily Telegraph*, February 16, 1991.
3. "A Peace Plan that Could Lose the War," *The Daily Telegraph*, February 20, 1991, p. 16; "Half a Peace Plan", *The Times* (London), February 21, 1991; "Back to Reality," *The Times* (London), February 23, 1991; "No Cease Fire Until Terms Met in Full," *The Daily Telegraph*, February 23, 1991, p. 14.
4. "The Moscow Proposal," *The Daily Telegraph*, February 23, 1991; "Faltering Steps Toward Peace", *The Times* (London), February 23, 1991; "Moscow Strives to Produce Peace Plan US Will Accept," *The Times* (London), February 23, 1991;

"Gorbachev Plays the Great Game," *The Daily Telegraph*, February 20, 1991; and Mark Almond, "Russia's Role as 'Honest Broker'," *The Daily Telegraph*, February 18, 1991.

5. "Soviet Military Aiding," *The Washington Times*, January 25, 1991; John Lenczowski, "Gorbachev's Words Contradict His Deeds in Iraq," *West Watch*, October 1990, p. 6; "Soviet Recon Satellites Image Persian Gulf Area," *Aviation Week & Space Technology* (November 19, 1990); "Soviets Use War to Boost Spying," *The Washington Times*, January 21, 1991; and "U.S. Hears Russian Language in Iraqi Radio Communications," *The New York City Tribune*, December 3, 1990.

PART III

FORCE DEPLOYMENTS AND THE WAR

5: The Air War
by
Rod Alonso
with
Bruce George, MP, Raimondo Luraghi,
Tim Lister, James Piriou, and B.L. Cyr

Great Britain, the United States, and nine other nations responded to Saudi Arabia's request for aid in August 1990, in the most extensive projection of air power in history (see Part I, Appendix D). On the 7th, the Coalition had 323 fixed wing combat and support aircraft. This strength rose to 501 aircraft on the 12th; 1,220 on September 11th; 2,430 on January 17th; and finally 2,790 aircraft by February 24th.[1]

In terms of distance and time, the projection of U.S. air power from America and Europe to West Asia was the largest in history. The Air Force deployed 46 percent of its total combat force in the United States, a force equal to 10.4 tactical fighter wings. Twelve reserve squadrons with five C-5 and seven C-141 heavy lift transport aircraft established a U.S.-West Asian air bridge. On August 18th, the Civil Reserve Air Fleet (CRAF) was activated for the first time in its 38-year history; it had 95 passenger and 63 cargo planes. The airlift amounted to a Berlin Airlift every six weeks and sent 482,000 people and 513,000 tons of cargo to West Asia, "the equivalent of moving Oklahoma City – all of its people, vehicles, food, and household goods halfway around the world" (see Part VIII, Appendix D). Within theater, the 317th Tactical Airlift Wing (provisional) transported over 209,000 troops and 300,000 tons of cargo.[2]

U.S. air power was deployed in two phases. The first began with an Air Force fighter squadron that flew non-stop for 15 hours and 7,000 miles from the U.S. east coast to Saudi Arabia, and was aerially refueled seven times by Strategic Air Command (SAC) KC-10 and KC-135 tanker aircraft.[3] It was in Saudi Arabia and ready for combat less than 34 hours after the deployment order was issued by Washington, and joined those Coalition forces already there: the Royal Saudi Air Force and remnants of Kuwait's Air Force that had fled to Saudi Arabia when Iraq invaded. However, within four days, five fighter squadrons and an AWACS element were present, and by August 12th, these were reinforced by Royal Air Force aircraft and fighter aircraft embarked aboard U.S. Navy carriers. The first phase lasted five weeks and when finished, the Coalition outnumbered Iraq in both defensive and offensive aircraft. The second phase, from November 8th to January 15th, doubled the Coalition's aircraft.[4]

Concurrently, her Majesty's Government ordered forces to the Gulf on August 9th, and within 48 hours, a squadron of twelve Tornado F3 fighters was operational at Dharhan Air Base. Two hours after their arrival, two were airborne on an operational mission. Within the next 48 hours, a squadron of twelve ground attack Jaguars, with VC10K tanker support, were at Thumrait Air Base in southern Oman, and by the 16th, three Nimrod maritime patrol aircraft were further north at Seeb. These deterrent forces were later reinforced by a squadron of Tornado GR1s at Muharraq, Tornado F3s (with Rapiers and a Light Armored Squadron from the RAF Regiment to provide airfield defense) at Dhahran, and Tornado GR1s (some equipped with ALARM for defense suppression of enemy radars) at Tabuk. After Desert Storm had begun six Buccaneers equipped with Pavespike laser designators, followed later by a further six, were deployed. Also, Tornado GR1s in theater were modified to take the Thermal Imaging Airborne Laser Designator (TIALD) equipment. The Jaguars moved forward from Thumrait to Muharraq, and Puma and Chinook helicopters were deployed to Al Jubail for logistic support and casualty evacuation. By mid-January, the Royal Air Force had deployed 96 aircraft, 14 percent of its total force, including: 24 Tornado IDS aircraft from RAF Germany to Bahrain; 18 Tornado F3 (with Foxhunter A-124 radar) from RAF Lemming to Bahrain; a squadron of Tornado GR1s to Tabuk; a squadron of 12 Jaguar GR-1As from RAF Cottishall to Bahrain; six TR-1A early warning and reconnaissance aircraft from RAF Alconbury deployed to an undisclosed site; a detachment of C-130s; a squadron of 17 Chinook and a squadron of 19 Puma support helicopters from RAF Odiham and RAF Gutersloh; a detachment of VC-10 tanker aircraft to Seeb; four Nimrod MR2s from RAF Kinloss to Seeb, and an RAF Rapier and ground defense squadron.

The Air Transport Force (ATF) flew around 14 million miles to support Operation Granby and moved some 50,000 tons of freight. This peaked at some 600 tons per day, more than six times the RAF's normal worldwide peacetime average. Within theater, Chinook helicopters flew some 500 sorties and some 1,350 hours carrying over one million kilograms of freight and over 8,000 troops, and Pumas flew some 1,200 sorties and 2,200 hours carrying over 68,000 kilograms of freight, over 4,000 troops, and 161 casualties. During the war, the tanker force offloaded some 13,000 tons of fuel.

France contributed about 850 men and 43 combat aircraft, including five Mirage F1–CRs, 24 Jaguars, 12 Mirage 2000–2 D1s, four C 160 transports and two C135 FR refueling aircraft. In addition, operation *Metell* involved sending eight Mirage F1–Cs to Qatar, whilst 4,000 men and a squadron of ten Mirage F1–Cs were prepositioned in Djibouti. An air base was established at Ad Ahsa from which 2,472 sorties, including 1,387 combat sorties, were flown. The airborne division of operation *Daguet* arrived on October 3rd. For ten weeks before the start of the air campaign, French Mirage 2000s flew air defense missions over Saudi Arabia, and Mirage F1–CRs, DC8 Sarigues, and C160 Gabriels conducted reconnaissance against Iraq.

Italy's force to the Gulf was organized by the Air Force and Navy. A squadron of ten Tornado bombers, reserve teams, repair groups, and a group of engineers were sent to set up *Locust*, a base at Abu Dhabi, while the 46th Air Brigade provided two Hercules C-110 aircraft to transport men and supplies to and from Italy. The Canadians deployed 24 CF-18 aircraft, and several Arab nations contributed to the Coalition Air Force: Bahrain sent 12 F-16s; Kuwait, 18 A-4s; Oman, 20 Jaguars; Qatar, 12 Mirages; Saudi Arabia, 48 Tornados, 85 F-5s, and 42 F-15s; and the United Arab Emirates, 50 Mirages.

THE AIR CAMPAIGN

The air campaign had four phases. The goal of Phase I was to destroy Iraq's vital centers of gravity – its offensive and defensive air capabilities, including the entire Air Force and its integrated ground-based air defense system; its national communications, including television, radio and land lines; its nuclear, biological, and chemical weapons research and production capabilities; and its war production potential and transportation system including railroads and bridges, and oil distribution and transportation capabilities. The goal of Phases II and III was to neutralize the Iraqi Army in the Kuwaiti Theater of Operation (KTO) by cutting bridges and lines of communications to disrupt its resupply, destroying its armor and artillery, and killing and demoralizing its personnel. The goal of Phase IV was to win the air/ground campaign by providing intelligence, massive firepower as needed, and protective air cover for friendly ground forces.[5]

Before the air campaign began, deception operations were waged by flying routine E-3A AWACS flights near the border, which conditioned Iraqi personnel to consider such activity as normal.[6] However, on the night of January 17th, Coalition strike aircraft were aerially refueled just beyond Iraqi radar range, and when the air campaign began at 3 a.m., the AWACS vectored the strike aircraft to their targets and surprise was achieved.

The campaign began with Stealth F-117A and Tomahawk cruise missile strikes. Tomahawks reduced pilot exposure over heavily defended targets, especially during daylight hours, and the F-117As flew virtually undetected. Although the F-117As amounted to only 2.5 percent of all U.S. air power, they struck 31 percent of all Iraqi targets hit on the campaign's first day and opened corridors for strikes by other aircraft. RAF Tornado GR1 aircraft were involved in the first wave of attacks on Iraqi airfields using JP 233 airfield denial weapons, some 6,000 1,000-pound bombs (of which over 1,000 were laser guided), over 100 anti-radar missiles, and nearly 700 air-to-ground rockets. At dawn on the 17th, French Jaguars bombed Al Jaber air base and Scud missile silos. French Mirage 2000s flew defensive missions over Saudi Arabia and strikes on munition depots, naval bases, and other targets. Italian aircraft also struck targets and a Tornado was lost when it was hit by Iraqi 23–mm four-barreled machine gun fire. In the first 14 hours of the campaign, over 1,000 sorties were flown against Iraq's early warning system, fighter defense direction system, command and control structure, communications, air defenses, Scud missile sites, electrical power, and other related targets. Eighty percent of the sorties were effective, meaning that 80 percent of the aircraft reached their targets, delivered their ordnance, and returned. The others did not because of mechanical or weather problems that prevented the pilots from positively identifying their targets, which was required under the rules of engagement so that civilian damage was absolutely minimal. Having been surprised in the initial attacks, the Iraqi Air Force and air defenses were never able to recover. By the end of the first 24 hours, the Coalition had flown 2,107 combat sorties, fired 196 Tomahawk missiles, and lost a U.S. Navy F/A-18A, two U.S. Navy A-6Es, a U.S. Air Force F-15E, a U.S. Marine Corps OV-10A, an Italian and two British Tornados, and a Kuwaiti A-4. A U.S. Air Force F-4G crashed with mechanical problems. Iraq lost four MiG-29s, three F-1 Mirages, and a MiG-25 Flogger (see Parts III and IV of Appendix D).[7]

The French intensified their activities on the 23rd as part of a Coalition strategy that called for two daily raids, one that delivered 250–kilogram bombs, and a second that involved AS 30 missile attacks. Mirage F1 CR fighter bombers were committed to combat on the 26th, and by February 12th, the French FATAC (*Force Aerienne Tactique*) had delivered its thousandth 250–kilogram bomb. By the 18th, the Mirage 2000s had completed their thousandth hour of flight operations. Meanwhile, the Italian Air Force contingent conducted bombing missions and flew defensive air missions to protect Italian naval ships. The defensive mission required 2,000 flying hours, while the bombing offensive required 2,100 more, amounting to a total of 226 missions against Iraqi targets in the vicinity of Basra, the Iraqi-Kuwaiti border, and inside Kuwait.[8] Canadian operations were also notable; Canadian CF-18 aircraft flew a heavy schedule of sorties.

The Royal and U.S. Air Forces were the backbone of the Coalition's air campaign. The Royal Air Force made a significant contribution, flying 6,000 sorties, including 2,000 offensive sorties by Tornado GR1 and Jaguar aircraft, between January 17th and February 28th. RAF missions involved air defense, offensive counter air/air interdiction, tactical reconnaissance, and Nimrod maritime reconnaissance operations. In air defense, Tornado F3s flew more than 2,500 operational combat air patrol sorties, of which over 700 were flown during the war. In offensive counter air/air interdiction (OCA/AI) operations, about 1,500 Tornado GR1 operational sorties were flown of which about half were flown against OCA targets and half against AI targets in three phases: a one week night low-level OCA phase with JP233 and 1000lb lofted bombs; a two-three week period of night/day medium level AI, with some OCA operations using ballistic freefall 1,000–pound bombs; and a final three-week phase involving a concentrated day/night medium level OCA/IA campaign delivering exclusively 1,000–pound laser guided bombs (LGBs) designated by Buccaneer/Pavespike (day only) or Tornado/TIALD (day/night). Due to their night and all-weather penetration capability and their unique JP233 airfield denial weapons, the Tornado GR1s were well suited to offensive counter-air attacks against Iraqi airfields and were used intensively for that purpose in the early days. Initially, the RAF were tasked to harass enemy airfield operations rather than attempt to close a selected few and in those early days the GR1s carried out low level attacks with JP233s to crater runways. These attacks were carried out in the face of exceptionally strong Iraqi antiaircraft artillery and missile fire. However, within four days of the start of the war, the counter air campaign had driven the Iraqi Air Force into hiding, effectively destroyed its integrated air defense system, and freed the middle and upper air for Coalition use. The defeat of Iraqi air power allowed most of the subsequent Tornado GR1 sorties to be flown in daylight and above the reach of Iraqi anti-aircraft artillery. Initially, the medium-level Tornado GR1 sorties used freefall bombs to attack large area-type targets such as fuel storage dumps and air fields. The deployment of Buccaneers with laser designator pods enabled the Tornados to attack point targets such as bridges and airfield facilities, using laser-guided bombs. These successful LGB missions led to a decision to deploy additional Buccaneer aircraft with laser designators, which enabled more Tornado GR1s to concentrate exclusively on precision attacks during the last few weeks of the war. This process was further strengthened when Tornados were fitted with Thermal Imaging Airborne Laser Designator (TIALD). The Pavespike laser des-ignator used by the Buccaneers is a stand-alone, manually-con-trolled system that can be used only in daylight. In contrast the Tornado's TIALD pods are fully integrated into the aircraft's navigation and bombing system, and can be used at night. By the end of the fourth week of the war, some 60 percent of Tornado sorties were using Paveway laser guided bombs. Six Tornado GR-1s were lost in action, five of which were involved in loft or medium level attacks with 1,000–pound bombs, and one was lost on a low level JP233 mission.

To accomplish the battlefield interdiction and close-air support mission, Jaguar GR1As attacked supply dumps, surface-to-air missile sites, artillery, and Silkworm missile sites. Using the Canadian CRV-7, a high velocity missile with a very flat and thus accurate trajectory, the Jaguars proved extremely effective in attacks against Iraqi naval targets, destroying patrol boats and landing craft. Over 600 Jaguar sorties were flown.

The RAF also fulfilled a vital tactical reconnaissance mission. The Tornado GR1A reconnaissance variant with its Vinten Line-scan/Computing Devices integrated system was deployed just before the outbreak of the war. It is the first reconnaissance aircraft to be equipped with video recording sensors and provides a day/night reconnaissance capability. Some 140 Tornado TR1A operational sorties were flown on tactical reconnaissance missions. They operated mainly in pairs at night and at low level and for extended periods over enemy territory against Scud mobile missile launchers, enemy positions, supply routes, and bridges for damage assessment after laser guided bomb raids.

Naval Air Operations
Located much closer to some targets in Kuwait and Iraq than land-based Coalition aircraft, carrier-based aircraft were also used for strikes. EA-6B Prowlers disrupted Iraqi radar and communications, while A-6E Intruders bombed military command and control centers and ground troops, and F/A-18 Hornets and F-14 Tomcats flew combat air patrols to defend against enemy fighters. The F/A-18s, accompanied by Prowler jamming and Intruder attack aircraft, also flew into Iraq to neutralize most of Iraq's fire control radar. The Hornets had antiradiation bombs and missiles, such as HARM, that were designed to lock-on to radar beams and destroy targets.[9]

The carrier-based aircraft also were invaluable in covering friendly combatant ships in the Gulf area. In mid-January, they flew against Iraqi-held islands and oil platforms that were being used to spy on Coalition ships and to fire at Coalition aircraft. A unique combined attack was waged against Kura Island. Army helicopters and the frigate *Nicholas* launched precision-guided rockets at Iraqi positions on nine oil platforms, including the Dorra oilfield platform about 40 miles from occupied Kuwait. The platforms then were seized by Navy special forces. At the same time the frigate *Curts* and A-6 aircraft from *Roosevelt* attacked Iraqi positions on Kura Island.[10] After naval aircraft attacked the naval base at Umm Qasr on January 25th, hitting four Iraqi naval vessels, and hit two others in the Gulf, Iraq had lost at least 18 boats.

Meanwhile, two Nimrod sorties were flown daily in support of the *Midway* group in the northern Gulf. Tasked with locating and identifying Iraqi Navy ships and aircraft, they were very successful in making many of the initial detections and then directing attack aircraft, particularly Royal Navy Lynx helicopters, onto their targets. Nimrod also played an important role as an Airborne Command Center, acting as Scene of Search Commander as part of the search and rescue (SAR) organization.

U.S. naval aircraft focused on destroying Iraq's Silkworm antiship missiles that were a serious threat. The Chinese-made Silkworm is a short- to medium-range cruise antiship missile designed for shipboard and coastal defense. It has a maximum range of 62 miles and cruises at 100 feet above the water, dropping to about 50 feet for the attack. On January 27th and 28th, British and American aircraft hit two Silkworm launchers at Umm Qasr naval base while attacking patrol boats at Umm Qasr, two Iraqi naval ships in Bubiyan channel, and a patrol boat in Kuwait harbor. On the 29th, A-6s destroyed two Silkworm sites on Iraq's Faw Peninsula, just north of Kuwait, while also attacking an oil storage facility near Kuwait International Airport. On February 9th, a three-launcher Silkworm system and a control center were attacked and destroyed. This occurred after a missile narrowly missed the guided missile frigate USS *Nicholas* and exploded about 50 yards off her starboard bow. Shrapnel struck the ship's superstructure but caused no injuries or serious damage. The Iraqis then fired two Silkworms at Coalition ships operating in the northern Gulf. One fell into the sea, and the other was intercepted by Sea Dart rockets fired by the HMS *Gloucester*, which was escorting the battleship USS *Missouri*.[11]

The naval air campaign was continued; three Iraqi ships were damaged or destroyed in the Shatt al-Arab and northern Persian Gulf, and three patrol boats were struck near Umm Qasr. On the

30th, attacks were continued on Umm Qasr, a patrol boat was hit and left burning near Mina al Bakr, and 15 prisoners were taken from the oil terminal at Khor al-Amaya. By now, 46 Iraqi naval vessels had been sunk or disabled and 74 Iraqi naval personnel had been taken prisoner. At least three patrol boats were hit on February 1st, thereby eliminating the Iraqi Navy's Exocet missile capability. A-6 attack aircraft relentlessly struck Iraqi convoys. As Iraqi troops retreated from Kuwait, the pace of air strikes from carriers was so feverish that pilots said they took whatever bombs happened to be closest to the flight deck. By war's end 18,117 sorties had been flown from six carriers, of which 16,899 were combat or direct combat-support missions.

SPECIFIC ASPECTS OF THE AIR CAMPAIGN

The Iraqi Air Force and Air Defense Threats

Before the war, Iraq had the world's sixth largest Air Force, and had Soviet-made MiG-21 Fishbeds, MiG-23 Floggers, MiG-25 Foxbats, MiG-29 Fulcrums, Su-24 Fencers, Chinese-made MiG-21s, and French-built Mirage F-1s in its inventory. Although the Coalition estimated that it had about 1,000 fixed-wing aircraft, including about 750 combat aircraft, the actual numbers may have been slightly higher. It also had an impressive air defense system, including as many as 17,000 surface-to-air missiles and between 9,000 and 10,000 antiaircraft artillery pieces. The system's modern radar systems were fiberoptically connected to integrate the computer data link system, and its command and control links were located throughout the country. For greater survivability, many primary command and control nodes were buried and concrete covered to create hardened facilities.[12]

During the two weeks before the war, the Iraqi Air Force flew about 100 sorties daily, including about 60 combat aircraft sorties. It sustained a good effort for the first several days of the war, considering the state of its air defense command and control and the damaged airfields. On the first day, it flew 96 sorties, including 53 combat sorties, and on the second day, its sorties surged to 118, although combat sorties dropped sharply to 23. The number of combat sorties remained the same on the third day, but the total number dropped to 42. On the fourth day, combat sorties accounted for 58 out of the 60 sorties flown. Thenceforth, the number of sorties fluctuated but remained low until the sixteenth day, when the flying stopped. During the war, Iraq lost 35 aircraft in air-to-air combat, while the Coalition suffered no losses. The first half of these were lost early in the war and by January 21st, Iraq had lost 17 fighters (eight MiG-29s, six Mirages, two MiG-25s, and a MiG-23) in aerial engagements. The other 18 were lost as Iraqi fighters fled to Iran. Besides these, it is estimated that a further 227 Iraqi aircraft were destroyed on the ground.[13]

The Coalition gained total air superiority within a week, and it was almost suicidal to fly against Coalition aircraft. In order to protect their planes, Iraqi placed them in residential areas, close to religious shrines and historic sites, and in hardened aircraft shelters. When the Coalition began to destroy the shelters, Baghdad decided to fly them to Iran and other nations to protect them. Thus, about 148 – 115 combat aircraft (24 Su-24s, 40 Su-22s, four Su-20s, seven Su-25s, 24 F-1 Mirages, twelve MiG-23s, and four MiG-29s) and 33 civil transport aircraft (two Boeing 747s, a Boeing 707, two Boeing 737s, a Boeing 727, five Airbus 310As, an Airbus 300, 15 Il-76 Candids, two Falcon 20s, three Falcon 50s, and a Jetstar aircraft) were flown to Iran (see Appendix D). Units of the Iraqi Airways fleet also may have been flown to other nations.[14]

Command and Control

The Coalition was successful in integrating and coordinating all air power in mission planning, identifying ground targets for air strikes, and all the other details and requirements of the war. Air operations were controlled by the Joint Force Air Component Commander (JFACC), who used an air tasking order (ATO) to assign targets to specific units and direct the weapons used. He also provided "deconfliction mission data," to prevent coordination problems that could occur when such a large force operated in such a lucrative target environment. The ATO ideally maximized the effectiveness of Coalition air power.[15]

Satellites provided surveillance, weather data, navigation support of unprecedented accuracy, threat warnings, and timely and secure communications. The Defense Meteorological Support Program provided near real-time accurate target weather data, and the Global Positioning System (GPS) was invaluable in guiding forces to target areas with unprecedented accuracy. While the GPS will not be completed until fiscal year 1993, it provided three-dimensional coverage for 18 hours and two-dimensional coverage for 24 hours daily. The navigational data it provided made strike missions much easier to accomplish.[16]

There were communications problems. At first there was a shortage of satellite communications, and civilian and commercial satellites provided up to half of the satellite communications because the Defense Satellite Communications System (DSCS) was swamped. However, the Air Force Space Command shifted the orbit of a DSCS satellite from the Pacific to the Indian Ocean area, where it supplemented two other DSCS satellites. By the war's end, there were 128 DSCS terminals in theater, and a Joint Chiefs of Staff spokesman said, "In the first ninety days, we put in more communications connectivity than we have had in Europe over the past forty years."[17] However, the communications traffic load was horrendous, because super high-frequency communications were not only used for links between Washington and the theater, but also between military units in theater. Additional capability, ultra-high frequency communications, was provided by six Navy fleet satellite communications satellites. The nine satellites provided over 1,400 land and sea satellite terminals with secure communications. While communications requirements increased by a factor of 30 and DSCS continually provided tactical commanders with communications, Air Force Space Command's commander, Lieutenant General Thomas Moorman, said that, "space officials were unable to respond as quickly as needed because of the lack of advanced planning," and believed that "we need to work on integrating space into operations plans." It was concluded that the Air Force must develop a more detailed space doctrine to provide principles governing the use of space systems in war so that these became an integral part of all battle force resources.[18]

Air Intelligence
Intelligence was criticized unfairly for overestimating the number of Iraqi Army troops in the Kuwaiti Theater of Operations (KTO). There were a number of reasons for this. Realizing that it was very difficult to estimate Iraqi troop strength in the KTO, General Schwarzkopf asked for a "worst case" intelligence estimate, one that qualified as the worst situation that he would encounter. Second, normal procedure is to base estimates by identifying enemy units, since units are more easily identifiable, and each has a

standard level of manpower and equipment. However, there was
no accurate way of determining if Iraqi units in the KTO were
over or under strength. Thus, the intelligence estimate assumed
that all units were up to strength. After the war, it was learned
that many were not, accounting for the overestimation of troop
strength.[19]

Theater reconnaissance systems supplemented these satellites.
Unmanned aerial vehicles (UAVs), including Pioneers and
Pointers, JSTARS aircraft with synthetic aperture radar, and RF-
4C aircraft that have both a conventional imagery and an infrared
capability for day and night operations were used. The best theater
support was by the U.S. Air Force's TR-1 squadron that deployed
from RAF Alconbury, England. It had a ground station (a mobile
version of the Ford Aerospace tactical reconnaissance exploitation
demonstration system [TREDS] that is reportedly part of Loral)
that allowed down linking intelligence in near-real-time. It also
may have had the Ford Aerospace TRIGS system that has a secure
automated processing and dissemination capability. Video imagery
was provided by F-117As and F-111s, while RC-135 Rivet Joint
aircraft provided electronic intelligence (ELINT).[20]

The Mission Support System (MSS) allowed planners to prepare
a pilot for a mission in four hours, instead of the days that were
needed for a Vietnam mission. MSS was used to integrate charts,
maps, enemy threats, and other data in mission planning. However,
despite the overwhelming success of these systems, there were problems with untimely intelligence support; there were excessive delays
at the unit level and a shortage of tactical reconnaissance assets.[21]

The most sensitive targets were Iraq's nuclear, chemical, and
biological facilities. Coalition Air Forces seriously damaged the
nuclear research facility by destroying two of its operating reactors,
and seriously damaged their biological warfare and chemical
warfare production facilities.[22] By January 30th, aircraft and Tomahawks had attacked 31 nuclear, biological or chemical warfare
targets, and had either severely damaged or totally destroyed at
least half of them. CENTCOM had absolute confirmation that
eleven biological and chemical storage areas were destroyed and
that three other production facilities were destroyed or heavily
damaged.

The goal of Phase II was to: destroy the air defense radars and
missiles in the KTO; achieve undisputed control of the air; sever

KTO supply lines and isolate the KTO; and continue attacks on the Republican Guard. CENTCOM said that 26 leadership targets had been struck, with 60 percent of them severely damaged or destroyed. Telecommunications centers and electrical generating facilities were attacked, leaving 25 percent of the electrical facilities completely inoperative and another 50 percent with degraded outputs. The goal was not to destroy all electrical power because the Coalition wanted to leave Iraq's civilian population with some electricity. Seventy-five percent of Iraq's command, control, and communications facilities were struck, with 33 percent completely destroyed or inoperative. More than 800 strike sorties were flown to attack 29 Iraqi Air Defense "nerve systems" targets, which forced Iraq to use less effective and more easily targeted backup systems. Thirty-six bridges were targeted to destroy supply lines to southern Iraq and the KTO, and by January 30th, 790 sorties had been flown against 33 of them. This reduced the rate of supply by about 90 percent, from about 20,000 to about 2,000 tons daily. The Republican Guards were struck by about 300 sorties daily and were hit very heavily. For example, on January 29th, 21 B-52s dropped 315 tons of bombs on them, and on the 30th, 28 B-52's dropped 470 tons of munitions, while F-15Es, F-16s, and A-6s also attacked. Strike damage on an ammunition storage area in northern Kuwait was so large that a secondary explosion destroyed 125 storage revetments and reportedly surpassed an exploding volcano.[23] Forty-four airfields (16 primary and 28 dispersal fields) were originally targeted. Thirty-eight were struck simultaneously, and collectively, they were the target of 1,200 strike sorties. Many were hit at least four times and nine were rendered unoperational. These multiple strikes were necessary because it is relatively easy to repair damaged runways and to insure that airfields remained inoperable, it was necessary to strike them repeatedly at approximately 48 hour intervals.[24]

The Iraqi Scuds

The worst intelligence failure was the gross underestimation of the number of mobile Scud missile launchers. Intelligence was not aware that Iraq had converted trucks into launchers and there is still no accurate estimate of the total number of these converted launchers. The 36 fixed sites were easily targeted, but the mobile launchers proved to be a nightmare, because the Iraqis simply

launched missiles from them and then immediately moved them to
hiding places, such as buildings, aircraft shelters, culverts along
highways, and in other structures.[25] Besides Soviet-supplied mobile
launchers, Iraq had built its own launchers by adding missile rails
to trucks designed for hauling equipment, and there was no way to
determine how many had been made. To further complicate
matters, Iraq used decoys. The Coalition conducted armed road
reconnaissance with A-10s and placed F-15Es on airborne combat
patrol missions over areas, designated as Scud boxes, where Scuds
were operating. The F-15Es worked with the Grumman E-8A Joint
Surveillance Targeting Attack Radar System (JSTARS) ground
surveillance aircraft, which was still in its developmental test and
evaluation stages. Its synthetic aperture radar provided images of
fortifications and bomb damage assessments out to 93 nautical
miles, and it would identify 'suspicious' ground vehicles and divert
the F-15Es to attack them.[26] Their success against the mobile
launchers forced Iraq to move the Scuds to areas that severely
restricted their ability to launch against Tel Aviv and Riyadh.

The Scud's inability to hit a defined target precluded its use as
a military threat and it has been described best as a long-range
terrorist weapon (see chapters 12 and 13 and Appendix C). The
United States shared intelligence and provided warning of Scud
attacks to Israel in an arrangement agreed upon before the war.
Besides sending U.S. manned Patriot units to Israel at its
government's request, America trained Israeli crews on the Patriot
system. The first battery was airlifted to Israel within eleven hours
of Israel's request for the missiles. During the first ten days of the
air campaign, Iraq fired an average of five Scuds per day. However,
as air strikes and British and American Special Forces teams struck
and took their toll, this rate fell sharply, to one a day for the war's
last 33 days.[27]

The Baghdad Baby Milk Factory and the Amiriya Bunker

The destruction of the Baghdad baby milk factory and the Amiriya
command and control bunker caused significant reactions.[28] The
Coalition said that intelligence had confirmed that the factory was
a biological weapons plant and that assessing the bunker as a
command and control bunker was valid. The Amiriya reaction was
so strong that thenceforth targeting was controlled by Washington.
Retired U.S. Air Force Lieutenant General Leonard Perroots,

former Director of the Defense Intelligence Agency and a special consultant to that Agency during the war, said "... the American intelligence community had got it wrong when bombers attacked the baby milk factory outside Baghdad at the beginning of the allied air campaign," and "... admitted that intelligence information that led to the bombing of the reinforced bunker at Amiriya in Baghdad, killing 300 civilians, had not been accurate. It was not the most current information." Since Washington never recanted its story or provided the media access to the intelligence used to determine the status of two targets before they were attacked, serious questions persist.

Bomb Damage Assessments

In his testimony to Congress in June 1991, General Schwarzkopf said bomb damage assessment (BDA) – the analytical examination of targets that were struck to determine the amount of damage they sustained – was abysmal. BDA was critical because from it, planners would determine if a target had been destroyed or if additional strikes were required. While BDA in itself is difficult, two problems made it worse. The weather in the region was the worst it had been in 14 years, and video tape recorders in many fighters did not have sufficient quality for accurate BDA. Analysts confirmed less than one-half of the aerial kills with the recorders but believed that better recorders would solve the BDA problems.[29]

Weapons

Both precision guided and unguided weapons were used in the air war. Some precision guided munitions (PGMs) glide while others are self-propelled, and all have guidance systems to lead them to their targets. In laser-guided munitions, a target is illuminated with a laser and the weapon homes in on a spot of intense light. Of the U.S. aircraft, only the Air Force's F-15E, F-111, F-117A, and Navy's A-6E could laser their targets. Equally impressive was the electro-optically guided bomb (EOGB) that had either a television camera (GBU-15V1/B) or a night attack infrared sensor (GBU-15V2/B). Only the F-111 and F-15E had this system, which required a weapon system operator to steer the EOGB onto the target. F-15E aircraft were extremely effective with their Low Altitude Night Infrared Navigation System (LANTIRN) that was used with JSTARS.[30]

Acclaim for the Patriot missile was deserved. Patriot had been designed to destroy aircraft, not missiles, and thus did not have the pinpoint accuracy needed to guarantee destroying a Scud warhead in the air. Its innovative use against Scuds, while it did not completely destroy them, intercepted the majority of them, saving many lives and property.

In laser guided bombs (LGBs), the GBU-15 EOGB and GBU-10 Paveway II were patterned after the standard Mk-84 2,000–pound general purpose bomb. (GBU-15 is a precision modular glide bomb for use against heavily defended targets.) Probably the most effective of the PGMs was the GLU-109/B, a 2,000–pound bomb with a hardened steel case. Built like a large armor-piercing round, it could penetrate 28.8 feet of reinforced concrete before exploding. It could be fitted with the GBU-10 Paveway II LGB kit and possibly the GBU-15 EOGB. Mk-82 and M118 demolition bombs were also adapted with laser guidance kits.[31] Use of PGMs minimized collateral bomb damage.

The Royal Air Force deployed half a squadron of Pave Spike-equipped Buccaneers to enhance their LGB capability. Pave Spike enabled the RAF to switch from low altitude attacks where anti-aircraft artillery fire was especially deadly, to safer medium altitude stand-off deliveries. Each Pave Spike Buccaneer could carry four LGBs, could conduct strikes alone, could act as a target (laser) designator for Tornado GR1s and Jaguar GR1As, or could deliver Anglo-French television-guided anti-radiation Martel missiles. The RAF's JP233 Low Altitude Airfield Attack System was used effectively against Iraqi airfields by cratering runways and laying down area denial weapons (delayed explosives) that were a continuing threat to Iraqi repair crews and vehicles. The JP233 has 30 SG357 cratering weapons and 215 HB876 denial weapons in each weapon dispenser, and each Tornado carried two JP233s, mounted in tandem on shoulder pylons.[32]

Among the tactical weapons the Coalition used were cluster bombs (CBUs) that were effective on close-air-support missions where targets were well spread out on the battlefield. CEMs (Combined Effects Munitions), patterned after a 1,000–pound tactical munitions dispenser (TMD) that releases a variety of submunitions, were also used. Each contained 202 three-pound BLU-97/Bs that could penetrate 118 millimeters of armor. One B-52 with its 40,000–pound bomb load capacity could deliver over 8,000 BLU-97/Bs.

For the most part, the B-52s focused on bombing Iraqi Republican Guard Divisions.[33]

Coalition aircraft obtained "catastrophic kills" 80 percent of the time with their air-to-ground Maverick missiles, about 100 of which were fired daily. The primary Maverick used was the Hughes/Raytheon AGM-65D/G infrared imaging version. F-15E, F-16, and A-10 aircraft had LAU-88 triple missile rail launchers that enabled them to carry six Mavericks.[34]

LESSONS LEARNED

The first lesson is a reaffirmation of the traditional belief that good leadership, training, discipline, and morale are vital to a war effort. The best weapons are of questionable value when these qualities are absent. This was stated admirably by General Schwarzkopf when he said that the Coalition would have won even if the sides were reversed, even if the Coalition had Iraq's manpower and equipment and Iraq had the Coalition's. The heart of the matter, he said, was that "the Coalition came to play, and Iraq didn't." In this context, the war reaffirmed the importance of rapidly gaining air superiority and ultimately, air supremacy, in a combat theater. This gave the Coalition freedom to maneuver on the land, sea, and air.[35]

The air campaign completely devastated Iraq's Army. Despite the outcome of World War II, before Vietnam, some still believed that air power could be enough to win wars. This theory was discredited in that war, but it must be considered again. Indeed, for the first time in history, air power was the major determinant in a large-scale war between two formidable forces with field deployed armies. Had the ground war been delayed and the air war continued, the deadly air strikes would have decimated Iraq's Army. This view will be argued at length by military strategists and historians in the future and is not meant to lessen the significant contributions of Coalition ground and naval forces. However, the inescapable conclusion is that air power virtually brought Iraq to its knees, and the air war showed that air power may be enough to win some conflicts.

The third lesson is that, working with a single concept of operations and clear and concise objectives that made best use of the unique capabilities of the component air forces, the Joint Force Air

Component Commander (JFACC) afforded the needed command and control of the disparate component air forces. The result was both a unity of purpose and a flexibility in execution that would not have been possible otherwise.[36]

The Gulf War demonstrated undeniably the value of the F-117A Stealth fighter. It continually struck Iraqi targets with a lethality never before known in warfare, while never being hit despite heavy Iraqi anti-aircraft artillery and surface-to-air missile defenses.[37] The value of conventional precision guided munitions (PGMs) was shown. Their striking hardened targets without causing collateral damage to civilian property was remarkable, proving that PGMs can surgically provide awesome destructive power in conventional air strikes. The B-52 bombers showed that despite their age, they can successfully deliver high conventional munitions tonnage against targets over long distances on very short notice and are an important part of the U.S. Air Force's global reach capability.

The Coalition's ability to conduct nighttime operations was successful in denying Iraq's forces respites after sundown. The systems used demonstrated that air forces can now operate in a nighttime combat environment with almost as much accuracy as in daylight. The high overall mission capable rates sustained during the war reflected excellent training and maintenance. It ensured mission capable rates during the war that exceeded those in peacetime. Finally, new high-tech systems such as JSTARS, space systems, AWACS, and the like were of immense value in providing information on the battlefield situation.[38]

Finally, as in any war, there were problems. Many complained of the excessive time needed to get intelligence to their units and that there were not enough theater reconnaissance systems to provide all the necessary intelligence. Second, the U.S. Air Force deployed to the West Asia without enough training munitions. This precluded them from taking full advantage of the training time afforded during Desert Shield. Finally, the U.S. military space commands were not able to respond promptly to the crisis because of an obvious absence of advanced planning. More comprehensive space doctrine and principles governing the use of space systems during wartime must be developed. [39]

NOTES

1. General Merrill A. McPeak, Chief of Staff, U.S. Air Force, *Department of Defense News Briefing (DoD News Briefing)*, Pentagon, March 15, 1991 (hereafter referred to as McPeak).

2. *White Paper*, pp. 8, 10; McPeak; "Twelve Reserve Squadrons Activated to Help MAC with Saudi Airlift," *Aviation Week and Space Technology* (hereafter referred to as *AW&ST*) (September 3, 1990): 36; Donald B. Rice, Secretary of the Air Force, *Air Force Posture Statement to Congress* (Washington, DC, 1991); and Department of the Air Force, *White Paper: Air Force Performance in Desert Storm* (hereafter referred to as *White Paper*) (Washington, DC, 1991). In addition, support aircraft included SAC's KC-135 and KC-10 refueling aircraft deployed to Mount de Marsan in southeast France to support SAC's B-52 operations from RAF Fairford in the United Kingdom.

3. About half of SAC's 600–tanker force supported the deployments.

4. McPeak; *White Paper*, pp. 2, 9; and Department of the Air Force, *Operation Desert Shield/Storm Overview* (Washington, DC, 1991).

5. "Unleashing Desert Storm," *The Economist* (January 19, 1991): 21; *Operation Desert Shield/Storm Overview*, p. 2; and McPeak.

6. McPeak.

7. "Who's Winning?" *The Economist* (January 29, 1991): 13; *DOD News Briefing*, January 18, 1991; and January 19, 1991.

8. "Il Capo di Stato Maggiore della Difesa nel Golfo Persico," in *Informazioni della Difesa*, 1(January-February 1991): 2 ff.

9. "US Carrier in 'Desert Storm'," *Jane's Defence Weekly* (January 26, 1991); and "SLAMs Hit Iraqi Target in First Combat Firing," *AW&ST* (January 28, 1991).

10. Michael Braunbeck, "'Desert Shield': The First Lessons Learned," *Naval Institute Proceedings* hereafter referred to as *USNIP*) (January 1991); Glen Montgomery, "When the Liberation of Kuwait Began," *USNIP* (January 1991); George Rodriques and Robert Ruby, "Taking Down the Oil Platforms," *USNIP* (April 1991).

11. Michael Kennedy, "Defense Chief Dampens Speculation on Assault," *The Los Angeles Times*, January 28, 1991, p. A1; J. Edward Cody and Barton Gellman, "Cheney Says Iraqis Still Strong," *The Washington Post*, February 10, 1991, p. A1; and George Esper, "Guard 'Being Beaten'," *Associated Press*, February 25, 1991.

12. "Finishing Saddam," *The Sunday Times*, February 3, 1991, p. 11; McPeak; "Reviewing the Troops: How the Sides Measure Up," *Newsweek* (August 20, 1990): 25; "Iraq's Superbase Program," *JDW* (February 2, 1991): 133.

13. McPeak; *DOD News Briefing*, January 20, 1991; and January 21, 1991.

14. McPeak; and "Iraq Says 148 of Its Planes Flew to Iran," *Reuters*, April 12, 1991.

15. *White Paper*, p. 10; and Stanley R. Arthur and Marvin Pokrant, "Desert Storm at Sea," *USNIP* (May 1991): 86.

16. *White Paper*, pp. 10–12.

17. Vincent Kiernan, "Cooper Lifts Veil of Secrecy To Applaud DSP," *Space News* (April 1–7, 1991): 6.

18. Vincent Kiernan, "War Shows Military Need for Space Doctrine," *Space News* (April 21, 1991): 4; Craig Covault, "Desert Storm Reinforces Military Space

Directions," *AW&ST* (April 8, 1991); and Kiernan, "Cooper Lifts," p. 6.

19. Covault, p. 44; "Recon Satellites Lead Allied Intelligence Effort," *AW&ST* (February 4, 1991): 25–26, 42; "Spacecraft Played Vital Role in Gulf War Victory," *AW&ST* (April 22, 1991): 91; and Kiernan, "Cooper Lifts," p. 6.

20. Bruce D. Nordwall, "U.S. Relies on Combination of Aircraft, Satellites, UAVs for Damage Assessment," *AW&ST* (February 4, 1991): 24–25; and "'Filtering' Helped Top Military Leaders Get Proper Intelligence Information," *AW&ST* (April 22, 1991): 85.

21. *White Paper*, p. 14.

22. Cheney; and *DOD News Briefing*, January 24, 1991, p. 15.

23. Schwarzkopf, January 30, 1991; and *DOD News Briefing*, January 30, 1991.

24. Schwarzkopf, January 30, 1991.

25. Cheney; *DOD News Briefing*, January 18, 1991, p. 6; and January 21, 1991, pp. 5, 12; and McPeak.

26. *DOD News Briefing*, January 19, 1991, pp. 8, 10; and January 21, 1991, pp. 2, 5, 12; Nordwall, p. 24; David A. Fulghum, "Desert Storm Highlights Need For Rapid Tactical Intelligence," *AW&ST* (February 11, 1991); and McPeak.

27. Schwarzkopf; *DOD News Briefing*, January 19, 1991; 2–3; January 22, 1991, p. 5; and McPeak.

28. *White Paper*, p. 12; and McPeak.

29. *DOD News Briefing*, January 19, 1991 and January 21, 1991; McPeak; and *White Paper*, p. 14.

30. Bill Sweetman, "Modern Bombs in the Gulf," *JDW* (February 9, 1991): 178; and *White Paper*, pp. 3–4.

31. Michael Evans, "Bridge Bombing Campaign," *The Times* (London), February 8, 1991, p. 4; and Sweetman, p. 178.

32. Cheney, January 23, 1991.

33. *DOD News Briefing*, January 20, 1991 and Schwarzkopf, January 30, 1991.

34. "On Their Way," *The Economist* (February 9, 1991): 19; David Hughes, "USAF Firing 100 Mavericks Per Day in Current Air-to-Ground Missions," *AW&ST* (February 11, 1991): 24; and Sweetman, p. 178.

35. *Operation Desert Shield/Storm Overview*, pp. 3–4; and McPeak.

36. *Operation Desert Shield/Storm Overview*, p. 3; *White Paper*, p. 1; and McPeak.

37. *Operation Desert Shield/Storm Overview*, p. 4; and McPeak.

38. Ibid.

39. *White Paper*, p. 14; Kiernan, p. 4; and Covault, p. 43.

6: The Ground War
by
Peter Tsouras and Elmo C. Wright, Jr,
with
Bruce George, MP, Tim Lister, James Piriou,
and Joe Sanderson

Eighteen nations sent ground forces in response to Saudi Arabia's request for assistance (see part I, Appendix E). The heart of the Coalition's ground power would be the American and British forces. The United States deployed over 500,000 men and about 2,000 tanks, while Great Britain sent about 35,000 troops or 23 percent of her ground forces and 210 tanks or 16 percent of her tank forces. The French ground forces contingent came from the "Armee de Terre" section of the Force d'Action Rapide (FAR), composed exclusively of professional soldiers.

As a result of Secretary Cheney's visit to Riyadh on August 6th, President Bush gave orders for the despatch of troops to Saudi Arabia. The first of these, the 82nd Airborne Division Ready Brigade, began arriving by air on August 8th. Two days later the Arab League also voted to send ground troops, and by early September Egyptian, Syrian, Moroccan, Pakistani, and Gulf Co-operation Council forces were deployed in support of the Saudi ground forces.

In the meantime, the U.S. ground force buildup continued, with the remainder of 82nd Airborne Division, 101st Airborne (Air Assault) Division, 11th Air Defense Artillery Brigade, and elements of the 1st Marine Expeditionary Force (MEF) being deployed. The main American weakness in the early weeks was lack of armor, with only a single battalion of U.S. Marine Corps M60 tanks being present. This was rectified once the 24th Mechanized Infantry Division, with its 200 M1A1 Abrams tanks and its Bradley Infantry Fighting Vehicles (IFVs) began to arrive at the end of September. Further heavy elements became available when the British sent their 7th Armoured Brigade from Germany also at the end of September. This was put under the operational control of the 1st

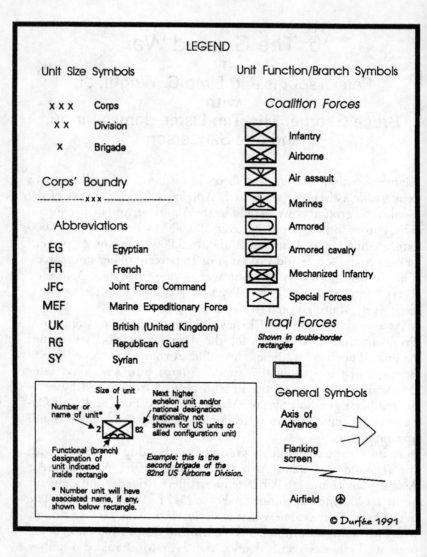

LEGEND

Unit Size Symbols

x x x   Corps

x x   Division

x   Brigade

Corps' Boundry

-------------- x x x --------------

Abbreviations

EG   Egyptian

FR   French

JFC   Joint Force Command

MEF   Marine Expeditionary Force

UK   British (United Kingdom)

RG   Republican Guard

SY   Syrian

Unit Function/Branch Symbols

Coalition Forces

Infantry

Airborne

Air assault

Marines

Armored

Armored cavalry

Mechanized Infantry

Special Forces

Iraqi Forces

Shown in double-border rectangles

General Symbols

Axis of Advance

Flanking screen

Airfield

Size of unit

Number or name of unit*

Next higher echelon unit and/or national designation (nationality not shown for US units or allied configuration unit)

Functional (branch) designation of unit indicated inside rectangle

Example: this is the second brigade of the 82nd US Airborne Division.

* Number unit will have associated name, if any, shown below rectangle.

© Durfée 1991

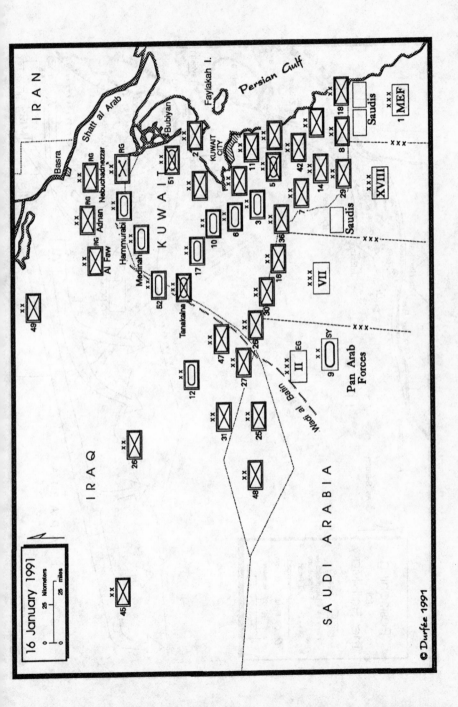

16 January 1991

© Durfée 1991

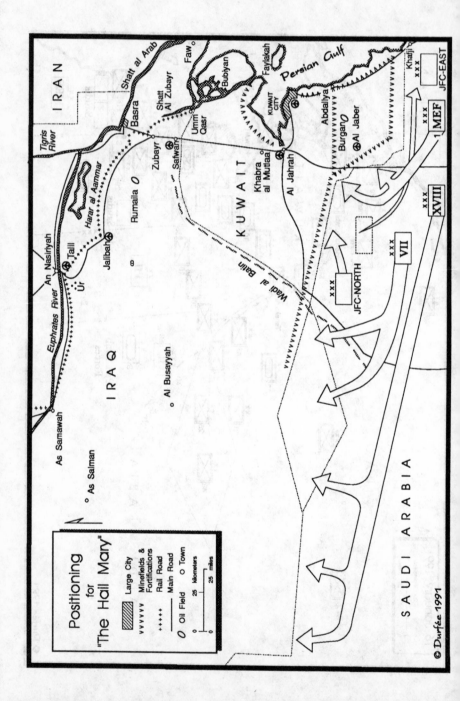

Positioning
for
"The Hail Mary"

Large City
Minefields & Fortifications
Rail Road
Main Road
Oil Field   o Town

0   25   kilometers
0   25   miles

© Durfée 1991

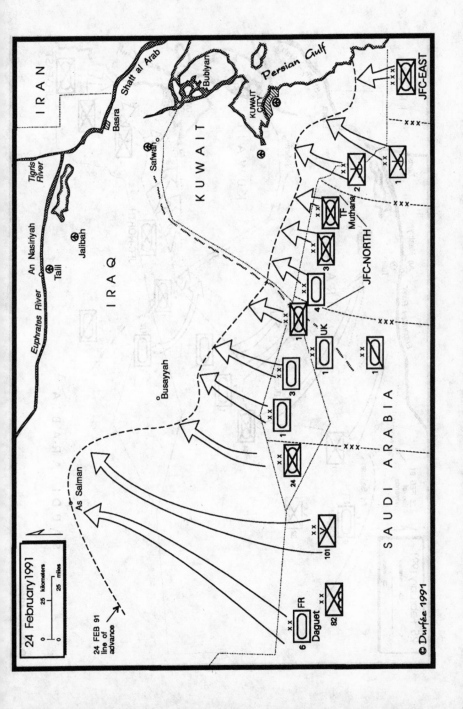

24 February 1991

0   25 kilometers
0   25 miles

24 FEB 91
line of
advance

© Durfée 1991

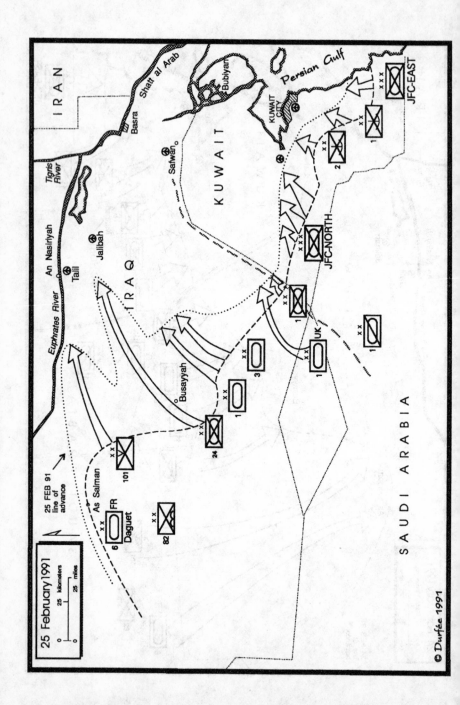

25 February 1991

0 —— 25 kilometers
0 —— 25 miles

25 FEB 91 line of advance

© Durfée 1991

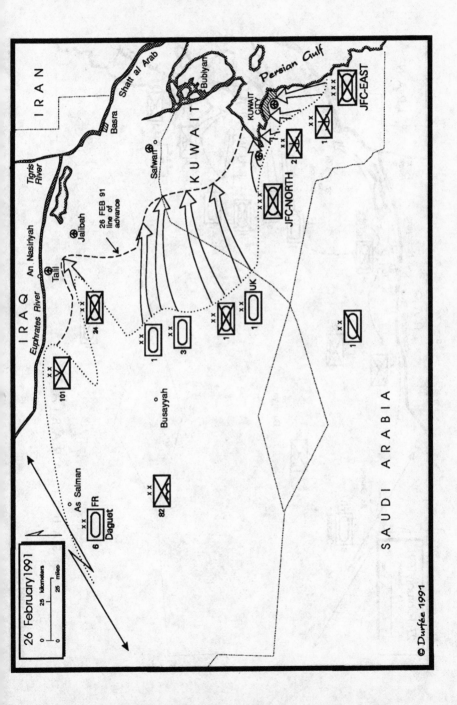

© Durfee 1991

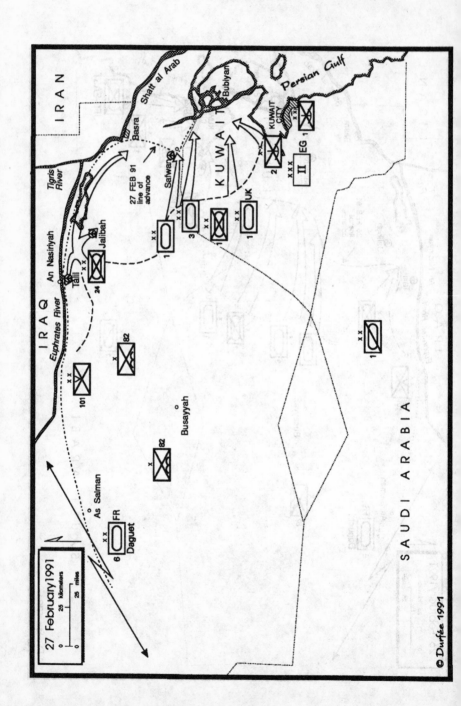

27 February 1991

© Durfée 1991

MEF. The French reacted even more quickly, with their first troops, 600 men, and 42 Gazelle and Super Puma helicopters, arriving on September 23rd. The Syrians also agreed to send an armored division and the Egyptians one armored and one mechanized division.

These initial deployments were completed by November 7th. Well before this time Saddam had, in the face of this demonstration of Coalition solidarity, given up any ideas he might have had of invading Saudi Arabia and was digging in on the Kuwaiti border. In view of his intransigence and the increasing likelihood that Kuwait would have to be wrested from him, the Coalition had to transform its planning from defense to offense. More than conscious of the spectre of Vietnam the CENTCOM planners were determined from the outset that the ground campaign must be short, sharp, and decisive, with minimum casualties. The first step towards this was to take maximum advantage of the Coalition's technological air superiority in order to persuade the Iraqis to withdraw from Kuwait, and, failing this, to prepare the battlefield for a ground offensive.

The planners also believed that it was essential to strengthen Coalition ground forces in order to achieve quantitative as well as qualitative superiority. Consequently, at the same time as Cheney's announcement on November 14th that 125,000 reservists were to be called up, the decision to deploy heavy divisions from U.S. Army Europe (USAREUR) was taken. U.S. VII Corps (1st and 3rd Armored Divisions, a brigade of 2nd Armored Division, and 2nd Armored Cavalry Regiment) was therefore ordered from Germany, and 1st Infantry Division (Mechanized) from Fort Riley, Texas. The French also agreed to reinforce their contingent to form the *Daguet* (6th Light Armored) Division and the British deployed another armoured brigade, the 4th, and other elements from Germany to form 1st Armoured Division. U.S. VII Corps would not, however, be complete in theatre until mid-February.

Other time factors which were to influence the launching of Desert Storm and the duration of the air campaign were that the region usually suffered a high incidence of sand and rain storms in late February and early March. Also, the Muslim period of fasting, Ramadan, began on March 17th. After this ended, summer would arrive, its high temperatures making it difficult for Western forces to operate effectively. Thus, it became clear to the planners that the optimum time for mounting the ground offensive was during the last two weeks of February.

During the Desert Shield period the bulk of the Coalition forces were positioned on the Saudi-Kuwaiti border. Arab forces largely held the front line, with the Syrians being responsible for much of the defense of the Saudi-Iraq border. The Syrian and Pakistani governments made it clear, however, that their forces had a strictly defensive role and would not take part in any offensive operations against Iraq.

THE SETTING

The Iraqi Design for the Battlefield

Iraq's defense in the Kuwaiti Theater of Operations (KTO) was influenced strongly by the borders that had been drawn arbitrarily in order to establish rights over water and oil, rather than to provide defensive military advantages. Having control of the known productive oil fields around Burgan and the brackish water fields both there and further westward accounted for the bend in Kuwait's border with Saudi Arabia. The boundary then ran due west to the Wadi Al Batin, a terrain feature that runs generally southwest to northeast. The border followed the wadi northeastward for lack of any better guidance until it began to approach the ancient lands of the river delta once under the control of Ur. There it curved over to the coast near the outlet of the Shatt Al-Zubayr, the secondary outlet to the Gulf from the confluence of the Euphates and Tigris rivers. Except for the coastline, none of the boundaries were marked along militarily significant terrain.

Iraqi Strategy

Iraq deployed its forces defending Kuwait so that they also served as the forward defense of Iraq. The key terrain was Kuwait City and Basra; Kuwait City because almost all of Kuwait's civilian population and almost everything of material value except for the oil were located there; and Basra because it was Iraq's second largest city, an oil processing center, a military logistics support center, and the terminus of lines of communication from Iraq's interior.

Iraq calculated that the Coalition would not attack from the desert interior because: no attack had ever been made from there;

the major roads were near the coast; there were few interior roads; and the types of desert soil varied, with exceptionally rocky and sandy places that were almost impassable to vehicles. Therefore, it concentrated its defenses along three lines: on the coast road, the direct route from Saudi Arabian cities to Kuwait City; on the bend in the border of Kuwait, the closest distance from Saudi territory to Kuwait City; and along the road parallel to the Iraq pipeline to Saudi Arabia (IPSA), on the western side of the Wadi Al Batin, the most direct route to Basra from the Saudi Army Base at King Khalid Military City.

Iraq's military experience in the Iran-Iraq War had fostered the following key beliefs: air power was not very effective in supporting ground operations, but was important as a "force in being," held back as a strategic counterweight to threaten the enemy, but losing all value when aircraft were lost in action; large ground forces were the most important part of military power; dense fortifications and heavy artillery barrages were needed to stop enemy attacks; and the strategic defense was a good means of draining an attacker's willpower. In the Gulf War, the Iraqis tried to replicate the defensive network that was effective against the Iranian infantry in the Iran-Iraq War, but the Kuwaiti environment was advantageous to the Coalition. Iraqi General Headquarters (GHQ) never saw that it was different when oriented to the south against the Allies, than when it was oriented to the west toward Iran.

Turning to strategy, Iraqi GHQ believed the Coalition would take a direct route, focusing on Kuwait City and Basra. Iraq layered its forces on the Saudi border and on the coast, putting several conscripted infantry units forward and keeping a smaller amount of armor units in reserve that would counterattack if the forward defenses were breached. The defense's strength lay in the massive amount of firepower that could be brought to bear on attackers hung up in mines and wire. The further northward the Iraqi defenses went, the better the quality of the units, and the elite Republican Guards, the center of gravity of the Iraqi defense, served as a theater reserve (see map 2).

Iraqi engineers barricaded the Saudi border. Drawing on Soviet defensive warfare doctrine, they used millions of mines as the heart of the barrier system, and then built anti-tank ditches and fire trenches. These obstacles ran from the Kuwaiti coast to beyond the Wadi Al Batin. Rows and rows of mines were bounded by barbed wire and augmented to their front (south) by fire trenches, and to the rear of the obstacles were direct and indirect fire weapons. They began a second layer behind the first, and the Allies named the entire defense "the Saddam Line" (see map 3).

The obstacles were more varied along the coast from the Saudi border northward to Kuwait City. There were underwater electric cables, wire, and mines on the approaches to the beaches and wire and mines laid between the coastal highway and shore. Wire and mines were also laid on the northern side of Kuwait Bay, under the heights of the Mitla ridge, and in the channel between the mainland and Bubiyan Island. Besides the delta marsh itself, roads in the delta region of the Shatt Al Arab and Shatt Al Zubayr at the head of the Persian Gulf were built on top of berms above the marsh, thus also acting as barriers to mobility.

State of the Iraqi Army Prior to the Ground Campaign

Coalition intelligence began assessing the condition of the Iraqi Army long before the ground campaign began. Here, human intelligence was particularly helpful. The Coalition's air campaign had been so effective that it convinced hundreds of Iraqis to surrender. These line crossers confirmed the Iraqi scheme for force deployment, the lack of logistic support for the forward infantry, a lack of combat training or knowledge about Coalition actions and deployment, and the weak points in Iraq's obstacle system. Additionally, several good human intelligence sources gave the Coalition cause to believe that the ground campaign might not be as difficult as it had expected. The line crossers reported that Iraqi soldiers were afraid to man their military equipment because so much of it was being hit with such frequency and precision. Indeed, the air campaign was blinding the Iraqis.

Deception and Reality: The Hail Mary Play

General Schwarzkopf called it the Hail Mary play, and it involved going around Iraqi defenses rather than through them. For deception, it used the U.S. Marines to fake the major thrust into the middle of the Iraqi line along the coast while the XVIII and VII Corps raced left, beyond the Saddam Line. Coalition ground forces were held in place as long as possible, and then dummy headquarters continued to fake the electronic signature of old locations. On the 16th, all CENTCOM ground forces were arranged east of a line running from Hafr Al Batin to the Saudi-Kuwaiti-Iraqi tri-border juncture. That squeezed all U.S. divisions fairly closely together. Under cover of air attacks and devastating artillery raids, U.S. Marine units swapped places with Saudi-Kuwaiti forces in the east, VII Corps moved to the end of the Saddam Line, and XVIII Corps took a giant leap westward. The 24th Infantry Division moved two weeks after the air campaign started.[1] Units of VII Corps were on its right flank, while the *Daguet* Division was on its left (see map 3).

Khafji and the Border Raids: Confirmation of Incompetence
Almost unnoticed in the initial rain of devastation from allied bombing in the air campaign were the artillery duels and small scale ground engagements that occurred along the border. Coalition ground forces were concerned about Iraqi probes. Saddam was certainly resourceful and capable of the unexpected, and if the first ground combat engagement went against the Coalition, it could affect significantly subsequent ground operations. Thus, Coalition forces on the border were on alert for a preemptive attack by Iraq's forward units.

Because of the static nature of Iraq's defense, Coalition intelligence knew precisely where the key Iraqi elements were located. Using the Global Positioning System, (the British system is called Trimble), to good effect, Coalition artillery batteries employed a "shoot and scoot" tactic; they would move up quickly so as to be within range of their target, fire, and then quickly move back out of range of any return fire. Between January 17th and 30th, U.S. Marine 155mm howitzers fired on the Iraqis, while the Iraqis fired back but never caused any significant damage. Similar actions were occurring in the VII Corps and Pan Arab sectors.

Khafji was the most intense of several small engagements that occurred before the ground campaign began on February 24th. In four separate actions from January 30th to February 1st, the 5th Iraqi Regular Army Division was rendered ineffective, losing over 500 killed, wounded, or taken prisoner. On the night of the 30th, five Iraqi T-55 tanks and 150 infantry moved into the outskirts of the town, while three simultaneous incursions were made at other points on the border. A twelve-man U.S. Marine reconnaissance unit in the town called in fires from Harriers, Cobras, and 155mm howitzers. Early the next morning, two Iraqi mechanized brigades with 4,000 troops and 80 tanks moved to contact. A column of reinforcements lost over 100 vehicles when A-10s systematically destroyed it.

On the 31st, the Qatari battalion and Saudi Army National Guard (SANG) 7th and 8th Battalions, supported by members of 5th Battalion, King Abdul Azziz Brigade, and 1st Marine Division, launched an attack to retake the town. Some observers were surprised that the U.S. Marines did not immediately launch a counter-attack, but this was because it took the Saudis over 24 hours to mount the operation. The Marines were spoiling for a fight, but at this point in the war, America did not want to appear as the only Coalition member engaged in ground force operations. Restraining the Marines from leading the counterattack paid public relations and military dividends, since the Arab forces led and repelled Iraqi forces. Although Saddam proclaimed the battle at Khafji a great victory, General Schwarzkopf described it as the time he "really began to think we are going to kick this guy's tail."

Two other actions that occurred just days before the beginning of the ground campaign forecast what would occur in that combat. On February 21st, a U.S. company assaulted an Iraqi armor and artillery position. The Iraqis lost five tanks and 20 artillery pieces, while the Americans lost one Vulcan, two Bradleys, and suffered one person killed in action and seven wounded in action. Seven Iraqis were captured. This battle loss ratio heavily favored the United States, although the ratio in the ground campaign would be even more favorable.

The Iraqis' utter lack of will to fight was manifested in the second action, which also occurred on February 21st. In it, two Apache helicopters operating with a Kiowa observation helicopter attacked and destroyed from 13 to 15 bunkers, and 450 to 500 Iraqi soldiers came out and surrendered. They were flown back to Saudi Arabia on Chinooks, and they brought the number of Iraqi prisoners of war to over 2,500.

Special Operations Forces

There are numerous claims concerning which force first struck Iraqi defenses. Eight Apache helicopters took out Soviet-made radars and special operations forces were credited with direct actions against Iraqi air defense sites. Members of the British Special Air Service (SAS) infiltrated into Iraq just before the air campaign began. They like their U.S. counterparts in special operations, the Green Berets, performed deep reconnaissance missions to designate targets for air-dropped precision guided bombs. Their weapon of choice was the laser designator. Communicating with the rear over scrambled circuits and stealing close to high value targets such as command bunkers or air defense radars, the SAS would beam lasers, "warming" or "painting" targets, at a prearranged time so that airborne aircraft such as AWACS could pick up the signal. AWACS would then direct strikes on the target. Special operations led to at least 16 mobile missile launcher kills.[2]

One report credited the SAS with direct action missions, going deep behind Iraqi lines to capture prisoners for interrogation. The SAS picked up at least 30 documents that gave the details of weapons employment plans and logistics capabilities. Other direct action missions included mining bridges, destroying communications facilities, clearing mines in the Gulf, and contaminating Iraqi aircraft fuel. One source credited the SAS with infiltrating into Baghdad and other large metropolitan areas.[3] Other officials said that none of these special forces were allowed to enter Iraq before the coalition's November decision to prepare for offensive action.

One interesting report concerned a U.S. reconnaissance team in western Iraq taking part in the great Scud hunt,[4] providing round the clock surveillance in the desert wastelands of western Iraq to augment the satellite passes overhead. These were an important indicator to Israel of the Coalition's commitment to the Scud hunting effort, and knowing that Coalition troops were in the area served to deter Israel from taking military action. The Special Operations Command of Central Command (SOCCENT) performed another important mission that reduced casualties by coordinating all Search and Rescue (SAR) missions to recover downed pilots.[5]

While it will be a while before we know of all the special operations that were conducted, American and British special forces made a significant contribution to the war effort. This was reflected on June 28, 1991, when it was announced that the British special forces had been awarded 52 medals and other honors for their actions during the Gulf War. Their main task was to counter the threat of Iraqi Scud missiles, and they performed in extremely brutal conditions – the cold was so intense that the diesel fuel froze, and some may have died of hypothermia.[6] We can assume that U.S. special forces were similarly active and that they made a similar contribution to the Coalition's victory.

SUNDAY, FEBRUARY 24, 1991

Careful timing is a basic element of any sound operations plan, and Desert Storm was no exception. Two simultaneous blows were to be struck at 0400 at either end of the long front. In the east the 1st Marine Expeditionary Force's (MEF's) two divisions and the Joint Forces Command-East would strike through the barrier system toward Kuwait City. This was a strategic deception to focus Iraqi attention on the direct approach. The second blow would fall simultaneously but more silently far to the west where the Iraqis were less alert. There XVIII Airborne Corps would make one of the great encirclements in warfare, a deep sweep that would place it in the Iraqi rear and across the route of any retreat up the Euphrates Valley (see map 4). These flank attacks would support the great crushing blow aimed at the center of the front by the VII Corps, the strongest armored corps ever assembled.

The details of this plan were changed from hour to hour almost up until the attack was begun, and eight or ten "branches or sequels" of it were drafted in order to deal with several possible contingencies. In what would become a recurring theme, timetables would be rapidly advanced and then advanced again. Because they were skilful and confident, the Coalition's military leaders used timetables as the control tools that they are meant to be. The only measure became to exploit opportunities in time by moving as fast and as far as possible.

1st Marine Expeditionary Force (MEF) and the Joint Forces Command – East (JFC-East)

The first blow of the ground campaign was struck by 1st MEF and JFC-East as they began the breach of the Iraqi barrier system in southeastern Kuwait. To meet this attack the Iraqis brought their operational reserves forward, deep into the trap CENTCOM had prepared for them. Before the attack, the 16,000–man 2nd Marine Division had been quietly redeployed from its positions near the coast farther westward to the left flank of 1st Marine Division. A deception unit had been left behind to simulate the departed division under the codename Task Force Troy. Instead of attacking due northward from near the coast, 1st MEF would attack the so-called "elbow" of Kuwait where the border with Saudi Arabia turns northward and the "armpit" where the border turns westward again. To give 1st MEF (1st and 2nd Marine Divisions) a greater armor punch, 2nd "Tiger" Brigade of the Army's 2nd Armored Division was attached. JFC-East, consisting of two Saudi, one Omani, and two composite Arab brigades, attacked directly northward from its positions along the coast.

Under darkness Marine artillery moved to the Saudi-Kuwaiti border to begin an intensive pre-assault bombardment of the Iraqi defenses, while at 0100 the 16-inch guns of the battleships USS *Wisconsin* and USS *Missouri* began raking Iraqi defenses. At 0400 1st Marine Division began its breaching operation followed at 0530 by 2nd Marine Division. Mine-breaching teams cut through the minefields. Iraqi artillery was sporadic and ineffective because the air campaign had damaged artillery units so badly that they were often less than half strength and many of the gunners were so afraid of air strikes that they refused to man their guns. Air strikes had also so shredded Iraqi communications that they could not accurately read the battlefield to find targets, and desertions among troops in forward observation positions had also blinded the Iraqi artillery. There was no one to call in fire missions and few gunners left to fire them if they had been received.

The Marines found the first defensive belt abandoned, but the Iraqi second line put up some resistance, which was defeated by circling Cobra gunships, Marine AV-8B Harriers, Navy F/A-18 Hornets, and 155mm howitzers. The Marines added to this firepower with highly accurate TOW missiles that could be fired well outside the range of the older Soviet-built tanks, and this second line quickly cracked. Iraqi tank crews abandoned their vehicles and surrendered, joining the surviving infantry who came rushing out of their bunkers waving white flags. The two Marine divisions had broken through the Iraqi barrier system with ease, shattering the 7th, 14th, and 29th Iraqi Divisions in the process. However, one regiment of the 2nd Marine Division suffered so many mechanical breakdowns that it did not successfully breach the barrier system until the second day.

As everyone did, Lieutenant General Boomer, commander of the

U.S. Marine forces in the Gulf, kept waiting for the other shoe to drop. Where was the Iraqi resistance everyone had expected? "We're taking on eleven Iraqi divisions with two Marine divisions. Our force ratios are horrible. We don't want him to know that. We're bypassing a lot of [Iraqi] folks because I have got so few forces." Prisoners were indeed the biggest problem faced by the 1st MEF. A situation report from the 2nd Marine Division commander did not ask for reinforcements or resupply but said, "We need a lot of help with POWs. I have a couple of thousand. We can't take care of them."[7]

Meanwhile, JFC-East made good progress against the Iraqi 18th Division. The Saudi Arabian National Guard (SANG) that spearheaded the attack, as it had at Khafji, was far more aggressive and efficient than the Saudi Army which "struggled to stay up with the National Guard and operated like a garrison army, highly dependent on Filipino bottle washers and Pakistani mechanics." The SANG was lightly armed compared to the Army and was recruited on a tribal rather than a national basis. Also, unlike the Army that had kept foreign advisors at arm's length, the SANG had been actively trained by U.S. advisors. "The Army was supposed to be more modern, but the SANG proved more open to reform than the Saudi land forces."[8] However, JFC-North's advance was slower than the Marines who began to worry about their increasingly unprotected western flank.

Once through the barrier system, the Marines drove inland bypassing large numbers of Iraqi troops. By day's end, 1st Marine Division had seized Al Jaber airfield and Al Burgan oilfield, destroying 21 tanks and taking over 4,000 prisoners. At Burgan, bypassed Iraqi tanks had come out of the burning oilfields to fire on the surprised Marines who recovered quickly enough to destroy them all.

To the west, Task Force Ripper of the 2nd Marine Division defeated the first Iraqi operational level counterattack in a tank battle, the first heavy fighting of the day along the entire front. The Iraqi tank column supported by the heaviest artillery fire of the day had issued from Kuwait City. By the time it had been beaten, 2nd Marine Division had 5,000 prisoners, while its losses were two destroyed tanks and three wounded Marines. Cobra gunships and fixed wing aircraft attacked and stopped several more Iraqi columns attempting counterattacks from Kuwait City.[9]

XVIII Airborne Corps

The XVIII Airborne Corps had the most complex mission and the farthest to travel of any of the ground forces. The French *Daguet* 6th Light Armored Division reinforced by the 2nd Brigade of the 82nd Airborne Division would seize As Salman and protect the corps' flank by intercepting any Iraqi attempt to reinforce the KTO down the Euphrates River Valley. The 101st Airborne Division would fly northward to seize blocking positions at Nasiriyah to sever Highway 8. The 24th Infantry Division would strike in the direction of Talil Air Base and then eastward toward Basra to envelop the Iraqis pressed back upon them by the VII Corps attack. The paratroopers of the 82nd Airborne were to secure forward operating bases for the ground forces. The 3rd Armored Cavalry Regiment screened the corps' dangerous right or inner flank to intercept any Iraqi forces counterattacking from the east. Before the attack, six Special Forces teams were sent deep into the Iraqi rear – four north of the Euphrates River and two west of the French zone – to keep a watch for reinforcements. Two were spotted by the Iraqis and were extricated quickly. XVIII Corps sent out about 15 of its own long-range surveillance detachments to report on the Iraqi.[10]

In the Corps' first offensive action, 2nd Brigade of the 82nd secured the highway that cut through the escarpment that paralleled the Saudi-Iraqi border early on the 24th. French mobile forces bounded through the escarpment bridgehead at 0530 toward their objectives at As Salman, headquarters of the 10,000-man Iraqi 45th Division. To their mortification, 2nd Brigade followed the trailing French units in buses. The 82nd Airborne Division (1st and 3rd Brigades) also followed the French, both divisions crowding down a single main supply route (MSR) in competing rather than prioritized convoys. This complete breakdown in traffic management had no unfortunate consequences due to the speed of the advance, off-road trafficability, and a lack of Iraqi interference.

Once on the road, *Daguet* took maximum advantage of the division's speed, flexibility, and firepower. The French used the "iron fist" tactic of advancing continuous waves of Gazelle helicopters armed with HOT antitank missiles, 1st and 3rd Regiments de'Helicoptere de Combat (RHC), and Jaguar aircraft, matched on the ground by an elite two hundred-man reconnaissance and action commando shock force, and French AMX 10 RC high speed wheeled reconnaissance vehicles. The French advance guard easily sliced through Iraqi defenses on the road to As Salman and conducted reconnaissance and antitank missions 60 kilometers forward of *Daguet's* operational front. Typically each regiment flew two squadrons abreast with a mix of ten antitank, six cannon-armed, and four reconnaissance Gazelles followed by Pumas to recover casualties and downed aircraft. A number of tanks were engaged early in the operation; toward the end most targets were trucks. The necessity to maintain the integrity of the aerial advance and the problem of sand obscuration caused the Gazelles to fire their HOTs well within the missile's 4,000–meter range and while on the move. Aircraft could not stop and hover to engage targets, resulting in distances as short as 1,500–2,000 meters from aircraft to target by the time of missile impact.

The need for accurate navigation was another reason for keeping tight formations. The French Nadir navigation system uses a Doppler-radar with a greater error potential than the Global Positioning System used by other Coalition aircraft. The French aircraft also did not have a night-vision capability because the Nadir system and an absence of radar altimeters did not provide sufficiently accurate navigation for night operations. Had there been more determined resistance, this could have been a serious problem.[11]

The only serious obstacle that the French faced that Sunday was a sandstorm that forced a short halt in their advance. Other than the absolute stopping power of this elemental force of nature, the sand and heat were not as severe a mechanical problem for the French helicopter force, because French equipment filters were developed for the coarser and more abrasive sand of Chad. Sand ingression did not cause the loss of a single engine in the 1st RHC, while normal maintenance servicing routines were kept during the operation.[12]

In the corps center, A-10 attack aircraft and Apache gunships raced ahead of the 101st Division. Four hundred helicopters followed, bearing an air assault brigade of 2,000 men and 50 Humvees and howitzers in the largest airmobile operation in history. Another brigade was transported overland in an operation that transported as many troops as the 101st had when it dropped on Normandy on June 6, 1944.[13] In order to better support its advance to Highway 8, the Division established a 60 square mile forward arming and refueling point (FARP) at Objective Cobra, which lay 50 miles inside Iraq.

The 3rd Armored Cavalry Regiment and the 24th Infantry Division were positioned on the right flank of XVII Airborne Corps. *Daguet* and the 82nd and 101st Divisions had advanced so rapidly that Lieutenant General Luck, the Corps Commander, advanced the H-Hour of these armored forces from 0600 on February 25th to 1500 on the 24th.

Four hours ahead of the main attack, the reinforced 2nd Squadron of the 4th Armored Cavalry Regiment (2/4 Cav) slipped through the breaches to scout out the division's two main supply routes (MSRs) and screen the main body's advance. The squadron had been reinforced from 550 to 1,235 men, mainly by the addition of an engineer company, an intelligence company, and a chemical warfare platoon. They were followed by the division's 1st Brigade with two armor battalions abreast, the 1st and 4th Battalions of the 64th Armor Regiment. Each battalion was reinforced by cross attachment to a strength of 900 men in two armor companies, two mechanized infantry companies, and an engineer company.

The division raced north cutting through blinding sandstorms and rain storms. It had 290 M1 Abrams tanks, 270 Bradley Fighting Vehicles, 72 155mm howitzers (4 battalions), 18 203mm howitzers (one battalion), nine multiple-rocket launcher systems (MLRS), 18 Apache attack helicopters, and 6,000 wheeled vehicles. It had more firepower and would plunge further – 250 miles from the Saudi border to the edge of Basra – than Patton's Third Army in 1944. The artillery alone could put 24 tons of ammunition on a target simultaneously.

This huge force was supported by an equally impressive logistics force that carried 2.5 million gallons of fuel and 17,000 short tons of ammunition. As added insurance, the division commander, Major General Barry McCaffrey, had loaded the division itself with 1.2 million gallons of fuel, enough to get it all the way to its destination.

VII Corps

The VII Corps' mission was the heart of the war plan. It was to strike a killing blow at the Iraqi Army's center of gravity – the heavy divisions of the Republican Guard, the two tank and one mechanized divisions lavishly outfitted with the most modern equipment possessed by the Iraqis. Reinforced with three Iraqi Regular Army tank divisions, these were the mass of maneuver that could counterattack any breaching forces still hung up in the defensive barrier system. The Corps' mission required a rapid breach of the barrier system and an immediate exploitation that would allow U.S. and British armor to engage the Iraqi heavy divisions in a maneuver battle. On the surface, a simple outflanking of the western end of the barrier system would have seemed sufficient. The problem was that the Iraqi heavy divisions were stacked up behind the last sector of the barrier system and could threaten the vulnerable right flank of VII Corps with their own southern flank protected by the barrier system. The plan therefore called for a simultaneous outflanking movement and a breach of the last sector of the barrier system that would grind the Iraqis from two directions at once. The breaching force would be the U.S. 1st Infantry Division, and the exploitation force would be the British 1st Armoured Division. Their mission was first to engage and destroy the 12th Tank Division and then the other two Iraqi tank divisions to the north. The 1st Infantry Division would regroup and follow the British, align itself on their right flank, and push northward with them. The outflanking forces would be the U.S. 1st and 3rd Armored Divisions. As soon as the two U.S. armored divisions had burst through the scattered Iraqi defenses, the 2nd Armored Cavalry Regiment would shoot through the breach to find the Republican Guard. The U.S. 1st Cavalry Division would demonstrate to the east in front of the Wadi Al Batin to draw the Iraq's attention while really acting as corps reserve. Once through the barrier system, the corps with its divisions on a broad front would swing northward then eastward to drive the Iraqi heavy divisions into a vice. These five heavy divisions of the joint U.S./British VII Corps had 1,300 Abrams and Challenger tanks, the largest concentration of armor in any corps in history.

Because of the unexpectedly rapid advances of the XVII Airborne Corps in the west and the Marines in the east, Schwarzkopf advanced the VII Corps attack from the evening of 24-25 February to the afternoon of the 24th. That afternoon, VII Corps sent the 1st Infantry Division's combat engineers and maneuver battalions into a breaching assault on the 26th Division's defenses. Luckily this attack struck almost on the seam between the 26th Division and the 48th Division to the west. Not since the Korean War had the U.S. Army conducted such a major breaching operation against such formidable defenses. However, incessant air strikes and an artillery preparation that dropped more ordnance on the Iraqi defenders than the 8th Army had fired at Rommel at El Alamein had practically paralyzed the defenders. There was very little defensive fire and most of that was poorly directed. U.S. reconnaissance teams were airlifted over the Iraqi sand berms to ambush counterattacks while bulldozers broke through the berms. The 1st Infantry Division conducted a breaching operation with sixteen lanes over a two mile front. They were followed by tanks to defend the first breaches with their heavy guns. Next came the combat engineers, who fired "snakes" over the minefields to clear lanes. These "snakes" were 200 yard-long high-explosive cords whose blast detonated mines and tore away barbed wire. The engineers followed the scorch marks and fired again until the minefields had been breached. They were followed by other engineers on foot marking the lanes for the passage of the following maneuver units. Other vehicles dropped modern fascines – bundles of pipe – into antitank ditches to allow tracked vehicles to cross. These were later covered with earth for the wheeled vehicles.[14] On the heels of the combat engineers came the maneuver battalions, the armor and mechanized infantry of the division, which fanned out to form a large and deep bridgehead and eviscerated the understrength 26th Division. Striking west to enlarge the bridgehead, the 1st Infantry Division hit the unsuspecting 48th Division.

The 26th Division, like most of the Iraqi divisions in the defensive barrier system, had already been abandoned by most of its officers. Only recently raised from reservists and recruits, the division had only two brigades and had never really come together as a cohesive unit. First Infantry Division's attack disintegrated it immediately. Like clockwork, the British 1st Armoured Division streamed through the breach over the stricken 26th. The armor-heavy 7th Brigade, the famed "Desert Rats", led the advance followed by the 4th Brigade. 1st Armoured Division had one reconnaissance regiment (16th/5th Lancers) equipped with Scimitar tracked reconnaissance vehicles and Striker tracked vehicles mounting Swingfire ATGW systems. The mechanized infantry was part of the two armored brigades, with 7th Armoured Brigade having two armor and one mechanized infantry battalions and 4th Armoured having one armor and two mechanized infantry battalions. The

only really significant increase to 1st Armoured Division's estab-
lishment was in artillery. Its immediate objective was to destroy
the Iraqi 12th Tank Division that had been deployed immediately
behind the 26th Division as a corps operational reserve. Remark-
ably, the Iraqis did not move out to immediately counterattack,
but seemed in a daze from the ceaseless air campaign and artillery
strikes. Within the first hour 7th Brigade's lead battalion, the
Queen's Royal Irish Hussars, had driven 25 kilometers into Iraq.
Following behind, the rest of 1st Armoured and its 2,500 armored
vehicles cleared the breach and burst into Iraq like an expanding
torrent. The Challengers and Warriors sped through the breach.

If deeds can summon the shades of man back to earth, surely 1st
Armoured at that moment recalled to this world a retired captain
of the Great War, one Basil Liddell Hart. In their dash and skilful
maneuver of the next few days, they were to prove his spiritual
heirs. Perhaps some of the Allies' high technology instruments might
have enabled someone to see the faint ghostly shimmer of the thin,
English scholar, waving 1st Armoured on.

Once through the barrier the division's two brigades wheeled to
strike 12th Tank Division from the west. The lead brigade, the
armor heavy Desert Rats, formed the left flank of the division's
attack while the following and lighter 4th Brigade formed the
southern or right flank. Initially there was only minor resistance,
but this changed when 7th Brigade's Royal Scots Dragoon Guards
Battle Group reached a large Iraqi communications complex near
Objective Copper. The Scots advanced on the complex just after
dark and staged a dismounted attack under absolutely appalling
conditions – pitch black and raining – quickly destroying a number
of tanks and several companies of Iraqi infantry in their bunkers.
The attached A Company, 1st Staffords, cleaned out the bunkers,
and the battle group then quickly moved on to its next objective,
a waterhole, reportedly defended by more infantry and dug-in
tanks. However, the British commander requested permission to
delay the assault until first light so that he could verify reports of a
hospital located there. [15]

As the Scots were at Objective Copper, the Queen's Royal Irish
Hussars and the 1st Staffordshire Regiment struck Objective Zinc.
A Milan anti-tank guided missile struck the rear of a T-55, and
"the force of the explosion literally lifted the back end of the T-55
off the ground, and the commander shot 40 feet into the air still

holding onto his hatch."[16] A 23–minute artillery barrage defeated the Iraqi defenders, and the survivors were mopped up easily. Night had fallen and Brigadier Patrick Cordingly, the 7th's commander, received permission to halt. The 7th was having difficulty picking up global positioning satellite signals, which made navigation difficult, especially in these conditions of poor visibility. Also, the Iraqi positions were much more extensive and varied than the British had been led to believe.[17] But the battle had taken on a life of its own. Within an hour, the two battle groups were advancing on "hot spots" identified by thermal sights. The brigade's forward movement toward the enemy had taken it to Objective Platinum sooner than expected.[18]

While the Desert Rats were making their wide strike through objectives Copper and Zinc, 4th Brigade's attack was keeping pace along 7th Brigade's southern flank. It engaged a number of T-55s, and one of the first was knocked out by the commanding officer of the 14th/20th King's Hussars in his Challenger. It and the 3rd Battalion Royal Fusiliers overran an infantry brigade taking large numbers of prisoners. The Royal Scots destroyed an artillery battery.[19]

Meanwhile, the two U.S. armored divisions had run over the light Iraqi forces in front of them and were driving deep into Iraq. The 2nd Armored Cavalry Regiment had passed through the armored divisions and advanced 45 miles before being ordered to stop to let the heavy divisions catch up.

Joint Forces Command (JFC)-North

To the west of 1st MEF was Arab JFC-North, the Coalition's largest and most effective concentration of Arab ground forces. From west to east were arrayed the Egyptian II Corps (4th Armored Division and 3rd Mechanized Division), the Syrian 9th Armored Division, and Task Force Muthana. The Syrian forces did not take part in the offensive for political reasons. Thus, it only initially guarded Muthana's flank, a composite unit of only two brigades – the Saudi Army 20th Mechanized and the Kuwaiti 35th "Al-Shahid" (Martyrs) Mechanized. Task Force Muthana's mission was to attack toward Kuwait City. On the 24th, it was the first to advance with the inexperienced but determined Kuwaiti brigade in the lead. The Egyptians were due to attack 24 hours after the Marines and Arabs to their east. Their II Corps was to advance on Kuwait City

to isolate the Iraqi III and IV Corps defending southeast Kuwait
from the strategic reserves deployed further to the north. Their
schedule was suddenly advanced by 14 hours due to the unexpected
successes of the Marine/Arab forces and XVIII Airborne Corps.
Surprised by the new orders, they did not begin the attack on
time, but when they did, their attack cleared away two screening
battalions that were defending a sector of the barrier system
described as more formidable than that faced by the Marines. Some
Egyptian tank and APC columns were momentarily halted, unsure
of the way through the minefields, and Iraqi artillery began firing
on them. This was the purpose of the Soviet-designed barrier
system; to hang-up the attackers in the mines and obstacles and
decimate them with artillery, but weeks of air bombardment and
the Egyptians' own strong artillery preparation had broken the
Iraqi artillery. Shelling was sporadic, and none scored a direct hit.
The defending Iraqi Division surrendered that afternoon, and at a
cost of 14 dead and 120 wounded, the Egyptians had breached the
most difficult part of the barrier system and destroyed most of an
Iraqi division.[20]

MONDAY, FEBRUARY 25, 1991

1st MEF and Arab Forces

On the morning of the 25th, Lieutenant General Boomer left his
forward headquarters in northern Saudi Arabia. Switching his
operation to a light armored vehicle, he joined a small convoy that
swept through a breach in the Iraqi defenses. He would command
from the move for the remaining three days of the campaign.
Meanwhile, 1st Marine Division completed destroying Iraqi units
around Al Jabar airfield, while on their left flank, 2nd Marine
Division and the attached U.S. Army "Tiger" Brigade broke free
and drove northward (see map 5). They met the 5th Mechanized
Iraqi Regular Army heavy division at Abdallya, quickly defeated
them, and moved on. Regimental Landing Team 5, the ground
element of the 5th Marine Expeditionary Brigade (MEB), was
flown in to become the MEF reserve since 1st MEF had pushed all
its maneuver units forward.[21]

The lack of Saudi and Kuwaiti operational experience began to
show in a collapse of traffic management and traffic snarls that
slowed their advance to a crawl. The 1st Marine Division extended

its right flank to keep in contact with JFC-East and in the process completed the isolation of the Iraqi 8th Division. Inland to the west, II Egyptian Corps finally crushed the remnants of 26th Division and moved northward toward Kuwait City. As the day ended, the blackness was deepened by the smoke from burning oil wells, and Marine commanders were forced to halt the advance from sheer blindness. Lieutenant General Boomer's convoy inched along, guided by red flashlights held by Marines along the road until finally the darkness forced him to halt as well. His convoy was isolated that night, his vehicle surrounded by two dozen Iraqi POWs. In one transmission to the rear he radioed, "It's really black out here with smoke, but everybody's okay ... There are a lot of little fights. There are EPWs [enemy prisoners of war] everywhere, including with us in the pitch dark .... I'm really pleased with the way the day went as far as I know."[22]

XVIII Airborne Corps

By the morning of the 25th the French had surrounded As Salman and by evening, had destroyed the 45th Division, capturing 2,500–3000 prisoners at a cost of two dead and 25 wounded.

From Cobra, the vast new forward operating base, the 101st Airborne Division launched an assault toward the Euphrates River Valley near Nasiriyah. 300 helicopters lifted a brigade of 3,000 men 130 miles to the north, cutting Highway 8, one of the main highways into the KTO. By the cease fire, the 101st had 8,000 men on the Euphrates, only 100 miles from Baghdad. Incredibly, this appears to have taken Saddam's High Command completely by surprise.[23] Having focused on the defense of Kuwait and now confused by the destruction of their communications system, they apparently failed to notice that an enemy corps of almost 100,000 troops had penetrated on a broad front 90 to 300 miles into Iraq. The first 32 hours after the 24th Infantry Division shot through the border berms were spent in speeding northward to a series of brigade objectives coded-named Red, Brown, and Grey. Objective Red, allotted to 1st Brigade and the battalion task forces of the 64th Armored Regiment, was furthest north, 200 miles into enemy territory. 1st Brigade reached it at 2100 hours on the 25th. By now, the 24th Mech was 36 hours ahead of schedule, and it conducted final refueling and refitting for half a day before making the leap into the Iraqi rear.[24]

VII Corps

The British 7th Armoured Brigade duly attacked Objective Zinc at 0500 hours on Monday morning. Rather than there being a hospital there, information came through that Zinc was a major Iraqi headquarters with a high ranking officer in command. A U.S. psychological operations (psyops) loudspeaker vehicle was therefore brought up to broadcast a surrender demand in Arabic. This and some warning shots flushed out 300 prisoners, but Zinc proved to be no more than a logistics site and the high ranking officer a more prosaic ordnance major.

By midday the brigade was poised to tackle its next major objective, Platinum. The western half of this was overrun by the Queen's Royal Irish Hussars. They then acted as a firm base for the Staffords, who attacked the eastern half from the north. The brigade then tackled Lead, which lay east of Platinum. Here the Staffords came up against unexpectedly stiff resistance from an Iraqi infantry battalion. Brigadier Cordingly described the engagement as "the fiercest fighting of the whole of our battle ... " Nevertheless, by first light on Tuesday the Iraqis had been defeated and over 1,000 captured, and the brigade was firm on Phase Line Smash. The Staffords had one soldier killed by an RPG 25.[25]

The Staffords had not only their own objective within Platinum to worry about but also enemy forces that spilled over from their sister battle group. As Lieutenant Colonel Charles Rodgers, Commanding Officer of the 1st Staffords, described it:

At Platinum, when the Queen's Royal Irish Hussars went through, a lot of enemy vehicles came out and tried to interfere with us, partly to counter-attack us and partly to get out of the of QRIH – like bloody pheasants bolting!

Then Milan engaged and there was quite a lot of carnage because when it hits armoured personnel carriers everyone inside is killed.

Some interesting things were happening at this time. The engineer squadron attached to us were following-up, blowing tracks and cutting barrels of Iraqi tanks to prevent them from being used. As a sand storm blew up it became quite exciting as actions took place when people bumped into each other in the darkness ... .Two T-55s came out of the murk and surprised the sappers. It was like Wacky Races as they rushed off with the T-55s in pursuit.

Mobile Milan took out lots of things – tanks, APCs, bunkers – and even took an Iraqi brigadier prisoner . . . .By the time the action was over, we had taken more than 600 prisoners. It became more and more apparent that the Iraqis did not want to fight, so there was less and less carnage. That would have been slaughter for slaughter's sake, but we are not in that business.[26]

Meanwhile, 4th Armoured Brigade had, after overrunning the southern part of Objective Copper and the smaller Objective Bronze on the first night, engaged in a pursuit operation before closing to its next objective, Brass. The Brigade secured this by noon on Monday, and the 3rd Royal Regiment of Fusiliers battle group pushed on to attack Steel. Here tragedy struck when two of its Warriors were hit by U.S. A-10s. Nine men were killed and 13 wounded. Nevertheless, Steel was secured. The Brigade was now ordered to attack Iraqi artillery positions on the edge of the Wadi Al Batin, up which the Iraqis had expected the main armored thrust to come. Codenamed Tungsten, this was subjected to a ten minute bombardment by over 100 guns and MLRS before the Royal Scots and Fusilier battle groups went in. This snuffed out virtually all resistance and many more prisoners were captured, including a general and a number of brigadiers.

For the first two days of the ground campaign, VII Corps honors had gone largely to the British 1st Armoured and the U.S. 1st Infantry, which had burst through the Iraqi defenses and now were pushing up the western edge of the Wadi Al Batin, attacking Iraqi heavy operational reserves. In doing so, they fixed Iraqi attention on their attack and prevented interference with the maneuver of the other VII Corps armored divisions. The corps had feared that Iraqi heavy units would slice across the rear of the divisions and savage their long logistics trains, but this had been prevented with a fast and aggressive attack. Von Moltke had said that a rain of blows is the best defense; VII Corps had found just the right forces to administer them.

In retrospect, the British had every reason to be pleased with their performance. From the first, British commanders had been given clear mission orders and sufficient firepower to do the job. Most importantly, each level had been allowed to fight its own engagements without undue supervision. First Armoured put to rest the British Army's reputation for the slow and methodical offensive. The brigades and battle groups had raced from one objective to another, overwhelming each in turn with a combination of firepower and assault. The willingness to risk the uncertainty of night operations when opportunities beckoned is a good case in point. British equipment also proved highly effective. The Milan AT missiles were so powerful that no second shot was required, and Challenger tanks also proved to be adept at open field running and fighting despite the reservations of many before the fighting.[27]

To the west of the British-1st Mechanized Infantry action, the 2nd Armored Cavalry Regiment continued its race northward followed by the U.S. 1st and 3rd Armored Divisions. Scattered Iraqi elements were easily overrun when the U.S. 1st Armored Division captured the road hub at Al Busayyah after nightfall and the corps' left flank had been secured. Now the Coalition's armored juggernaut would turn eastward, straight for the unsuspecting heavy divisions of the Republican Guard.

TUESDAY, FEBRUARY 26, 1991

1st MEF and Arab Forces

The third day of the ground campaign saw the final disintegration of Iraqi forces in southeastern Kuwait. First Marine Division fought its way to Kuwait International Airport where it surrounded the Iraqi 3rd Tank Division and destroyed about 100 Iraqi tanks (see map 6). Led by the Tiger Brigade, 2nd Marine Division bypassed Kuwait City to the west, seizing the chokepoint town of Al Jahra, cutting Kuwait City off from Iraqi forces to the north. The surviving 11th Iraqi Division disintegrated without contact with Allied regular forces. The honor of entering Kuwaiti City was reserved first for the Kuwaiti forces themselves and then for their fellow Arabs. Task Force Muthana was steadily grinding its way north through the Iraqi 16th, 21st, and 36th Divisions and would not arrive until the 27th.[28]

XVIII Airborne Corps

The 24th Mechanized Division rolled northward, but by 1400 when they crossed the line of departure (LD), they were in a sandstorm that reduced visibility to 25 meters. The division kept going until it reached Objective Gold, a large logistics center in the Euphrates Valley five kilometers from Highway 8 and halfway between the Iraqi airfields at Talil and Jalibah. This enormous complex contained 1,700 bunkers filled with munitions, weapons, petroleum, and other war stocks. It was defended by a four-battalion Iraqi commando brigade that was entrenched in a series of bunkers. "We must have caught them off guard," said a platoon sergeant of the 4/64 Armor, SFC Genett, "It was probably because of the storm; we came right out of the edge of it."[29]

The Iraqis recovered and attacked with small arms and RPGs. The division's first battle had begun. Abrams and Bradleys slugged through the bunker system, taking prisoners where they could and snuffing out defiant bunkers with direct 120mm main gun rounds. Iraqis swarmed around the vehicles with small arms and RPGs-below the depression angle of coaxial and turret mounted machine guns. The crews found themselves fighting back from open turrets with pistols and rifles.[30]

The division's debouch into the Euphrates valley was supported by a devastating use of artillery. Major General McCaffrey had concentrated his artillery well forward during the advance, just behind the lead 1st Brigade. His orders were clear: "Don't waste time or ammunition on targets less than a battalion in size, but when you find a suitable target, bring everything to bear with an immediate, crushing bombardment – then move out." Division artillery fired a 30 minute preparatory bombardment of all guns. The MRLS and 203mm howitzers ranged for the deep targets resulting in the complete destruction of three Iraqi artillery battalions. The four 155mm howitzer battalions provided close support to the maneuver battalions.[31]

After crushing a defending brigade, 24th Division moved a few kilometers from Objective Gold and was astride Highway 8 by early evening. Now both the air assault infantry of the 101st and the 24th had interdicted the Iraqi escape route and nothing in the Iraqi Army had the power to force them off.[32]

VII Corps
Tuesday was the day U.S. armored divisions of VII Corps would engage the heavy divisions of the Republican Guard. In their path were the Tawakalna "Trust in God," Mechanized Infantry Division and the Guard's Medinah Tank Division, as well as several Regular Army heavy divisions. The corps was disposed as follows: 1st Armored was to the north; while 3rd Armored Division and the 2nd Armored Cavalry Regiment merged with the British 1st

Armoured Division and the 1st Infantry further southward. The southern edge of the wave struck the Tawakalna Mechanized Division lines of revetments at the same time as the Shamal, a blinding northwesterly windstorm, making the conditions appalling. An ungodly mix of sand and rain swept over both sides, throwing a murk over the battlefield that defeated the naked eye. The Republican Guards sat and waited, many not even aware that the battle had come to them. Iraqi reconnaissance had long since lost any ability to see the battlefield and the weather lulled them into a false sense of security.

However, the combination of high levels of technology and training helped Coalition tankers overcome the elements. In a tactical tour-de-force that illustrated the synergism of that combination, a tank company of the U.S. 3rd Armored Division destroyed an Iraqi force over ten times larger. The U.S. soldiers sighted an entrenched line of Iraqi vehicles from 3,000 meters away without being detected. The Global Positioning System device gave the company commander his own location, and he matched his position to the intelligence overlay of Iraqi positions that had been passed electronically. According to the template he had come across the Tawakalna. Putting his own tanks on line, he ordered the end platoons to work toward the middle and his center platoon to work from the center outward. Secondary explosions of ammunition loads confirmed that the targets were armored vehicles. In minutes, 144 pieces of equipment in the Iraqi line were destroyed, and surviving Iraqi crewmen stated they had never even seen where the rounds had come from.

The battle rippled southward along the front. The 2nd Armored Cavalry Regiment, on the southern flank of the two U.S. armored divisions, was experiencing the same weather conditions. It attacked Iraqi tanks dug into revetments. Sergeant Sam Clements of I "Iron" Troop recalled, "You could just see the top of the turret over the berm. So I started shooting two or three feet down from the top. We were shooting sabot rounds right through the berms. You'd hit it, and see sparks fly, metal fly, equipment fly. We were lucky that their fighting positions were facing the other way." Another sergeant added, "We were told before the battle that you've got to hit 'em in a certain place, but anything you shot 'em with, they blew up. Usin' sabot, we blew one turret out of the hole about 20 feet. It landed upside down. And we just said, 'Yeah!'"

In five hours, 3rd Squadron, 2nd Armored Cavalry Regiment, had destroyed a Tawakalna brigade with the loss of two wounded and one Bradley lost. This action marked the end of the fighting for 2nd Armored Cavalry Regiment as it took up position behind the 1st Mechanized Division as corps reserve.[33]

As 3rd Armored Division and 2nd Armored Cavalry Regiment were destroying Tawakalna, the U.S. 1st Armored Division struck the Medinah Tank Division which was deployed in the middle of a major Iraqi training area. What ensued was described by soldiers and commanders as a feeding frenzy, and the 100 Abrams and Bradleys of 1st Brigade accounted for at least 100 Iraqi T-72s and BMPs. The accuracy of Iraqi gunners was so poor that some rounds landed at least 300 meters short of their targets. Iraqi prisoners later said that they were reduced to firing at the flashes from U.S. guns. In scenes repeated all along VII Corps' front, one observer recorded:

> Near an asphalt road that marked the center of the battlefield, Iraqi Soviet-made T-72 tanks and BMP armored personnel carriers lay charred and broken, their parts strewn for hundreds of yards in explosions that had sent flames about 80 feet into the air.
>
> Trucks had run off the roadway and now lay in battered heaps, some ripped apart by tank rounds, others crashed head-on into poles and even into one another amid what must have been the terror and confusion of the five-hour fight.
>
> Some corpses lay atop the asphalt. But other Iraqis appeared to have died in their vehicles as they burned, or were wounded and hauled away by others, their boots, gas masks and helmets scattered at road's edge and deep into the desert,the legacy of American tanks that fired killing blows from two miles away.[34]

By the day's end, Tawakalna and an attached Regular Army tank division had ceased to exist, while the Medinah Division was fleeing to the northeast with less than half its strength. Iraqi losses were 309 tanks and 318 APCs with hundreds of trucks and guns, and as many as 10,000 men. In contrast, 1st Armored Division, for example, lost two killed and 36 wounded and only four tanks and two Bradleys.[35]

Now in the extreme south of the VII sector, the British 1st Armoured Division swung east once more and closed up the Wadi Al Batin and crossed it that afternoon. There was now some confusion as to what its next task would be, either to clear the Wadi of Iraqi forces still trapped there or to continue to advance eastward in order to cut off the forces fleeing northward from Kuwait City. Major General Rupert Smith, commanding the Division, now became concerned over the danger that his armor might clash with 1st and 3rd Armored Divisions to the north to produce what he later called "one of the biggest blue on blues in history." Consequently, the British were ordered to halt where they were.[36]

WEDNESDAY, FEBRUARY 27, 1991

1st MEF and Arab Forces

Having surrounded the Iraqi 3rd Tank Division at Kuwait International Airport the night before, 1st Marine Division closed in and destroyed it in the morning. In the two-day battle at the airport, the Marines claimed 320 tanks destroyed. Almost at the same time they had to prepare for a passage of lines by the Kuwaiti 35th Mechanized Brigade. The Kuwaitis returned to their city at 0900 followed by the RSLF 20th Brigade and U.S. Special Forces, while Arabs of the JTF-East entered from the south.

Although the honor of liberating Kuwait City went to Arab forces, the Marine 2nd Reconnaissance Company also had entered surreptitiously to secure the U.S. embassy. To their surprise, the Stars and Stripes were still flying from the command flagpole, and the gates were still padlocked. At the embassy a Marine pulled another American flag from his shirt. It had been given him 23 years before, pressed into his hands by a dying buddy at the Battle of Hue in Vietnam. Now, he hung it upon the embassy gate. It was a symbol of faith and redemption; the Marine had kept faith with his friend; and the United States had redeemed its honor.

To the north of Kuwait City, 2nd Marine Division formed the southern half of the box that caught much of the Iraqi rout on the highway leading to Basra (see map 7). That afternoon the Tiger Brigade reached al-Mutlaa police station on the 6th ring road west of Kuwait City which later turns into the highway running north to Basra. The highway was covered with thousands of fleeing Iraqi troops. Initial shelling blocked the highway itself with destroyed vehicles, trapping more than 2,000 Iraqi vehicles and countless troops. Then the brigade's lead battalion, 3/67 Armor fell upon the Iraqi tanks and APCs guarding the access to the highway at the police station. In endless relays, Coalition Air Forces attacked the 25 mile traffic jam. By night the flames of the burning mass of vehicles lit the sky along the newly renamed "Highway of Death."[37] The ceasefire was announced that night. The plan of the campaign had succeeded brilliantly. The large and well-armed enemy garrison fled out of Kuwait City without a fight and then was trapped in a classic slaughter.

At the end of the day Lieutenant General Boomer drove his command convoy through the streets of Kuwait. Crowds of joyous, flag-waving Kuwaitis thronged around the vehicles shouting their thanks and throwing candy, turning the drive into an instant victory parade. Not since the liberation of Paris in 1945 had American troops been so greeted. For Boomer it was one of the most emotional moments of his life. "It was fun – and I can't remember the last time I had fun."[38]

XVIII Airborne Corps

On Wednesday the division would have that rare and heady experience of being an armored force stampeding in the enemy's rear. McCaffrey and the 24th would join a select club – Rommel and his Ghost Division in France in 1940; Guderian and his Panzer Corps in Russia in 1941; and Patton and his Third Army in France in 1944. At 0400 hours the brigades of the 24th Mechanized were moving in three directions along the Euphrates River. 1st Brigade moved eastward down Highway 8, defeating the eternally surprised Iraqis; the 197th Mechanized Brigade headed westward to overrun Talil Air Base; and 2nd brigade attacked southward toward Jalibah Air Base. Preceded by an artillery barrage, 2nd Brigade's tanks raced across the runways at Jalibah at dawn, destroying ten MiG jet fighters, and a dozen helicopters. Forty miles to the west along Highway 8, near the ancient Sumerian ruins of Ur, the 197th Brigade demolished the air base at Talil. Next to the ziggurat of Ur, one of the great archaeological treasures of the world, the Iraqis had tried to hide some of their jets from the Coalition air campaign.[39]

The 1st Brigade roared a hundred kilometers down Highway 8 towards Basra, running over retreating Iraqi columns. Scores of blazing, twisted Iraqi vehicles were left burning along the highway. Later that day the 24th Mech engaged the Hammurabi Tank

Division about 20 miles from Basra. Before the Hammurabi broke and fled back toward Basra, it had lost six battalions.[40]

VII Corps

The previous day's hammer blow from VII Corps had sent the remnants of the Republican Guard and Iraqi Regular Army heavy divisions fleeing northward and eastward, and the two U.S. armored divisions ran over every Iraqi attempt to conduct an organized retreat. The Iraqis tried tank ambushes and leapfrogging back one element through the other's overwatch, but nothing worked. Because of their superior training and aggressiveness, the small U. S. units were always eagerly seeking the enemy. Superior tank thermal sights ensured early acquisition of Iraqi ambushes through haze, smoke, and sand; and superior tank gunnery skills meant that these units fired the classic first shot desired in tank engagements – the killing shot. And over the ground battle Apache helicopters and Thunderbolt aircraft hunted with equal aggressiveness despite the heavy obscuration. Eight hundred tanks drove the Iraqis eastward and northward. Only 300 tanks remained from the Hammurabi, Medinah, and Regular Army heavy divisions. During the ground campaign Iraqi tanks had sparked and flamed, dying one after another as unit integrity wilted, then collapsed entirely. The arrogant Republican Guard became a mob running for safety.

In the Battle of Medinah Ridge, the 2nd Brigade of the Medinah Division, augmented by elements of an army mechanized division, was thrown across VII Corps' path in a desperate rear guard effort. The Iraqis had positioned themselves in a revetted defensive line six miles long to strike VII Corps tanks after they had crossed a ridge to their front. Rain came down as the tanks of the 2nd Brigade, 1st Armored Division approached the ridge. They stopped at 2,500 meters and began to pick their targets. Iraqi fire fell well short. T-72s quickly began turning into fireballs. A hit on a T-72 would cause an "initial splash of sparks as the depleted uranium round penetrated the armor of the tank. Then there would be a huge secondary explosion as the ammunition stowed inside the Iraqi tank detonated and the turret would usually pop off." One battalion commander said, "It was like driving through Dante's inferno." The 40–minute battle cost the Medinah 60 T-72s, nine T-55s, and 38 APCs. With grudging respect, 2nd Brigade's commander,

Colonel Montgomery Meigs said, "These guys stayed and fought."[41]

The British 1st Armoured Division had been unleashed once more at 0630 hours on Wednesday. They had, however, used the pause to good effect in order to organize their logistics support so that it could meet any eventuality. The Division was ordered to cut Iraqi egresses from Kuwait City, and arrived on its objective virtually as the ceasefire was announced. The only concern that the British had during this final phase was that Soviet-built vehicles of the Pan-Arab forces on their southern flank might be mistaken for Iraqi forces, an event that fortunately did not occur.

LESSONS LEARNED

There were many lessons to be gleaned from the ground campaign. In command and control, General Schwarzkopf and his planners developed an ambitious and imaginative plan, reflecting the General's confidence in his forces to execute it. Considering the diverse nature of the Coalition's ground forces, they meshed surprisingly well. In contrast, the success of the air campaign in disrupting Iraqi C^3 left their forces unable to move, let alone to operate effectively. This was reflected when the Iraqi generals sent to negotiate a ceasefire showed total surprise when Schwarzkopf revealed to them how much of southern Iraq had been overrun. Given, however, the high speed of the Coalition's operations, it was inevitable that at times the information flow, in spite of excellent communications, could not keep up with what was happening on the ground and it was this that really caused the "blue on blue" encounters.

The Coalition's use of deception was highly successful, probably reflecting the attention paid in recent years by NATO forces to the use of *Maskirovka*, especially in World War II.

Another lesson concerns fixed defenses. They have often been of value, but as has often been demonstrated in history, their weakness is that a determined enemy, given sufficient time and study, can always overcome them.

The ground campaign proved once again (as if further proof were necessary) that well trained, well motivated, and well led forces will prevail over poorly trained, poorly motivated, and poorly led troops. No matter what scientific and technological advances are made on the battlefield, this axiom holds true from the highest to the lowest ranks of an army and must never be forgotten.

Concerning equipment, the war proved the effectiveness of Abrams, Bradley, Challenger, and Warrior on the battlefield. However, this conclusion should be qualified by the caveat that equipment is only as good as the troops who operate it, and the competence of Coalition personnel was as important as the equipment in producing such a startling victory.

Logisticians certainly provided Coalition forces with the sustainability necessary to achieve a quick and decisive victory. However, if the air situation had been one in which the Coalition did not enjoy total air supremacy, then the Allies might have had problems. Certainly, they would not have enjoyed the luxury of despatching long columns of nose-to-tail vehicles to travel along roads in daylight. Tribute, though, must be made to the logisticians for their achievements in moving the vast quantity of supplies when the *Schwerpunkt* was switched to the west.

As the United States learned in Vietnam, today's telecommunications are such that they have heightened the interrelationship of the political and military aspects of a war, to the extent that the two are now very symbiotic, and an occurrence in one realm can prompt a reaction in the other that will, in turn, impact on the first. The best example in the Gulf War was the "Highway to Hell." Undoubtedly it was the television coverage of the carnage on this which persuaded President Bush to call a halt when he did. In retrospect, there perhaps was a good argument for carrying on to destroy the remainder of the Republican Guard in the Basra area, but at the time the belief was that public opinion might have been disgusted by this. By then the objective of the war – the liberation of Kuwait – had been achieved and to go beyond this would have been exceeding the UN remit.

On the other hand, retreat is an operation of war and no firm evidence has come to light that the seeming rabble escaping from Kuwait City tried to surrender before they were hit. For example, although the cease fire went into effect on the 28th, the Iraqis were still not entirely convinced of their predicament. In a brazen attempt to save their remaining Republican Guard heavy division elements, they tried to brush past the 24th Infantry Division and escape across a causeway over the Euphrates. Just before dawn Iraqi forces trying to clear a path to the causeway fired on the mechanized infantry of the 24th's 1st Brigade. Artillery and Apache and Cobra gunships struck back, and one Cobra blocked the causeway by destroying the lead tank with a TOW missile. Then 1st Brigade pressed in from three sides, leaving a trail of shattered and burning Iraqi vehicles in its wake. The two armor battalion task forces, 1/64 and 4/64 Armor, trapped the Iraqis along a path between Highway 8 and a large lake to the north – the Harar Al Hammar. Survivors fled into the marsh again, leaving the tell-tale Iraqi sign of defeat – hundreds of pairs of boots and shoes on the water's edge.[42]

Concerning special forces, the lesson is that they are most effective when they are used to further the strategic rather than the operational plan. This was so in the Gulf, both in their operations against Iraqi C^3 and against the Scud launchers.

NOTES

1. Dennis Steele, "Tanks and Men: Desert Storm from the Hatches," *ARMY* (June 1991).
2. Paul McEnroe, "Commandos in Iraq Guide Allied Bombers," *Minneapolis Star-Tribune*, February 21, 1991.
3. Spike Van Pelt, "SAS Dares in the Gulf", *Soldier of Fortune* (July 1991); and R. Jeffrey Smith, "U.S. Special Forces Carried Out Sabotage, Rescues Deep in Iraq," *The Washington Post*, March 4, 1991.
4. Authors' conversation with CPT Brian LeSieur, U.S. Army, June 10, 1991.
5. Smith.
6. Michael Evans, "SAS Mission to Cripple Scuds Earns 41 Awards," *The Times*, June 29, 1991.
7. Molly Moore, "Commander Waged War From Battlefield Convoy," *The Washington Post*, March 3, 1991, p. A32.
8. David Ottaway, "For Saudi Military, New Self-Confidence," *The Washington Post*, April 20, 1991, p. A14.
9. Edwin H. Simmons, "Getting the Job Done," Naval Institute *Proceedings* (May 1991).
10. "Outflanking Iraq," *The Washington Post*, March 18, 1991.
11. Murray Hammick, "Gazelle HOTs Extend French Anti-Armor Reach," *International Defense Review* (5/1991): 456.
12. Ibid.
13. John Pomfret, "In 'Bodacious Action,' 300 Copters Lift 2,000 Troops 50 Miles Inside Iraq," *The Washington Post*, February 25, 1991.
14. Peter David, *Triumph in the Desert* (New York: Random House, 1991), p. 84.
15. "The Thrust Into the Unknown," *Soldier* (April 1, 1991): 9–10.
16. Mark Banks, "Back from the Dead," *Soldier* April 1, 1991): 13.
17. Robert Fox, "The 100–Hour Battle," *Daily Telegraph Magazine*, April 20, 1991.

18. "Thrust Into the Unknown," p. 10.

19. Harvey Elliott, "Border Corps Paves the Way," *The Times*, February 28, 1991.

20. Ottaway, p. A14; and Patrick Bishop, "Slowly But Surely, Egyptians Topple Iraqi Troops," *The Washington Times*, February 26, 1991.

21. Moore, "Commander Waged;" Frank Chadwick, *Gulf War Factbook* (Bloomington: GDW, Inc., 1991); and Simmons, p. 96.

22. Moore, "Commander Waged," p. A33.

23. John Pomfret, "101st Flies 8,000 Soldiers into Iraq, Cuts Major Road," *The Washington Times*, February 28, 1991, p. B1.

24. Galloway.

25. "Thrust Into the Unknown," p. 10; and Charles Rodgers, "Courage and Luck Amid All the Carnage," *Soldier* (April 1, 1991): 12.

26. Rodgers, p. 12.

27. "Thrust into the Unknown," p. 11.

28. Chadwick, p. 83.

29. Steele.

30. Ibid.

31. Robert H. Scales, Jr. "Accuracy Defeated Range in Artillery Duel," *International Defense Review* (5/1991): 481.

32. Steele; and Scales.

33. William H. McMichael, "Iron Troop's Trial by Fire," *Soldier* (June 1991): 8–12.

34. Douglas Jehl, "Truce Halts Tanks On Brink of Battle," *The Washington Post*, March 2, 1991, p. A11.

35. Ibid.

36. Fox.

37. Tony Clifton, "Move Forward and Shoot the Things," *Newsweek* (March 11, 1991): 46; and Moore, "Commander Waged."

38. Moore, "Commander Waged," p. A33.

39. Galloway, p. 33.

40. Rick Atkinson, "Outflanking Iraq: Go West, 'Go Deep'," *The Washington Post*, March 18, 1991, p. A14.

41. Michael R. Gordon, "G.I.'s Recall Destruction of Powerful Iraqi Force," *The New York Times*, April 8, 1991, p. 6.

42. Atkinson, p. A15; and Steele, p. 33.

7: Naval Operations
by
B. L. Cyr, Bruce W. Watson, Raimondo Luraghi, Bruce George, MP, Tim Lister, and James Piriou

ASSEMBLING THE COALITION NAVIES

The U.S. and British navies were the first to respond to the invasion of Kuwait, and they would continue to detail ships until the war ended. Other nations' navies would join in a multinational navy that would accomplish the following missions: enforce the sanctions against Iraq; keep the Gulf free of mines and protect the seaborne delivery of supplies; conduct shore gunfire support and surface-to-surface missile strikes against land targets; defeat Iraq's Navy; conduct bombing sorties and provide close air support for ground troops with its sea-based air power; and prepare for a possible amphibious assault.[1]

Even after the naval presence east of Suez ended, the Royal Navy maintained the Armilla Patrol, which was begun in 1980 to protect British merchant shipping during the Iran-Iraq War. It was continued after the war ended and thus was close by when the invasion occurred. One of three ships in the Armilla Patrol, the Sea Dart-armed destroyer HMS *York*, was already in the Gulf, while the other two, the frigates *Battleaxe* and *Jupiter*, had been visiting Penang and Mombasa. They and their oiler, the Royal Fleet Auxiliary (RFA) *Orangeleaf*, returned rapidly. To bolster this patrol and provide a needed mine warfare capability, three *Hunt*-class mine countermeasures vessels (MCMVs), *Atherstone*, *Hurworth*, and *Cattistock*, were sent from Great Britain. They were supported by HMS *Herald*, a survey ship that was to serve as the headquarters and control vessel for mineclearing operations. Three Royal Air Force Nimrods that arrived at Seeb, Oman ten days after the invasion provided maritime air support (see chapter 5). The RFA tanker *Olna* and repair ship *Fort Grange* were deployed, while the repair ship *Diligence* was sent from the Falklands. A fourth escort, the guided missile destroyer *Gloucester*, was sent to joint the Armilla force before the end of August. The escorts were relieved in October by the frigates *London* (flagship of the British commodore in theatre) and *Brazen*, and the destroyer *Cardiff*, a veteran of the Falkland Islands War. These ships and *Gloucester* were the cutting edge of the Navy's presence in the Gulf during the war. Their reliefs, the destroyers *Manchester* and *Exeter* and the frigates *Brave* and *Brilliant*, arrived shortly before the end of hostilities. Like *Cardiff*, *Exeter* and *Brilliant* had seen successful Falklands service, during which the three ships had downed a total of seven hostile aircraft.

Two more *Hunt* MCMVs arrived before the end of 1990, as did the helicopter training ship *Argus*, which was used as a "primary casualty receiving ship," a forward ambulance station with none of the protection offered by hospital ship status. Due to the peculiarities in the Royal Navy's system, the *Argus* was an RFA, not a commissioned unit, but this did not preclude her use in the forward area, where her four Sea King transport helicopters were used for mine-spotting and her deck and maintenance facilities supported the escorts' Lynx attack helicopters. Another RFA used on the front line was the LSL *Sir Galahad* (one of four LSLs that ferried 7 Armoured Brigade vehicles to Saudi Arabia) that gave technical support to the *Hunts* after delivering an Army cargo.

On August 2nd, the U.S. Middle East Force was already on station in the Persian Gulf, providing a modest naval presence. However, the carriers *Eisenhower*, on station in the Mediterranean and *Independence*, near Diego Garcia, were both redeployed so that by the 8th, *Eisenhower* was on station in Red Sea and *Independence* was in the Gulf of Oman. If required, *Independence* could have launched long-range strikes as early as the 5th. On the 22nd, *Saratoga* and two guided-missile destroyers passed southbound through the Suez to relieve *Eisenhower*, while the battleship *Wisconsin* passed through the Strait of Hormuz into the Persian Gulf on the 24th. *Independence's* entrance into the Gulf on October 1st was the first time that a U.S. carrier had been there since *Constellation* in 1974, and the timing of her entrance was meant to coincide with Iraqi National Day on the 3rd. The Navy hoped to avoid sending aircraft carriers into the Gulf because it is narrow and shallow, which limits significantly the sea-room needed for flight operations, because carriers must steam into prevailing winds to launch aircraft, and extended steaming in any direction except on the northwest-southeast axis in the Gulf would bring a carrier into shallow water.

Airspace constraints were equally important if the aircraft were to remain outside Iranian territorial limits. Still, the carriers had to be sent into the Gulf because the range limitations of the F/A-18s meant that if they were launched in the Arabian Sea, they would have to refuel in flight or at a land base to reach Kuwait and Iraq.[2]

At the beginning of the air campaign on January 17th, there were 108 U.S. Navy warships in the region: 13 ships, including three cruisers and two destroyers, in the eastern Mediterranean; 25 ships, including the *America, Saratoga, Kennedy*, and *Roosevelt* carrier battle groups, in the Red Sea; about 40 ships, including the *Midway* and *Ranger* carrier battle groups, the battleships *Wisconsin* and *Missouri*, two command ships, four cruisers, five destroyers, and two hospital ships in the Persian Gulf; and about 30 ships in the northern Arabian Sea. There were also 13 attack submarines; eight conducted reconnaissance and provided warning screens for the carriers as they voyaged the Mediterranean en route to the Gulf, and five more, including two that conducted submerged submarine-launched cruise missile attacks against Iraq, were added after the war began.[3]

A mission of the Coalition navies was to protect seaborne deliveries of equipment. During the war, U.S. Military Sealift Command (MSC)-controlled ships delivered 3.4 million tons of cargo and 6.8 million tons of fuels. This accounted for over 90 percent of all cargo transported into the theater and was four times the cargo moved across English Channel in support of the D-Day invasion, and over six times the peak force build-up during a similar six month period of the Vietnam War.[4]

France responded with operations *Artimon* and *Salamandre*. Seven ships were sent to the Hormuz Strait, while the aircraft carrier *Clemenceau* and three frigates were also deployed, and French naval units patrolled key areas off Hormuz Strait and the Straits of Bab-el-Mandeb and Tiran. 6,800 naval personnel and 34 ships with their helicopter detachments, about a tenth of the entire French Navy, participated in the war. Italy's naval response was a squadron composed of 20th Group, consisting of a destroyer, five frigates, three corvettes, two supply ships, and one support ship. Under the command of a Rear Admiral, this 2,400–man contingent included several troops from the "San Marco Battalion," the Italian equivalent of Marines. All Italian forces in the Gulf were under the command of an Army general who operated from a small command post with a group of Carabinieri (military police) at Abu Dhabi. Other Italian ships were in the Mediterranean to guard against Libyan or other hostile action.

Other Coalition nations also committed naval power to the force so that it was eventually composed of ships from 16 nations (see Appendix F).[5] Communications were established with the U.S. Navy, other NATO/WEU allies, and with Royal Australian Navy using NATO procedures and cryptographic systems. Other nations procured equipment to communicate, but the only means to talk with Soviet, Pakistani, Argentinean, and Arab maritime forces was through signalling and VHF communications.

THE EMBARGO

Since several nations differed as to how the blockade should be upheld, the first issue was to develop rules of engagement. Some wanted to operate in the Gulf, while others preferred the Red Sea. Some allowed their ships to fire warning shots or let their crews board suspicious ships, while others did not. On August 14th, the United States said it would block ships carrying cargo to or from Iraq, justifying its actions on the basis that the exiled Kuwaiti government had requested aid, and that under Article 51 of the UN Charter, nations are entitled to act in self-defense. The Royal Navy's ships and helicopters assisted in implementing the embargo from its inception and Australian ships joined the blockade, pledging that they would stop and search all ships seeking to trade with Iraq. France joined, but would not stop ships breaking the blockade because that would make her a co-belligerent. A major concern was evidence that Iraq had set up Silkworm antiship missiles in Kuwait. A Chinese-made missile with a 60–mile range, it could attack warships as they tried to stop ships in the Gulf from approaching Kuwaiti or Iraqi ports.[6]

Overall coordination of maritime interception forces fell to Commander, U.S. Middle East Force. The Navy was to board and search cargo ships and tankers, and could use minimum force, such as shots across the bow, or take ships into custody to prevent them from reaching port. The term "intercept," meant that the directive fell short of a blockade, which potentially would have been an act of war against Iraq. On the 17th, the guided-missile cruiser USS *England* and the frigate USS *Bradley* stopped two Iraqi coastal ships in the Gulf, but allowed them to proceed when it was determined that they were empty. These were the first ships inspected during the official blockade. The first U.S. shots fired in the confrontation came from USS *Reid*, which fired a warning salvo across the bow of an Iraqi tanker.[7]

Italian forces began to participate in the embargo in August, as their naval ships stopped, identified, and inspected merchant ships voyaging in the area. Joint co-ordination with the Western European Union (WEU) was extremely efficient during the Gulf War and, under French Presidency, it was very successful in directing the Union's naval embargo. French ships conducted more than 7,500 missions, of which 160 involved checking suspect ships and four required stopping ships. The embargo was quite successful. By May 1, 1991, over 29,700 merchant ships had been challenged, more than 1,200 boarded and inspected, and at least 67 diverted for carrying prohibited cargo. As a result, Iraq's GNP was reduced by one-half.[8]

THE MINE WARFARE CAMPAIGN

Essential to the allied strategy was the U.S. amphibious force that threatened the Iraqi's seaward flank in Kuwait. As a precursor to any landing, and to maintain the enemy's belief in the likelihood of assault from the sea, it was necessary for the allies to clear a channel through the extensive minefields believed to have been laid in the approaches to Kuwait Bay and the offshore island of Faylakah. On February 16th, Royal Navy MCMVs and U.S. Navy minesweeping helicopters began to clear a route towards the Kuwaiti coast, initially to provide a secure area from which U.S. battleships could bombard Iraqi positions. The only other modern minehunter available was the USS *Avenger*; like those of the three 1950s-vintage MSOs that made the remainder of the U.S. Navy's surface minehunting contribution, her crew was relatively inexperienced in this form of warfare.

The mine warfare battle was waged with the forces available. On January 21st, four U.S. Navy A-6s in the northern Gulf attacked an Iraqi T-43–class mine warfare ship that was capable of laying 20 mines, and Navy aircraft later attacked three unidentified Iraqi boats in the same area, sinking one of them. On the 23rd, A-6s attacked an Iraqi patrol boat, tanker, and hovercraft, sinking or disabling all of them, while Coalition forces destroyed 24 free-floating mines in the Gulf. Saudi and British forces then destroyed two Iraqi minelayers near Qurah Island, which was an Iraqi forward command post. U.S. naval personnel then took the island, killing three Iraqis and capturing 51 in the process. On the 25th, the Sea Island Terminal off Kuwait was set afire during a skirmish between U.S. Navy ships and an Iraqi ship that was laying mines.

The mine clearance task was complicated by the Iraqi's "mix" of buoyant moored contact mines and influence mines on the seabed and delayed from time to time by Silkworm warnings that required temporary withdrawals. That there was a very considerable risk was shown by the mining, in the early hours of February 18th, of two major U.S. warships, the assault helicopter carrier *Tripoli* and the guided-missile cruiser *Princeton*, that strayed from the swept channel and were severely damaged. *Tripoli* struck a mine with the explosive force of 1,500 pounds of TNT, and about three hours later, *Princeton* was damaged by an influence mine that was designed to lie on the bottom and explode when triggered by sound, water pressure, or a ship's magnetic field. She suffered structural damage to her hull near the stern and to a propeller, forcing the captain to shut down one of her two turbines.[9] By the 23rd, a fire support area was cleared and the first battleship was able to take up this bombardment station in readiness for the beginning of the land offensive. A Royal Navy Type 42 missile destroyer was permanently allocated to "ride shotgun" for the air defense of the battleship, and early on the 25th, HMS *Gloucester* proved the necessity of this task, and the effectiveness of the "Sea Dart" system, by destroying the only Silkworm surface-to-surface missile to approach allied forces.

During the days that followed, the MCMVs expanded the fire support area in preparation for landings on Faylakah, approaching to within 21,000 yards of the Kuwaiti coast. The swift collapse on the land front rendered an assault on the island unnecessary, but the obvious threat posed by the Marines had contributed to the brief campaign, for it had tied down substantial numbers of enemy troops who continued to face seaward up to the beginning of their withdrawal. By the ceasefire on the 28th, the MCMVs had located and disposed of 191 mines. The clearance work continued and a channel was driven through to the coast. On March 12th, HMS *Cattistock* led a small allied convoy into the first mainland Kuwaiti port to be reopened. Throughout, the MCMVs and their support ships were protected by Type 42 destroyers and Type 22 frigates. Not far behind, and barely beyond the extreme range of the Silkworms, *Argus* provided invaluable helicopter support facilities for the British and U.S. Navies alike, the repair ship *Diligence* provided assistance that included advice to the damaged U.S. Navy ships, and other RFAs provided replenishment. During the final days of fighting, the goalkeeper for this "second line" group was the frigate *Brilliant*, the first ship deployed to a combat area to include members of the Women's Royal Naval Service (the "Wrens") in her ship's company.[10]

The complexity of Iraq's sea mining became clear when Iraq provided charts of its minefields to the Coalition after the war. It had laid over 1,200 mines centered in ten separate areas but in two mine belts, one inside the other, in concentric arcs that extended 40 miles off the Kuwaiti coast. The fields had bottom influence mines that were activated by a ship's noise or magnetic field, and contact mines suspended below the surface on cables attached to anchors, and were set to explode on contact. By March 26th, more than 270 mines had been destroyed. The British flotilla clearly had the most advanced knowledge and is perhaps the best force in the world today. U.S. and British forces were later joined by French, Belgian, Dutch and German ships to clear the ten fields, and by April 14th, 633 mines had been found.[11]

THE SEA CONTROL CAMPAIGN

From January 18th, a well coordinated U.S. Navy-Royal Navy offensive was waged against the Iraqi Navy which, though small, had a significant number of fast attack craft armed with a mix of combat-proven Soviet and Western anti-shipping missiles. U.S. carrier aircraft attacked the naval base at Umm Qasr and mined the channels leading to it, thus forcing out the small craft while bottling-up large ships. Once in the waters off Bubiyan Island, the ships were exposed to direct attack by American and British aircraft, Royal Navy destroyers' and frigates' Lynx helicopters. Eleven days after the outbreak of the war, Iraqi ships attempted to break out of Umm Qasr en masse, apparently hoping to seek asylum in Iranian ports, but were continuously and repeatedly attacked. Those that survived this attempt repeated the experience in mid-

February; thereafter, to all intents and purposes, the Iraqi Navy ceased to exist. RAF Nimrod patrol aircraft, operating well north of the Saudi-Kuwaiti border, were instrumental in locating many targets and Royal Navy helicopters, operating as the teeth of Anglo-U.S. Lynx/SH-60 "hunter/killer" teams, enjoyed considerable success with their Sea Skua air-to-surface missiles. They claimed hits on 17 Iraqi ships and craft between January 28th and February 16th, including five TNC 45 Exocet-armed FPBs, two T-43 mine-sweepers, two Polnocny LSMs, two Spasilac patrol boats, two Zhuk boats, and two assault boats, amounting to the largest share of anti-surface action in the war.

Throughout the allied offensive, the Royal Navy's Type 42 guided missile destroyers operated in the northern Gulf, usually as the most advanced allied units, on the forward antiaircraft screen. Fully integrated into the U.S. Navy's antiair warfare defensive organization, they controlled carrier fighter combat air patrols (CAPs) for local defense and for "de-lousing" returning strikes, to ensure that Iraqi aircraft were not attempting to use the allied formations to cover a surprise attack. At the same time, they were ideally positioned to make the best use of their missile-armed Lynxes in the inshore game.

Italian naval ships were also tasked with protecting U.S. carriers and were ready to support amphibious operations. The embarked helicopters flew a total of fifty missions protecting ships, identifying mines, and checking suspected naval craft. The Italian contingent was replaced on April 15th by a contingent of three minesweepers, two frigates and one support ship.

ANTI-SHORE OPERATIONS

Beginning with a Tomahawk firing from *San Jacinto* in the Red Sea (the first combat firing of Tomahawk) and moments later from *Bunker Hill* in the Persian Gulf, U.S. battleships *Missouri* and *Wisconsin*, cruisers, destroyers, and submarines fired more than 100 Tomahawk land-attack cruise missiles in the first 14 hours of the war. With a 2,500–kilometer range and a circular error probable (CEP) of 280 meters, Tomahawks destroyed air defense systems and fortified military complexes, such as command and control centers, fixed Scud sites, and nuclear and chemical weapons plants. By the end of the war's second and third days, a total of 196 and

216 Tomahawks, respectively, had been fired at reinforced targets, including Iraqi nuclear facilities that were completely destroyed. During the war, 288 Tomahawks were fired from the Red Sea, Persian Gulf, and eastern Mediterranean from nine cruisers, five destroyers, two battleships, and two nuclear-powered attack submarines, at targets in and around Baghdad. The submarine *Louisville* fired the first submarine-launched Tomahawk in combat while submerged on patrol in the Red Sea on January 19th, and the *Pittsburgh*, on patrol in the Mediterranean, fired Tomahawks that flew over Turkey before hitting Iraq.[12] Tomahawk proved to be an extremely reliable weapon, effectively destroying vital Iraqi air defense systems, which made Coalition fighter and strike aircraft operations much safer. However, at issue is its accuracy. The Navy said that Tomahawks hit more than 85 percent of their targets, which, while impressive, also means that about 43 of these high tech weapons did not hit their targets. While it was known before the war that the Tomahawk's route must be intricately programmed if it is to hit its target, the war showed the missile must fly over distinct terrain in order for its guidance system to work properly. As the terrain features that guided the Tomahawks were destroyed in the war, the missiles could not find their targets. According to a senior Navy official, "It has to fly over certain kinds of terrain to work. If you fly it over flat desert it doesn't work."[13]

Concerning shore bombardment operations, at Normandy in 1944, the Germans had considered Allied naval gunfire as great a problem as Allied air supremacy and the same held true for Iraqi forces. On February 3rd, the battleship *Missouri* fired her 16-inch guns for the first time in combat since the Korean War, and on the 6th, *Wisconsin* fired her 16-inch guns in battle, also for the first time since the Korean War, targeting an Iraqi artillery position. With this action, *Missouri* and *Wisconsin*, joined *New Jersey*, which had bombarded positions in Lebanon in 1983, as having fired their guns in combat in recent U.S. naval reactions. In the 33 missions that *Wisconsin* fired and the 47 *Missouri* fired, they fired 324 and 759 rounds, respectively, for a total of 1,083 rounds. The total ordnance they delivered was about 2,166,000 pounds, equal to 4,322 Mk 82 bombs or 542 A-6 missions. The types of targets they engaged included: 17 artillery targets; 13 small boats (1 mission); 10 antiair warfare sites; 10 bunkers; 8 engagements against infantry in bunkers; 6 ammunition storage sites; 5 SAM/SSM rocket launchers;

5 radar/communications/SIGINT sites; 4 command/observation posts; 4 engagements against troops in the open; 3 logistics sites; 3 tanks; 2 buildings; 2 minefields; a pier; and a truck. Battle damage assessments were available for only 41 missions or 68 targets; 32 percent were damaged light to moderately; 26 percent were damaged heavily; 10 percent were neutralized; and 32 percent were destroyed.[14] The value of the battleships was in their multipurpose roles – they effectively fired Tomahawks against Iraqi targets at the start of the war, and later laid down these large and effective barrages of firepower against targets that were defended by SAMs. Finally, they pounded beach emplacements to soften the enemy for the amphibious landing that never came. After the war, the Pentagon announced that the battleships would be retired because of funding cuts. This was unfortunate since the ships had again proven their worth and versatility. More than one seasoned warrior said that he would much rather face a missile attack than a 16–inch barrage from one of these battleships.

The Navy's Stand-off Land-Attack Missile (SLAM), a long-range precision surgical strike weapon, was used in combat for the first time on January 25th. Deployed from carrier-based aircraft, SLAMs use targeting data loaded into the missile before take-off, Global Positioning System mid-course guidance aid and video aim-point control to provide a precision strike capability that minimizes collateral damage. This attack was successful, destroying an Iraqi hydroelectric plant. During the attack two SLAMs were fired in succession from two A-6E aircraft. The first blasted a hole in the target and the second then entered the target and destroyed it from within.[15] A Harpoon derivative with a 500–pound high explosive warhead, SLAM has an infra-red seeker that is activated one minute before impact. It can be launched at low altitude, at less than 50 nautical miles from the target, and has an accuracy of 16 meters CEP. After launching a SLAM, plane crews operate a joystick in the cockpit to aim it with pinpoint accuracy as it approaches the target. Although it was still under evaluation, the Navy deployed it aboard *Kennedy* and *Saratoga* and used it during the war on A-6E and possibly on F/A-18 aircraft, thus using the war as a proving ground for a system that had not yet finished the development and acquisition process. The fact that it was used in combat before standard operational evaluations were completed indicates the Navy's high degree of confidence and expectation of success. Its performance in the war was described as "superior," although exact data are not available on the success or failure rate. However, the Navy and McDonnell Douglas, the manufacturer, are considering a wide-range of modifications to improve its performance and lethality.

THE AMPHIBIOUS DECEPTION

The Coalition strategy of secretly moving large numbers of troops westward along the Saudi border during the air war and then enveloping Iraqi forces from the West is fully discussed in chapter 5 and need not be repeated here. An important part of this deception was to convince Iraq that a major amphibious assault would occur so that Baghdad would commit significant forces to the coast and away from the real point of assault.

Preparations for such an assault began in August 1990. On the 7th, 2,500 Marines from Camp Lejeune, North Carolina, sailed for the Mediterranean aboard the amphibious ship *Inchon*. At the same time Marine units afloat off Diego Garcia, Guam, and in the Atlantic began steaming toward the Persian Gulf, and Marine preposition ships, five from Diego Garcia and four from Guam, prepared to steam to the Gulf with supplies. In mid-August, the Pentagon said that a 15,000–man Marine Expeditionary Brigade on 13 amphibious ships would depart the U.S. east coast for the Persian Gulf. In the Autumn, the embarked Marine forces received prominent press coverage as elements of operation "Imminent Thunder" conducted amphibious exercises in the Gulf. By mid-January there were about 17,000 Marines on ships in the Gulf and the force included elements of the Fourth and Fifth Marine Expeditionary Brigades and Amphibious Task Groups 2 and 3, while the amphibious force included eight amphibious ships inside the Gulf and another 25 in the northern Arabian Sea, just outside the Gulf's entrance.[16] On the 17th, the Coalition announced that aircraft would soon strike Kuwaiti beaches to soften up defenses and clear the way for a Marine amphibious assault. On the 25th, it was announced that the current amphibious forces exercises in the Gulf were the "largest since Korea," and on the 28th, A-6s from *Ranger* struck Iraqi warships in Kuwaiti waters, ostensibly to open an approach for a beach assault by Marines aboard the amphibious ships. U.S. special forces conducted mineclearing operations off the Kuwaiti coast as though an amphibious landing were imminent, while battleships pounded Iraqi positions and amphibious landing rehearsals continued. By February 22nd, naval mine-sweeping operations moved closer to Kuwait's beaches to clear the way for a Marine landing. As many as 80,000 Iraqi troops reportedly defended the beaches. On the 25th, Marine helicopters repeatedly flew missions along the Kuwaiti coast while the 13th Marine Expeditionary Brigade feigned an attack on the Kuwaiti coast, hyping up Iraqi coastal defense forces. On the first day of the ground offensive, Radio Free Kuwait claimed that Marines had landed on Faylakah Island. The deception was continued even after the ground invasion began. Elements of the 4th and 5th Marine Expeditionary Brigades simulated a full-fledged beach landing, and Navy SEALs conducted reconnaissance, probing the beaches for suitable landing sites for heavy equipment and scouting for minefields and submerged high-voltage wires.[17]

This deception was highly successful. Six of Iraq's 42 divisions were massed along the Kuwaiti coast in anticipation of a Marine amphibious assault, and captured Iraqi equipment and plans showed that Baghdad had expended considerable resources preparing for the assault that never came. In doing so, it wasted resources that could have considerably bolstered Iraqi defenses along the Kuwait-Saudi border and have made the Coalition ground assault more difficult.[18]

LESSONS LEARNED

Although the Coalition navies played a supporting role in the war, they nonetheless conducted significant operations and learned some important lessons. The reaffirmation of a well-known lesson was that naval power remains unique in its low-visibility, promptness, flexibility, and sustainability. Naval power from around the world was brought to bear in the Persian Gulf and conducted significant operations in the war. The value of battleships was again seen in their 16-inch gun bombardments and Tomahawk strikes. *Iowa*, *New Jersey*, *Missouri*, and *Wisconsin* provide a unique and formidable capability, and it will be sad if the Navy must retire them because of budget constraints. The war demonstrated recent U.S. Navy investments were well spent, and the combat effectiveness of many expensive high tech systems, such as Tomahawk, SLAM, satellites, and modern electronic warfare systems, was proven. Nonetheless, as in any combat situation, lessons are learned, and many systems, including Tomahawk, will be improved based on this wartime performance.

As in any conflict, not all of the lessons were positive. The difficulties in forming the armada, deciding on rules of engagement, and other organizational problems demonstrated the command and control difficulties that occur when an armada is formed from naval forces of so many different nations. This was simplified in the end because only the Royal Navy and U.S. Navy, which are familiar with each other's procedures and operations, were involved in the actual fighting and the Royal Navy was easily integrated into the U.S. Navy's air defense arrangement. Additionally, Iraq's mine warfare demonstrated again how difficult it is to combat these weapons. The Royal Navy had spent its money well and made a great contribution to the Coalition Navy's minesweeping campaign, but the U.S. Navy saw once again that it is necessary to bolster its minesweeping force, one of the low-priority items on its procurement list.

NOTES

1. "Chronology of War," *The Washington Times*, March 1, 1991, p. B4; Michael Pocalyko, "Desert Shield: The First Lessons Learned," U.S. Naval Institute *Proceedings* (hereafter referred to as *USNIP*) (October 1990): 58; and Carla Anne Robbins and Peter Cary, "Top Guns of Desert Storm," *US News and World Report* (February 11, 1991): 42.

2. Andrew Rosenthal, "Baghdad Warns Diplomats Against 'Act of Aggression'; Hussein Shows off Hostages," *The New York Times*, September 16, 1990, p. F-52; John H. Cushman, Jr., "Inside the Arsenals," *The New York Times*, September 16, 1990, p. F-52; "Preparing for the Worst," *The New York Times*, August 26, 1990, p. D-1; "Carrier Moves into Persian Gulf," *Navy News*, October 1, 1990; and "US Carrier Force Back in the Gulf," *Jane's Defence Weekly* (hereafter referred to as *JDF*) (October 13, 1990): 685.

3. "Freedom of the Skies and Seas Speeds War's Third Phase," *The Times* (London), February 5, 1991, p. 2; James Gerstenzang, "U.S. Will Double Force in Gulf," *The Los Angeles Times*, November 9, 1990, p. A1; and James Longo, "U.S. Subs Played Surveillance, Recon Role in Gulf War," *The Navy Times*, April 8, 1991, p. 24.

4. Department of the Navy, *The U.S. Navy in "Desert Shield"/"Desert Storm"* (Washington, DC: Department of the Navy, 1991), pp. 28–29.

5. "Blockade Tightens Vise on Hussein," *The Washington Times*, August 14, 1990, p. A1.

6. Michael R. Gordon with Eric Schmitt, "Much More Armor Than U.S. Believed Fled to Iraq," *The New York Times*, March 25, 1991, p. 1; R.W. Apple, Jr., "Ships Turn Away From Ports as Iraq Embargo Tightens," *The New York Times*, August 14, 1990, p. A1; and James Gerstenzang and David Lauter, "Bush Says Hussein is Backed Into a Corner," *The Los Angeles Times*, August 11, 1990.

7. R. W. Apple, Jr., "Confrontation in the Gulf," *The New York Times*, August 18, 1990, p. A1; "Bush Briefs Legislators on Crisis and They Back His Gulf Strategy," *The New York Times*, August 29, 1990, p. A1; John H. Cushman, "Inside the Arsenals," *The New York Times*, September 16, 1990, p. F- 52; William Claiborne, "U.S. Ships Fire Warning Shots at Iraqi Tankers," *The Washington Post*, August 19, 1990, p. A1; and Molly Moore and William Claiborne, "U. S. Warships Interrogating up to 75 Cargo Vessels Daily," *The Washington Post*, August 31, 1990, p. A18.

8. *The U.S. Navy in "Desert Shield"/"Desert Storm"*, pp. 22–27.

9. "Tuesday's Riyadh Military Briefing," *Associated Press,* January 22, 1990; Schwartz, "The Persian Gulf War," January 24, 1991; "Timetable," *JDW* (February 2, 1991): 135; "War in the Gulf: Military Briefing," *The New York Times,* January 28, 1991, p. A9; David Lamb, "Mines Damage 2 U.S. Warships in the Gulf," *The Los Angeles Times,* February 19, 1991, p. A1.

10. Eric Schmitt, "Gulf Is Swept for Mines In the Aftermath of War," *The New York Times*, March 19, 1991, p. 14; and John Boatman, Nick Cook, Tony Banks and Jori Janssen Lok, "Iraq Naval Threat Now 'Ineffective'," *JDW* (9 February 1991): 168.

11. Eric Schmitt, "Gulf is Swept for Mines In the Aftermath of War," *The New York Times*, March 19, 1991, p. 14.

12. Norma Zamichow, "'Forgotten' Navy Plays Up Its Exploits," *The Los Angeles Times*, March 19, 1991, p. 7; James Schwartz, "The Persian Gulf War," *The Washington Post*, January 19, 1991; Paul Woodward, "Operation Desert Storm," *The Washington Times*, January 21, 1991; "SSNs Launch Tomahawks," *JDW* (February 2, 1991): 133; Dan Balz and Ann Devroy, "Bush Warns Iraq Against Mistreating POWs" *The Washington Post*, January 22, 1991, p. A1.

13. Michael Gordon and Eric Schmitt, "Radios and Mine Sweepers: Problems in the Gulf," *The Los Angeles Times*, March 28, 1991, p. A19.

14. Robin Cross, "Execute Desert Storm," *The Daily Telegraph*, March 2, 1991, p. 6; and Schwartz, "The Persian Gulf War," February 5 and 8, 1991.

15. "With Testing Incomplete SLAM Scores Military Success," *Defense Aerospace Business Digest* (January 30, 1991): 4.

16. *The Los Angeles Times*, August 8, 1990, p. A1; August 17, 1990, p. A1; and January 15, 1991, p. A1; *The Washington Post*, August 8, 1990, p. A1; and *The New York Times*, January 25, 1991, p. A1.

17. Paul Bedard, "Sadam Bombs Israel," *The Washington Times,* January 18, 1991, p. A1; Richard C. Gross and Rowan Scarborough, "Saddam Talk of Deadlier Scuds," *The Washington Times,* January 29, 1991, p. A1; Schwartz, "The Persian Gulf War," February 27, 1991; George Esper, "Iraq Ignores Deadline," *Associated Press*, February 23, 1991; Edwin Chen, "Marines Are Still at Sea and Unhappy," *The Los Angeles Times*, February 28, 1991; and Tom Post, John Barry and Douglas Waller, "To the Shores of Kuwait," *Newsweek* (February 11, 1991): 28.

18. "Before the Storm," *Annapolis Capital*, February 28, 1991, p. A2.

PART IV
SPECIFIC MILITARY FACTORS

8: Command and Control
by
Joel H. Nadel

To be prepared for exigencies, the U.S. military has several joint headquarters. Coinciding with geographic areas, each plans and coordinates military operations, including battle planning, use of facilities, deployment, and training areas, logistics support, and contractual support, with U.S. allies in its area. Southwest Asia, including the eastern Mediterranean nations and the Persian Gulf, is under the aegis of U.S. Central Command (CENTCOM), headquartered at MacDill Air Force Base, Florida. When the Coalition deployed forces, CENTCOM deployed rapidly to a forward headquarters in Riyadh and established the initial command and control structure for deploying U.S. forces. It later became the multinational Coalition headquarters.

The Coalition's forces operated under both administrative and operational or warfighting chains of command, and General Schwarzkopf, Commander-in-Chief, CENTCOM commanded both. The administrative chain of command (figure 1) was organized with the various national forces under national command, but subordinate to CENTCOM. It coordinated administrative and logistics plans, procedures, and actions. Forces with specialized logistical missions, such as the Czechoslovakian chemical decontamination unit, the Polish field hospital, and the South Korean Air Force transportation squadron, were included in the administrative chain of command. More streamlined and flexible, the operational chain of command (figure 2) was designed to coordinate rapidly battle plans, orders, and actions.

Headquarters, Joint Forces CENTCOM had seven subordinate headquarters: 3d U.S. Army in Riyadh; Joint Forces Command

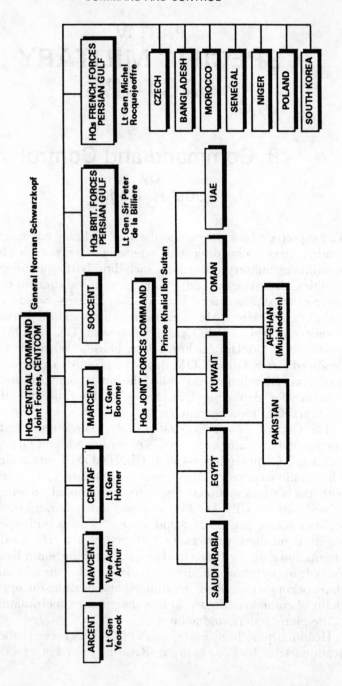

Figure 1. CENTCOM Administrative Chain of Command

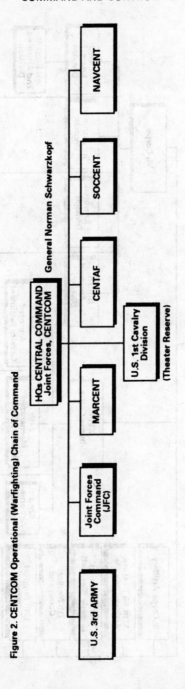

Figure 2. CENTCOM Operational (Warfighting) Chain of Command

Figure 3. U.S. 3rd Army Chain of Command

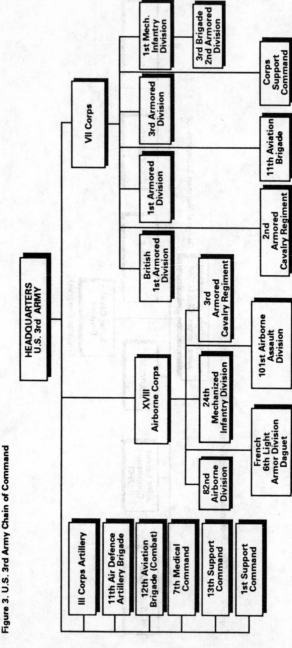

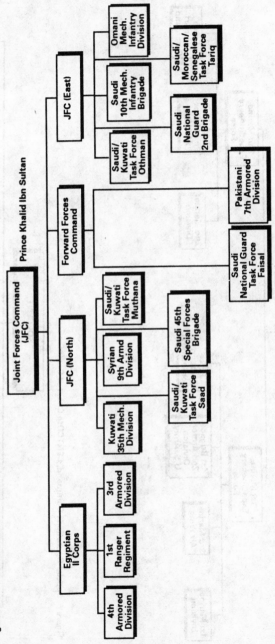

Figure 4. Joint Forces Command Chain of Command

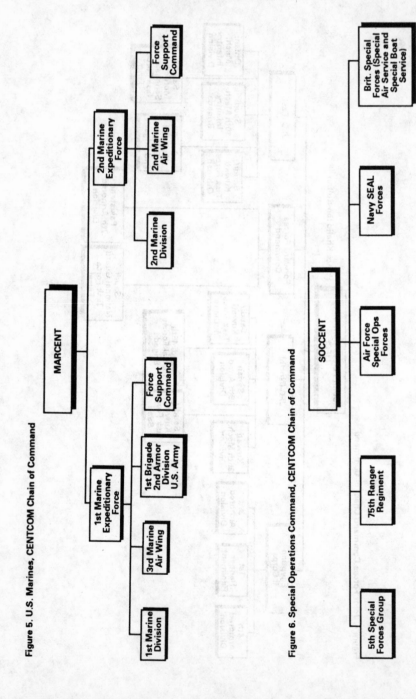

Figure 5. U.S. Marines, CENTCOM Chain of Command

MARCENT

1st Marine Expeditionary Force
- 1st Marine Division
- 3rd Marine Air Wing
- 1st Brigade 2nd Armor Division U.S. Army
- Force Support Command

2nd Marine Expeditionary Force
- 2nd Marine Division
- 2nd Marine Air Wing
- Force Support Command

Figure 6. Special Operations Command, CENTCOM Chain of Command

SOCCENT

- 5th Special Forces Group
- 75th Ranger Regiment
- Air Force Special Ops Forces
- Navy SEAL Forces
- Brit. Special Forces (Special Air Service and Special Boat Service)

Figure 7. Joint Naval Services, CENTCOM Chain of Command

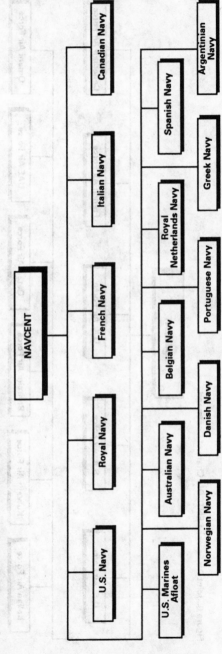

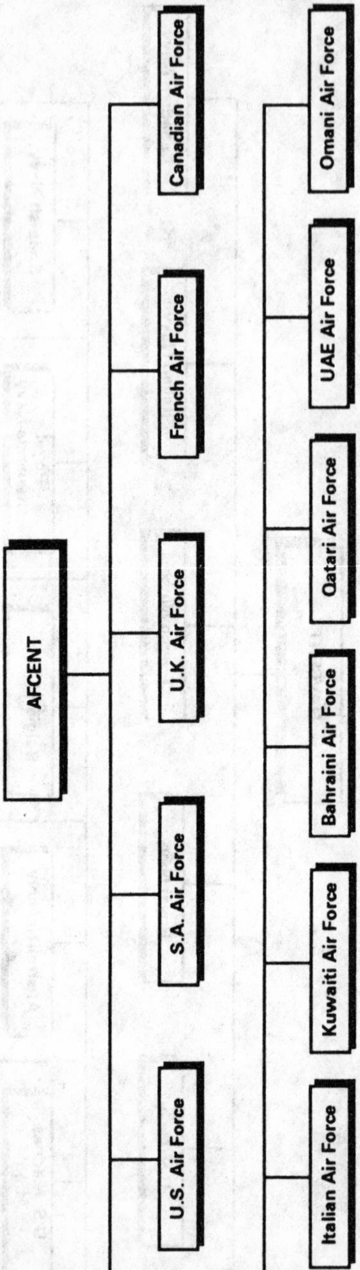

Figure 8. Joint Air Forces CENTCOM Chain of Command

(JFC) in Riyadh and Hafr al Batin; U.S. Marines, CENTCOM (MARCENT) in Khafji; Special Operations Command, CENTCOM (SOCCENT) in Dharhan; Joint Air Forces, CENTCOM (CENTAF) in Riyadh; Joint Naval Forces, CENTCOM (NAVCENT) in Dhahran; and 1st U.S. Cavalry Division in King Khalid Military City. Initially a theater reserve directly subordinated to CENTCOM, 1st Cavalry Division was resubordinated to 3d Army during the ground war. 3d Army (figure 3), commanded initially by Lieutenant General (Lt Gen) John Yeosock and later by Lt Gen Calvin Waller, was primarily composed of the U.S. XVIII Airborne and VII Corps. They were supported by III Corps Artillery, 11th Air Defense Artillery Brigade, 12th Aviation Brigade (Combat), 7th Medical Command, and 13th and 1st Support Commands. Also, the French 6th Light Armor Division was operationally subordinate to XVIII Airborne Corps, and the British 1st Armoured Division to VII Corps. These subordinations are excellent examples of how the administrative and operational chains of command differed. Under the administrative chain of command, the 1st Armoured Division and the 6th Light Armored Division were subordinate to Lt Gens Sir Peter de la Billiere and Michel Roquejeoffre, who were subordinate to Schwarzkopf.

Joint Forces Command (figure 4) was commanded by Prince Khalid Ibn Sultan, a member of the Saudi Arabian Royal Family. Its subordinate headquarters were the Egyptian II Corps, Joint Forces Command North, Joint Forces Command East and the Forward Forces Command. It had the most complex organization because there were so many different national forces. Egyptian II Corps had only Egyptian troops, JFC North had Kuwaiti, Syrian, and Saudi forces, and JFC East had Saudi, Kuwaiti, Moroccan, Omani, and Senegalese forces. Forward Forces Command had Saudi and Pakistani forces, and its operations were complicated by distrust among the Arab Coalition partners. Further complicating the command and control issue were the partners' differing national agendas that affected the operations of their military units. In one case, the Syrian 9th Armor Division was given an operational reserve mission within the JFC because the Syrian leadership would not commit to participating in an offensive to liberate Kuwait. The Pakistani contingent was even more restricted than the Syrians, being tasked with merely guarding Islamic shrines.

CENTCOM's U.S. Marine Corps component (MARCENT) (figure 5), commanded by Lt Gen Walter Boomer, consisted of 1st and 2d Marine Expeditionary Forces (MEF). Each MEF had a Marine Division, a Marine Air Wing, and a Force Support Command. The 1st (Tiger) Brigade of the U.S. Army's 2d Armor Division was subordinated to the 1st MEF, and the 4th Marine Expeditionary Brigade (MEB), the 5th MEB, the 13th Marine Expeditionary Unit (MEU), the 22d MEU, and the 26th MEU were on ships and subordinated to NAVCENT. Information on the organizational structure of SOCCENT (figure 6) is scarce due to the sensitive and classified nature of its missions and operations. The headquarters subordinated to SOCCENT were: 5th Special Forces Group, 75th Ranger Regiment, a U.S. Air Force Special Operations element, U.S. Navy SEAL (sea, air, land) forces, and British Special Forces (Special Air Service and Special Boat Squadron). SOCCENT units may have participated in joint operations with Egyptian, Saudi, and Kuwaiti units. Joint Naval Forces, CENTCOM (NAVCENT) (figure 7), was commanded by Vice Admiral Stanley Arthur. Joint Air Forces, CENTCOM (CENTAF) (figure 8), commanded by Lt Gen Charles Horner, had 1,820 combat aircraft from 11 different nations. Air missions were centrally directed by CENTAF, but were executed by the various components. However, U.S. Marine air operations were primarily in support of MARCENT ground force operations.

The nub of coalition warfare is balancing national interest with sound military warfighting strategy. Each nation had a link to its government and could object when displeased. In order to avoid this, major strategic decisions were not implemented until the White House had cleared them with other governments. Washington then issued military directives to CENTCOM.

Lessons Learned

Overall, the administrative and operational chains of command effectively ensured the necessary unity of command while accounting for national differences. The exception to this was the Joint Forces Command. However, its command and control problems were unavoidable given the diversity of nationalities in its composition and the lack of any formalized collective security arrangements. The Arab partners were not as familiar as their European and U.S. allies with coalition warfare procedures. No doubt, if they had a collective security structure of some sort prior to the war, they would have had significantly fewer command and control problems. Clearly, in light of the problems encountered by the Joint Forces Command, forming a Middle East collective security organization should be an imperative for them. Their experiences may enable them to establish a coalition agenda vice their various national agendas in order to better ensure their collective security in the future.

9: Indications and Warning (I&W) and Intelligence Lessons
by
Gerald W. Hopple

Was the Gulf War preventable or foreseeable? Kuwaiti Army Colonel Said Matar, military attache to Iraq before the war, recounted subsequently that as early as April 1990 he warned in his reports of an Iraqi military operation, and on July 2nd, he pinpointed August 2nd as the invasion date, based on data from several sources confirmed independently by informants in the Republican Guard. No one in Kuwait heeded his warnings, and he was silenced by Kuwaiti army officers and the minister of planning while talking to the press, illustrating the common syndrome that those with intelligence prescience are seldom rewarded by their superiors. The invasion also caught virtually everyone in the Western intelligence community by surprise. That community documented the Iraqi buildup, but completely missed Baghdad's real intentions until August 1st. Walter P. Lang, the U.S. national intelligence officer for the Middle East and South Asia, warned of the Iraqi invasion, but his alert was ignored.[1]

Indications and warning, or I&W, is "successful" only if no shots are fired, if war is prevented altogether. The Coalition's impressive success should not obscure this basic I&W *sine qua non*. The evidence suggests that strategic I&W, from both Iraqi and Coalition perspectives, was far from "optimal."

THE POLICY CONTEXT

Referring to post-1980 U.S. policy toward Iraq as the "great American screw-up," international relations expert Professor Paul Gigot avers that a decade of consistent U.S. misjudgment could be traced back to Washington's reaction to Israel's bombing of Iraq's Osirak nuclear facility, which involved condemning Israel, while failing to see the threat from Iraq's potential nuclear capability.[2] The climax of this policy was the August invasion.

As Roberta Wohlstetter, an I&W expert, noted, it is very hard to separate genuine policy "signals" from the backdrop of "noise" in which they are embedded. Saddam's aggressive signals were heard clearly but were not used to change hypotheses about his intentions. It was simply assumed that his threats, designed to force concessions from Kuwait, did not constitute a precursor to (and *indicators* of) invasion. This led to the second mistake, failing to signal U.S. intentions. In fact, the pattern on mixed messages could plausibly be seen as appeasing Saddam.

The roots of this U.S. policy were anchored in the 1979 Iranian revolution that sparked a tilt toward Iraq. Pentagon analyst and National Security Council staffer Howard Teicher warned of the dangers of this and forecasted Iraq's invasion of Iran. During that war, Washington was a "silent ally," sharing intelligence with Iraq. Several years later, a 1985 memorandum by Teicher and the CIA's Graham Fuller stated that concerning Iraq's domestic terror, "change" might very well be cosmetic. No sanctions were imposed in 1988 in response to Saddam's chemical attacks on the Kurds, although Iraq had replaced Iran as the primary threat to U.S. regional interests, since Iran, weakened severely by its war with Iraq, could no longer offer a balance.

The Bush Administration explicitly rejected making overtures to Iran and issued a directive favoring detente with Iraq in mid-1989. From late-1989 to July 1990, Saddam issued many threats and hostile actions toward both Washington and various Arab states. His April 1989 threat to use chemical weapons on Israel sparked a reevaluation of U.S. policy. Limited sanctions emerged as an option, but this was never pursued seriously. Consistency characterized the messages during 1990. There were no threats to break relations and U.S. strategy clearly was one of placating Iraq. The now infamous July 25th meeting between Saddam and Ambassador Glaspie culminated in the statement that "we have no opinion on the Arab-Arab conflict, like your border dispute with Kuwait."[3] Washington never provided even the most basic signal that might have served to deter Iraq.

All of this demonstrates that policy preconceptions (and underlying state concepts, leader images, regional security frameworks, and other theoretical frameworks) shaped decision-makers' perceptions. This, of course, is natural and inevitable. However, when policy becomes the driver and controlling lens through which intelligence is processed and interpreted, failing to respect norms of analytical pluralism may lead to an egregious situation in which "policy without intelligence" dictates actual choices as well as assessing stimuli from the environment. This is one of several "models" for interpreting I&W performance.

MODELS FOR I&W PERFORMANCE ASSESSMENT[4]

All major I&W case studies that have accrued in strategic studies literature share a common trait in that military attacks typically generated many warning signals that were embedded in a maze of both noise and deception.[5] There often were several previous alerts that turned out to be false alarms. The Pearl Harbor case provides a dramatic example of this syndrome; after June 1940, there had been three distinct periods of huge tension and alerts in U.S.-Japanese relations, including the month of November 1941, a month prior to the attack.

It can be argued that the Gulf War fits this pattern, since warning signals of Iraq's attack existed. Such post hoc minority "prescience," it must be conceded, often turns out to be a false alarm. From Iraq's perspective, signals of Coalition intentions were potentially clear, although there was a failure to recognize them for what they were, and as is usual in such cases, the environment was pervaded by noise and potential deception. For example, the West's preoccupation with the end of the Cold War may have resulted in failing to heed the warning signals. A list of prior alerts was at least theoretically available; and as was the case with most Arab-Arab conflicts, the Iraqi claim on Kuwait had a lengthy history, as Iraq had threatened to seize Kuwait as early as 1961, when the latter became independent.

The Falklands case shows the central role of the model of *strategic assumptions* in the matrix of precrisis/prewar political and strategic intelligence indicators and analytical frameworks. Faulty Argentine and British strategic assumptions imply that the war may have been avoided, that more rational, better articulated strategic concepts may well have prevented it. Notably, finished intelligence data available to British decision-makers was much less alarmist than the raw material, giving at least indirect support for the belief that indicators and data were filtered through a particular strategic assumptions lens.

The logic of the British strategic concept was abysmal. Underlying the base line assumption that Argentina simply would not go to war was a higher order set of factors contained in London's fundamental defense strategy. A truism in strategic thinking is that a nation's political goals must be achievable with available military forces and strategy. Related to this in a transparent fashion is the deterrent value of forces on the spot. Only a token force was present in the region, signalling to Buenos Aires that Britain was not serious about defending the Falklands. Thus, from Argentina's vantage point, the base assumption was that the British would not fight but would indulge in posturing and harassment. This was a valid assumption, given the empirical signals and indications that the British sent. There were multiple signals that she would neither make a long-term military commitment nor diplomatically resolve the issue.

From the British perspective, Falklands was a decision or policy failure. Decision-makers rely on and extrapolate from preconceptions in the form of "facts" about their own potential, their opponent's capabilities, political and military intentions, and inferred or perceived risk calculations. Preconceptions or strategic assumptions obviously have a potential for extensive variation on the dimensions of quality, rigor, and validity. In more basic terms, Falklands also can be seen as an intelligence analysis failure, since there was compelling evidence of flawed analysis and key miscalculations on both sides and better analysis could have prevented the war.

Analogously, the Gulf War was perhaps not a failure of data (collection) but of interpretation and assessment (analysis), but before embracing this conclusion prematurely, the insidious nature of "hindsight bias" must be recognized. Wars often begin with surprise attacks, the pattern of August 1990. Postmortems in such contexts lead to the conclusion that an "intelligence failure" had occurred. However, the hindsight bias, a powerful and pervasive fallacy ("I knew it would happen all along"), leads to the facile and dangerous assumption that what we know after the fact could realistically have been foreseen. This almost universal human cognitive bias can lead to unwarranted inferences of intelligence or analysis failure. Hence a note of strong caution about premature or suspiciously enthusiastic assignments of "blame" for the war.

Grenada provides a textbook example of poor intelligence, since it was weak in both volume and quality. U.S. forces met more resistance than expected, the Cuban presence was severely underestimated, and there were few data on military hardware. Concerning capabilities and intentions, there was no defensible evidence to sustain the rationale that Grenada was being transformed into a base for exporting terrorism. Both pre-attack and tactical intelligence were deficient and there even was uncertainty about exactly who was in charge on the island.

Two somewhat contrasting models can be juxtaposed to explain inadequate performance. The first, *foolish intelligence*, occurs when estimates are flawed and other analytical errors and biases intrude. An example of this is the consistent underestimation of Soviet forces and intentions in strategic weapons. The second model introduces the notion of *policy without intelligence*, when decision-making occurs without the benefit of intelligence input. The U.S. decision to declare a Defense Condition 3 alert in response to perceived Soviet actions during the Yom Kippur War, when extreme secrecy precluded intelligence involvement, is a good example of this pernicious syndrome. In direct and striking contrast, the Cuban missile crisis illuminates the value of close cooperation between the intelligence and policy communities. There is undeniable evidence of foolish intelligence with respect to Grenada. Political intelligence, concerned with elite analysis (analyzing the actions and beliefs of leaders), bureaucratic politics interpretations, and internal societal trends, can increase lead time dramatically. The most noteworthy characteristic of political intelligence in this instance was its obviously poor quality, due to both the lack of HUMINT (human intelligence) and the paucity of genuine, rigorous analysis.

Even more evidence supports a policy without intelligence interpretation. Developments in Grenada were viewed in the context of overall Central American/Caribbean regional patterns as seen through a Cold War prism. This theoretical framework provided a constraining lens, analogous to the causal role of strategic assumptions in the Falklands case. The theoretical prism maximized the role of external Cuban and Soviet influence, despite the convincing evidence that the Grenadian revolutionary process was unfolding in line with a purely domestic trajectory. There is no support for the belief that alternative hypotheses were identified and considered, reinforcing the validity of the applicability of the policy without intelligence model. The cases and models surveyed here offer a basis for formulating some conclusions about the war. The pervasive hindsight bias warns against prematurely accepting any hypotheses relating to I&W shortcomings. With this, we now turn to a consideration of specific evidence about prewar intelligence and analysis.

Policy emerges as the driving primordial variable from the U.S. perspective. Offensive military planning began in September 1990.[6] On October 30th, Bush approved a timetable to launch an air war in mid-January and a large-scale ground offensive in February. The war led to victory, but prior to this officials lacked insight into Saddam's intentions, and no options to halt the invasion were seriously considered in the Summer of 1990.

Was the Gulf War avoidable? Hindsight is always perfect but the evidence and plausible reasoning suggest that war could have been avoided. America tilted consistently toward Saddam's regime, while completely misjudging his designs on Kuwait and allowing its addiction to cheap oil to distort its view of regional events. While satellite photos clearly showed Iraqi troops amassing on the border, the assessment was that Saddam was bluffing or at worst would make a limited grab for the oil rich islands off Kuwait.[7] This policy posture, which governed the intelligence analysis and estimation processes, was reinforced by the belief that Iran was the key regional threat (and, as is known in alliance research in international relations, "the enemy of my enemy is my friend"). Thus, U.S. intelligence and policy leaders ignored human rights abuses, shared intelligence during the war with Iran, and sold grain and large amounts of military equipment. All of this converges in a portrait in which America's "actor concept" of this regime was as inaccurate and misleading as Britain's strategic concept in the Falklands War.

The raw data were there, but interpretation was very deficient. Just as a dominant theoretical framework served as a lens which obscured events in Grenada, failing to inject nuances and subtleties into this process reflected deeper analytical problems. Specifically, a greater awareness of the region's complexities was needed. Grenada was refracted through an arbitrarily imposed Cold War/external environment prism. Likewise, in respect to the Middle East, two conflicting schools currently compete for hegemony. The first sees all events in terms of their impact on Israel; the second, "Arabist" perspective, says that a tilt toward

Israel and neglect of the Palestinian problem will result in permanent unrest.

Neither premise explained the Gulf War's alliance patterns, with "moderates" like Jordan linked to Baghdad and "hardliners" like Syria active partners in the Coalition. The "Arab world" is not as monolithic and predictable as is assumed. Cross cutting cleavages, complex shared interest patterns, and many historical Arab-Arab conflict axes and fissures (many unrelated to Israel) imply that intelligence analysis should be less framework-driven and that explicit analytical pluralism, with developing and juxtaposing multiple alternative hypotheses, is essential. The data were potentially available, but interpreting and the intervention of theoretical frameworks "biased" the assessments. Intelligence perspectives are always biased, although the term bias is used here to refer to a predisposing prejudgment, not in the more commonplace pejorative sense. The danger is not the intrusion of frameworks (all of which constitute "biases"), but the dominance of one particular theoretical perspective.

If we briefly shift from I&W to intelligence during the war, the picture is less bleak. There was certainly no breakdown in technical intelligence; during battles satellite photography was of such high quality that planes were capable of dropping leaflets which identified Iraqi brigades and divisions by name. Conversely, in other intelligence areas, there were problems. For example, since the war the Director of CIA has retired, which may indicate displeasure with the CIA's performance in the war. Specific problems concerning intelligence are just coming to light, but on June 13th, General Schwarzkopf testified before the U.S. Congress that intelligence reporting on bomb damage assessments was abysmal. There are rumors that Schwarzkopf was very dissatisfied with the intelligence support that he received from Washington's Intelligence Community, particularly the Defense Intelligence Agency, and that he eventually relied on Army intelligence organizations for intelligence inputs.[8]

Before the air war was launched, the reconnaissance focus was the strategic question: how large were Iraq's forces and where were they deployed?[9] When the war began, the need shifted to tactical intelligence or specifics and information was frequently delayed in "clogged circuits" between Washington and Riyadh. Photographic capabilities were good, but photos reached fighter squadrons within one to two hours, while the media, in contrast, moved pictures in only seconds. Due to intelligence shortcomings, there was a change of air tactics. F-16s patrolled individual 20x20–mile grids of terrain, instead of set targets. As the Republican Guard shifted equipment, a new problem arose: reconnaissance photos became outdated too fast. This led to the use of "Fast FACs" (fast forward air controllers). F-16s stripped of weapons except for phosphorous rockets led the attacks, looking for enemy equipment in new locations.

High technology space-based reconnaissance systems "proved their value in warning, communications, surveillance, and navigation, but the Gulf War strongly suggested that improvements in collecting and distributing surveillance data are needed."[10] Satellites warned of Scud launches and cued Patriot systems, but their dated architecture, involving a small number of ground stations that passed warnings manually to commanders in the field, should be upgraded to a system in which data are delivered to users automatically, perhaps directly from satellites.

Tactical intelligence recorded a number of successes and several failures. In I&W, the best interpretation of the failure to warn of Iraq's invasion (again, taking into account the inescapable impact of the hindsight bias and recognizing that warning is so extraordinarily difficult, in part because the events per se are so rare and noise is so pervasive), emphasizes a policy or decision failure as the culprit and, secondarily, an analysis failure. The same holds for the other I&W evaluation task of Saddam's estimate that the Coalition simply would dissolve and that there would be no U.N. offensive at all.

From the U.S. view, the policy failure can be attributed to the national security bureaucracy, including the President. Bush's immediate reaction to the invasion was anger; he had personally invested in the idea that Saddam's behavior could be moderated.[11] It was *assumed* all along that Iraq's sabre rattling should be seen as using threats to force concessions from Kuwait, a case of coercive diplomacy rather than the unfolding of a trajectory leading to war. This assessment led to a second key mistake: the failure to signal U.S. intentions.

Saddam ignored all of the warnings of a Coalition military response. Iraqi Foreign Minister Tariq Aziz told Secretary Baker at the January 9th Geneva meeting: "Your Arab allies will desert you. They will not kill other Arabs. Your alliance will crumble and you will be left lost in the desert. You don't know the desert because you have never ridden on a horse or a camel."[12]

Simplistic strategic assumptions thus account for I&W policy "failures" on both sides. The data offered an empirical basis consistent with a hypothesis of an Iraqi attack; the concept of analysis failure also enters into the equation. Saddam's failure to see warning signals in the noise of the environment can be interpreted in a straightforward fashion. A dictator in a totalitarian state easily becomes immune to external signals because of his own unchallenged beliefs and the complete absence of analysis and policy pluralism in the decision-making process; there are no devil's advocates or institutionalized dissenters in Baghdad.[13] In a totalitarian regime ruled by an egomaniacal (albeit pragmatic, but opportunistic) dictator, the price of dissent – or even rigorous reality testing, is too high to pay.

Dissenters in the U.S. intelligence and policy processes do not pay the price of death, but dissenters are still disturbingly rare. The evidence suggests that the Bush national security policy process unfolds along two tracks; the official bureaucracy such as the National Security Council, and a small coterie of advisors surrounding Secretary of State Baker. Concepts like devil's advocacy or multiple advocacy are alien to this process.

It should also be noted that there were some failures symptomatic of "foolish intelligence." The most dramatic occurred during the war, leading to the bombing of the Amiriya bunker in a Baghdad suburb, killing 400 civilians. As a result, the Pentagon reassumed some control over targets. Air Force General Dugan notes in an assessment of lessons of the war that some favor the use of space systems for almost all reconnaissance requirements.[14] However, rapidly unfolding tactics virtually dictate continuous intelligence updates; daily passes over the Baghdad bunker were insufficient to prevent the dynamic assessment/reassessment of the situation.

There were at least three major intelligence blunders. First, U.S. planners were told Iraq had moved 540,000 troops into the Kuwait theater, with more than one-half in Kuwait. The actual totals were 250,000 and 150,000, respectively. Iraq was estimated to have only 35 Scud missile launchers; the actual number was up to 200. Finally, intelligence reported that Iraq had moved chemical weapons into the Kuwaiti theater, setting off major efforts to discover and destroy them; none were found.

This implies suboptimal intelligence performance especially when other problems (such as the proliferation of technical data with a concomitant failure to conduct high quality *analysis*, the lack of HUMINT, and the obsolete architecture of the system for disseminating satellite-based warnings) were present. Very basic capabilities were misestimated dramatically, and intelligence performance was far from acceptable. The strategic and tactical intelligence processes and products were not quite as deficient as those for Grenada, but they were distant from any reasonable standard of success. Compared to Grenada and many previous I&W "failures," this situation lacked many of the typical ambiguities of collection and analysis barriers, suggesting that intelligence should have been of appreciably higher quality.

LESSONS LEARNED

The future of the Middle East will be debated extensively, and consequences and antecedents of the war are obviously multidimensional. America is in need of a long-term strategy in the Gulf region with respect to Iraq. Systematic analysis of the lessons learned and strategic policy planning will require high quality current, I&W, and estimative intelligence. Central to this is the indisputable need for more sophisticated intelligence analysis and analytical pluralism. Theoretical perspectives and policy assumptions can easily become analytical straitjackets. The hope (and expectation) is that warning (and other forms of) intelligence inputs to the policy process can be analytically grounded and sensitive to underlying causal forces in the Gulf region and to nuances and subtleties operating below the surface.

NOTES

1. Bob Woodward, *The Commanders* (New York: Simon and Schuster), pp. 205, 210, 216–218.
2. Paul A. Gigot, "A Great American Screw-Up: The U.S. and Iraq, 1980–1990," *National Interest* 22(Winter, 1990/91): 10. This section draws heavily on Gigot's article.
3. "Avoiding the Next Crisis: America Should Learn from Mistakes that Made Saddam's Invasion Possible," *Newsweek* (March 11, 1991): 60. It should be noted that Ambassador Glaspie's testimony before Congress in April 1991 amplified, if

not contradicted, the statement made here. At present, what occurred precisely at the Saddam-Glaspie meeting remains undetermined.

4. The discussion in this section draws extensively on Gerald W. Hopple, "Intelligence and Warning Lessons," pp. 97–125, in Bruce W. Watson and Peter M. Dunn (eds.), *Military Lessons of the Falkland Islands War: Views from the United States* (Boulder, CO: Westview Press, 1984). Also relevant is Gerald W. Hopple and Cynthia Gilley, "Policy Without Intelligence," pp. 55–71, in Peter M. Dunn and Bruce W. Watson (eds.) *American Intervention in Grenada: The Implications of Operation "Urgent Fury"* (Boulder, CO: Westview Press, 1985).

5. See, For example, Roberta Wohlstetter's comparative case study in "Cuba and Pearl Harbor: Hindsight and Foresight," *Foreign Affairs* 43(1965): 691–707.

6. Thomas L. Friedman and Patrick E. Tyler, "From the First, U.S. Resolve to Fight," *The New York Times*, March 3, 1991, pp. A1, A18.

7. "Avoiding the Next Crisis," pp. 58, 62.

8. Molly Moore, "Schwarzkopf: War Intelligence Flawed," *The Washington Post*, June 13, 1991, pp. A1, A40; and Molly Moore, "War Exposed Rivalries, Weaknesses in Military: Communications, Intelligence Flaws Cited," *The Washington Post*, June 10, 1991.

9. "The Secret History of the War," *Newsweek* (March 18, 1991): 36.

10. General Michael Dugan (USAF), "First Lessons of Victory," *U.S. News and World Report* (March 18, 1991): 35.

11. Friedman and Tyler, p. 18.

12. Ibid.

13. The reference to Iraq as a totalitarian state is intentional. In a scale developed to measure polyarchy (a concept close to political democracy), Iraq appears in the tenth category set (the lowest possible scale score), along with such closed regimes as Cuba, Ethiopia, Libya, and the USSR (based on 1985 data). Interestingly, Saudi Arabia is also included in this category; Kuwait (and Jordan) are in the sixth ranked cell of the typing scheme. See Michael Coppedge and Wolfgang H. Reinicke, "Measuring Polyarchy," *Studies in Comparative International Development* 25(Spring 1990): 51–72.

14. Dugan, p. 36.

10: Electronic Warfare Lessons
by
David C. Isby

Schwarzkopf was able to dismantle the electromagnetic spectrum [so that] he effectively closed Saddam's eyes and ears. He therefore made Saddam less mobile, less able to react, less able to gain intelligence-- basically, less able to orchestrate and put the air, land, and sea [elements] together.[1]

General John Galvin
Supreme Allied Commander Europe

During the Gulf War, the Coalition's electronic warfare (EW) systems, operations, and tactics may have lacked drama and media attention, but were vital to the success of the entire war effort.[2] The war demonstrated lessons in all the elements of EW: electronic support measures, countermeasures, and counter-countermeasures with a scope and sophistication that far exceeded anything seen before. The EW investment made in the 1980s defense build-up was intended for a Soviet-NATO conflict in central Europe. Refined in exercises such as the U.S. "Green Flag" series against a postulated formidable Soviet threat, allied EW triumphed against the much weaker Iraqis.

The Coalition's EW completely disrupted Iraq's command, control, communications and intelligence (C^3I) system. EW severed the command links from Baghdad to field forces, which led directly to the spectacular collapse of the Iraqi Army as soon as the ground offensive began. In the air war, EW increased the impact of Coalition airpower, which quickly defeated Iraqi air defenses, and lowered losses in Coalition aircraft. As one pilot said, "If it had not been for ECM ... 50% of our aircraft would not have returned."[3] EW also allowed the Coalition to look deep into the Iraqi operational and strategic depths, while denying them the same advantage, and the deception that accompanied the ground offensive was made possible by EW superiority.[4]

EW resulted in a low loss of Coalition aircraft despite the Iraqi air defense system, composed of 17,000 SAMs, nearly 10,000 AAA pieces, and a wide variety of sophisticated communications links. A major factor in this imbalance was the fact that the Iraqis were weakened by a limited EW investment. Iraq never faced a technically sophisticated air threat from Iran, and it was confident that it could deal with the threat posed by its other Arab neighbors. Thus, it had made limited investments in air defense system modernization.[5] Maintaining what some have described as the world's fourth largest war machine with a GNP about equal to Portugal's led to economy in EW: much was sacrificed to achieve and maintain the force structure. The vast force structure was built on a Third World economy, which meant that there were far too few technical personnel to support the military and its associated industries. To compensate, it relied on foreign advisors and technicians, particularly Soviet advisors, and when these were withdrawn, the military's EW capability was weakened.

ELECTRONIC SUPPORT MEASURES (ESM)

Electronic support measures (ESM) involve collecting and analyzing electronic emissions. The Coalition's ESM effort was extensive and yielded a comprehensive intelligence picture. Among its specialized ESM aircraft were three U.S. Air Force RC-135s, including RC-135V/W Rivet Joint models. U-2Rs were used to collect COMINT (communications intelligence), and some could relay intercept data in real time through a wideband satellite link. British RAF Nimrod R.2s deployed; and the French had a DC-8 Sarigue, an EC-160 Gabriel, and two modified SA330 Puma helicopters. EW combat aircraft, such as the U.S. Navy's EA-6B and Air Force's F-4G, EF-111A, and possibly RF-4Cs were used to refine the electronic order of battle before the war began. The U.S. Navy's EP-3E and EA-3B forces also reportedly had aircraft in the Gulf, and the Air Force's TR-1As were also used for COMINT collection and radar surveillance. These were supplemented by U.S. Army ESM aircraft, both fixed wing (including RC-12s and RV-1D Quick Looks) and helicopters (including EH-60A Quick Fix IIBs) that provided intelligence vital to the rapid outflanking movements of the ground campaign. At sea, eight U.S. submarines conducted surveillance and reconnaissance operations, presumably using ESM, and also provided indications and warning for carrier battle groups. Besides the ESM capabilities on its surface combatants and submarines, the Navy used "bolt-on" ELINT (electronics intelligence) and COMINT systems. The French electronic research ship *Berry*, reportedly configured for ESM duties, was also used against Iraq.[6]

The Gulf War was a space-age war in its unprecedented use of satellites for communications, navigation, and intelligence. Geostationary U.S. ELINT satellites – two Magnum and a Vortex – were stationed over the western Indian Ocean to provide information on Iraq. KH-12 imaging satellites also reportedly had a secondary ELINT capability. The ELINT satellites provided information to field commanders promptly because improved connectivity between U.S.-based processing facilities and theater headquarters had been provided by the mid-1980s Constant Source and TENCAP (Tactical Exploitation of National Capabilities) programs that had expedited the intelligence flow considerably. Ground-based strategic ELINT sites that probably were used in the intelligence effort against Iraq included U.S. stations in Turkey, Saudi Arabia, the United Arab Emirates, and Oman, British stations in Cyprus and Oman, and French facilities in Djibouti.[7]

The Coalition's ground force's ESM capability was enhanced considerably by the U.S. Army's Combat Electronic Warfare and Intelligence (CEWI) battalions of the heavy divisions. They had a broad range of EW capabilities and worked closely with corps-level military intelligence brigades. This integration of ESM with offensive EW, hard-kill weapons, and intelligence-gathering seen in the CEWI battalions was constant throughout the war. Iraq had extensive landline communications, including fiber-optic systems, to provide secure communications, and extensive back-up systems, including buried telephone lines and troposcatter radios. Land lines were targeted by special operations forces, forcing the Iraqis to use radio links that were intercepted by COMINT forces and were destroyed by hard-kill weapons.[8]

The most common ESM systems used were the radar homing and warning (RHAW) receivers carried by all tactical aircraft (with the possible exception of some A-4KV and Jaguar fighter-bombers) and many helicopters. The ESM problem seen in earlier conflicts – adapting systems and threat libraries of electronic signatures originally designed against Soviet threats to include Western-designed threats – did not re-occur. During the 1979 Iran Hostage crisis and the Falklands War, U.S. and British forces initially were unprepared to counter threats from Western-designed gear, but in 1991 there were equipment and tactics to counter systems such as captured IHAWK SAMs and Exocet ASMs and SSMs. This was due in large measure to the five months between the force deployments and the beginning of the war. In this respect, General Dugan said, "It's not clear that the U.S. will have time in future to train against friendly equipment and the lessons learned to others is don't give the U.S. five months to train."[9]

Iraqi ESM, consisting of Soviet- and Western-designed systems, proved difficult to totally destroy during the air campaign. Although the attacks rendered the Iraqi high command blind and deaf and unable to move forces in response to information, the residual Iraqi ESM capability required an extensive deception plan to cover the shift of Coalition forces westward before opening the ground offensive. Coalition forces were redeployed in radio silence, while bogus radio transmissions in the original assembly areas provided a flow of radio traffic that would indicate to Iraq that the units had not moved.[10]

Iraq used COMINT information to move its mobile SCUD missile systems away from incoming air strikes, to turn off radars from defense suppression strikes, and to ambush low-flying attack aircraft. Iraqi ESM detected Coalition standoff jamming before strike aircraft came over their targets, alerting AAA to open fire. This led the Coalition to cease jamming support for some F-117 strikes so that the aircraft remained largely undetected; while on other occasions jamming was used to trigger fruitless Iraqi AAA barrage firing. Iraqis also monitored the rescues of downed Coalition air crews, but were unable to use this intelligence to thwart these operations. Iraqi internal security forces also used ESM equipment against Kuwaiti resistance.[11]

Many sources noted that the Coalition was able to monitor Iraqi communications throughout the war and that this provided much valuable intelligence. This suggests that orders for using chemical weapons would have been intercepted had they been given and that such intercepts led to post-war Coalition warnings against the use of chemical weapons against the Shiite rebels.[12]

ELECTRONIC COUNTERMEASURES (ECM)

The most dynamic element of electronic warfare, electronic countermeasures (ECM), are intended to affect enemy electronic emitters. ECM consists of active countermeasures that involve radiating electromagnetic energy, and passive countermeasures that do not. Both were used widely in the war.

Active jamming was extremely heavy. With the possible exception of some non-Saudi Arab forces, every fixed-wing tactical aircraft that crossed the front lines had either an internal or a podded jammer. This let them operate largely at medium altitude, above the reach of visually-directed AAA and heat-seeking SAMs, thereby reducing aircraft losses. Many helicopters also carried on-board self-protection ECM gear.[13]

The most formidable ECM aircraft were the U.S. Air Force's EF-111A and the Navy-Marine Corps EA-6B. Both had the powerful ALQ-99 jamming system and were used throughout the war to escort air strikes, providing jamming support that enabled tactical aircraft to penetrate to their targets. The Navy and Marine Corps did not launch strikes without EA-6B support, and this prevented Iraqi SAMs from lock-on against strike aircraft.[14]

Air communications jamming was the mission of about eight U.S. Air Force EC-130H Compass Call aircraft (which also have a "spoofing" capability able to invade enemy communications nets) supported by U.S. Army RU-21 Cefire Tigers. These aircraft, surface-based jammers such as those in the CEWI battalions, and accurate air strikes severed the control links from Saddam's centralized national command authority to his troops. At the tactical level, air defense radars did not receive target data when they were jammed and had to light up and search, making them vulnerable to HARM missile attacks. This communications severance was very complete. The captured diary of one Iraqi air defense battery commander revealed that he had not heard from his superiors for the last three weeks of the war![15]

Iraq's active jamming was focused mainly on ground-based systems. It deployed a range of Soviet-designed and 1970 vintage French-designed ground-based jammers that had little effect. Also, its "Paint Can" van-mounted jammers were reportedly countered when it tried to jam E-3A AWACS radars before the war. Both AWACS and tactical aircraft overcame Iraqi jamming during the war itself.[16]

To defeat Iraqi C³I and air defense, the Coalition used ESM, hard-kill weapons, and ECM judiciously, so that each complemented the other's effects. Hard-kill weapons were vital, and the Israeli general who said "the most effective ECM is a bomb on a radar station" was proven correct. Hard-kill systems included U.S. Air Force F-4G "Wild Weasels," as well as F-117s and F-16s. U.S. Navy-Marine Corps EA-6Bs and F/A-18s also made extensive use of anti-radiation missiles (ARMs). During first ten days of the air campaign, U.S. forces alone flew over 1,000 sorties against Iraqi air defenses, expending about 600 HARM anti-radiation missiles (over 1,000 were used throughout the war), that supplemented Paveway laser-guided bombs. Royal Air Force Tornado GR1s fired over 100 ALARM ARMs. Attacks on the key nodes of the Iraqi C³ system in the first hours of the war were so destructive that Iraq never recovered. In the very first strike of the air campaign eight U.S. Army AH-64 Apache helicopters destroyed two Iraqi radars, opening strike corridors for fixed-wing aircraft going to repeat the process throughout Iraq. This was followed by many similar tactical aircraft strikes, led by U.S. Navy Tomahawk cruise missiles and Air Force F-117s and F-4Gs.[17]

The Coalition's passive countermeasures went far beyond the near-universal use of chaff (and their active-infrared countermeasures counterpart, flares) seen in earlier conflicts. U.S. Navy and Marine Corps tactical aircraft made extensive use of TALD air-launched decoys, and efforts were made to reduce the radar cross-section of a wide range of ships and aircraft.[18]

The U.S. Air Force F-117 Stealth fighter does not use passive countermeasures. It is a passive countermeasure and is the best example of how ECM has progressed from a peripheral "add-on" to an integral part of a system. While the F-117s represented only 2.5 percent of the Coalition's tactical air power, they struck 31 percent of the targets hit in the first day of the war and were assigned more than 40 percent of all targets. While they were not invulnerable to detection, they showed the increased importance of passive countermeasures in the face of modern weapons.[19]

Electronic Counter-counter Measures (ECCM)
The most basic ECCM tactic is emission control (EMCON) that reduces the radiation of electromagnetic energy that is vulnerable to

ESM or ECM. Radio or radar silence is its most intense application. Maintaining effective electronic discipline in the Coalition was sometimes difficult. While U.S., British, French, and NATO forces have spent years trying to minimize those lax operational communications security practices commonplace in the past, some Coalition forces, particularly the Saudis, did not have such discipline.[20]

Iraq made extensive use of EMCON. Before the war, the Iraqis minimized the use of their radios and air defense radars, thereby reducing the ELINT available to the Coalition. When hostilities began, Iraqi air defense radars were activated but were quickly silenced by Coalition attacks. There was 95 percent less radar activity on January 23rd than on the 17th. Frank Kendall, U.S. Undersecretary of Defense for tactical warfare programs was correct when he said, "the willingness to turn on your radars and fight didn't seem to be there."[21]

The Iraqis also practiced tactical EMCON and were quite good at controlling radar emissions from their missile sites until the last moment. Iraqi actions were similar to other Arab and Vietnamese users of Soviet-made air defense systems in that they switched to the less accurate back-up optical guidance mode for their SAMs and AAA.[22] The low number of aircraft lost to SAMs, mainly heat seekers, shows this method is less effective.

ECCM also was a factor in the success of secure, reliable Coalition communications and resolved interoperability problems that initially seemed insurmountable. Systems such as the U.S. Army's SINCGARS radio system, the Air Force's Have Quick radio and the Navy's Link 11 data link had integral ECCM capabilities. The Iraqis had first and second generation secure radios with ECCM capability, but they were not used effectively.[23]

Lessons Learned

EW is no longer just the "wizard war." Rather it is now so integral to effective war-making that it is difficult to isolate and analyze it as a separate entity. Sophisticated technology is a part of daily life, and fears that any level of technology higher than that of the mid-1960s would prove unsupportable in sustained combat were proven invalid in the Gulf War. The war showed that, if it is supported by quality people and good training, EW works.[24]

The war showed once again that having hardware and manpower does not translate directly into a militarily effective force, especially in the Third World. The Coalition's air campaign and EW turned the Iraqi military into an ineffective rabble.

There is the question of the role EW will play in the force-structuring and thinking of both the United States and "medium" forces, such as those of Great Britain and France, who saw EW's importance in the war, but are unlikely to have the resources in the 1990s to afford many of the new technologies, considering the deep defense cuts that are currently looming.

Finally, while EW did not win the war and may not have been used to its optimum advantage, the lessons remain clear. The Soviets saw the power of Western electronic war-fighting and the uselessness of many of their own systems in the hands of the hapless Iraqis; certainly disarming news in Moscow. The West saw that control of the battlefield means control of the electromagnetic spectrum.

NOTES

1. Theresa Hitchens, "One on One," *Defense News* (April 8, 1991): 30.
2. R. Jeffrey Smith, "Air War Wrecked Iraqi Ability to Detect, React to Assaults," *The Washington Post*, February 27, 1991, p. A-28; and George Wilson, "Iraqis Face Early Defeat, Officials Say," *The Washington Post*, February 26, 1991, p. A-18.
3. Bruce D. Nordwall, "Electronic Warfare Played Greater Role in Desert Storm Than Any Conflict," *Aviation Week and Space Technology* (hereafter referred to as *AW&ST*) (April 22, 1991): 68–69.
4. Eric Schmitt, "Why Iraqi Battle Threat Fizzled: Allied Strengths and Enemy Weaknesses," *The New York Times*, March 4, 1991, p. A-9.
5. Barbara Opall, "McPeak Says Iraqi Air Force in Ruins", *Defense News* (April 18, 1991): 36; Kernan Chaisson, "U.S. Must Refine EW Systems, Tactics," *Defense News* (March 11, 1991): 29–30; and "F-117, Joint STARS are Winners in Gen. Dugan's Desert Storm Scorecard," *Inside the Pentagon* (March 7, 1991): 6–7.
6. Bill Sweetman and Tony Banks, "Techint v. Humint: The Unseen War," *Jane's Defence Weekly* (February 16, 1991): 221; "Gulf Operations Begin," *MILAVNEWS* (February 1991): 9; Martin Streetly, "Allies Take Advantage of Electronic Support," *Flight International* (January 30, 1991): 10; Nordwall, p. 68; "Other Aircraft Used," *AW&ST* (April 22, 1991): 114; Barbara Staff, "Submarine Missions Detailed," *Jane's Defence Weekly* (April 6, 1991): 523; and Jean Guisnel, "Doubts About Efficiency of French Intelligence," *Liberation* (January 24, 1991): 8, in *FBIS Daily Report: Western Europe* (January 30, 1991): 20–21.
7. Barbara Starr, "Satellites Paved Way to Victory," *Jane's Defence Weekly* (March 9, 1991): 330; "Satellite Intelligence," *AW&ST* (February 25, 1991): 13; "Space-craft Played Vital Role in Gulf War Victory," *AW&ST* (April 22, 1991): 21;

Desmond Ball, *Intelligence War In The Gulf* (Canberra: Strategic and Defence Studies Center, Australian National University, 1990), pp. 2, 8; Bob Archer, "Month 1: The Air War," *Air Forces Monthly* (March 1991): 12; Sweetman and Banks, p. 221; and "Battle Ready," *AW&ST* (March 4, 1991): 4.

8. Neil Munro, "Enemy Silence Hampers Army Intelligence Efforts," *Defense News* (February 25, 1991): 36; Neil Munro, "Iraq Finds Little Advantage in Electronic Eavesdropping," *Defense News* (April 1, 1991): 9; and Neil Munro, "C3 Countermeasures Aid Swift Defeat of Iraqi Military," *Defense News* (April 15, 1991): 48.

9. Streetly; and "F-117, Joint STARS are Winners," pp. 6–7.

10. Hugh McCann, "Operation Desert Shield Electronic Warfare," *The Detroit News*, November 12, 1990, p. F-1; Ball, pp. 18–21; James Adams "Secret War," *The Sunday Times*, March 10, 1991, p. 9; Neil Munro, "C3 Countermeasures;" "Michael R. Gordon, "Desert Missions by Commandos Aided in Victory," *The New York Times*, March 1, 1991, pp. A-1, A-12; Ian Kemp, "100 Hour War To Free Kuwait," *Jane's Defence Weekly* (March 9, 1991): 326–327; Molly Moore, "Allies Used a Variation of Trojan Horse Ploy," *The Washington Post*, March 17, 1991, p. A-23; and Michael R. Gordon, "Before Ground War Began, Marines Were Inside Kuwait," *The New York Times*, March 17, 1991.

11. David A. Fulghum, "U.S. Searches for Electronic Equipment Used by Iraqis to Foil Allied Attacks," *AW&ST* (March 18, 1991): 27; Michael A. Dornheim, "F-117A Pilots Conduct Precision Bombing in High Threat Environment," *AW&ST* (April 22, 1991): 51–53; Munro, "Iraq Finds," and Ball, p. 19.

12. Neil Munro, "Allied Forces Cracked Iraqi Scrambling Systems," *Defense News* (April 15, 1991): 19; "Russian Spoken on Iraqi Wavelengths," *Liberation* (12 February, 1991): 4, translated in *Daily Report: Western Europe* (February 19, 1991): 30; and Bill Gertz, "Allies Plan Reply to Iraqi Chemicals," *The Washington Times*, March 11, 1991, p. A-8.

13. Streetly; Paul Beaver, "Figures That Add Up To Success," *Jane's Defence Weekly* (April 6, 1991): 529–531; Christopher Bellamy, "RAF Chief Tells How War Strategy Changed," *The Independent*, March 26, 1991, p.9; Craig R. Whitney, "B-52 Crews in England Tell of High-Altitude Strikes on Iraqi Targets," *The New York Times*, March 8, 1991, p. A-8; and "RN: Guarding the Gulf," *Jane's Defence Weekly* (April 6, 1991): 543.

14. Julie Bird, "Ravens Confound Antiaircraft Operators," *Defense News* (January 28, 1991): 31; and Nordwall, p. 68.

15. Munro, "C3 Countermeasures," p. 48; Tony Capaccio and Eric Rosenberg, "Iraqis Confounded by Jamming Fury," *Defense Week* (January 28, 1991): 1, 9, 12; and Douglas Jehl, "Diary from a Bombed Bunker: 'Shrapnel Everywhere'," *The Washington Post*, March 5, 1991, p. A-12.

16. Ball, pp. 19–22; Bill Gertz, "U.S. Breathes Easier As It Spots Iraq's Jamming Gear," *The Washington Times*, October 9, 1990, p. A-8; Jeffrey M. Lenorovitz, "AWACS Played Critical Role in Allied Victory Over Iraq," *AW&ST* (March 4, 1991): 23–24; and "F-16As Prove Usefulness in Attack Role Against Iraqi Targets in Desert Storm," *AW&ST* (April 22, 1991): 62–63.

17. Nordwall; Cappacio and Rosenberg, p. 1; Martin Streetly, "HARM and ALARM in the Gulf," *Jane's Defence Weekly* (March 30, 1991): 500–50l; "RAF Reports ALARM Success," *Flight International* (January 23, 1991): 23; Carole A.

Shifrin, "Britain's Gulf Role Highlights Value of Flexible Tactics, New Technology," *AW&ST* (April 22, 1991): 107; Joris Janssen Lok, "Fighting To Communicate – the USN's Biggest Problem," *Jane's Defence Weekly* (April 13, 1991): 586; Kieran Daly, "US Army Claims Gulf War Systems Success," *Flight International* (March 27, 1991): 6; David F. Bond, "Army Speeds Helicopter Enhancements In Response to Desert Storm Problems," *AW&ST* (April 1, 1991): 24–25; Stewart M. Powell, "Voices From the War," *Air Force* (April 1991): 36–42; and William B. Scott, "F-16 Displays High Reliability Under Demanding Wartime Schedule," *AW&ST* (March 4, 1991): 66–7.

18. David Foxwell, "Reaping the Benefit of Experience in the Gulf," *International Defense Review* 2(1991): 115.

19. Michael A. Dornheim, "Trapeze Gives F-117 Ability to Carry Variety of Weapons," *AW&ST* (April 8, 1991): 72; John F. Morton, "TACAIR – Lesson From the Gulf," *Defense Daily*, April 17, 1991, p. S-1–S-3; Bill Gertz, "Stealth Gave Allies Early Air-War Edge," *The Washington Times*, March 18, 1991, p. A6; "Flexibility of Attack Aircraft Crucial to Crushing Iraq's Military Machine," *AW&ST* (April 22, 1991): 46–47; Michael White, "Stealth Defence Pierced," *The Guardian*, March 25, 1991, p. 1; and O. Falichev, "Networks for 'Stealth Aircraft;' Can Our Radars Detect Stealth Aircraft?" *Krasnaya Zvezda*, January 30, 1991, translated in *Daily Report: Soviet Union* (February 11, 1991): 60–61.

20. Fulghum.

21. "Filtering Helped Top Military Leaders Get Proper Intelligence Information," *AW&ST* (April 22, 1991): 85; John D. Morrocco, "War Will Reshape Doctrine, But Lessons Are Limited," *AW&ST* (April 22, 1991): 41; and "Cheney, Powell Deliver First Major Briefing on Operation Desert Storm," *Desert Storm Report* (January 25, 1991): 5.

22. An example of this is seen in "Comment and Discussion: Two Seats-Until Now," Naval Institute *Proceedings* (April 1991): 14–15. Capaccio and Rosenberg, p. 9; John D. Morrocco, "Soviet Peace Plan Weighed As Gulf Ground War Looms," *AW&ST* (February 25, 1991): 22.

23. James W. Canan, "How to Command and Control a War," *Air Force* (April 1991): 16; Caleb Baker, "Army Finds Few Flaws in War," *Defense News* (March 18, 1991): 1, 9; Robert Holzer, "Long Buildup Allowed U.S. To Fill Gaps In Intelligence," *Defense News* (March 18, 1991): 5; "Filtering Helped;" and Munro, "C3 Countermeasures."

24. George Leopold, "Maintenance of Vital EW Gear in Gulf Worries U.S." *Defense News* (January 28, 1991): 31.

11: Logistics Lessons
by
Joel H. Nadel

There are four general categories of supplies required by any military organization to make war: ammunition, petroleum, spare parts, and food and medical supplies. There must be enough ammunition to conduct any operation that is required, and whether one is attacking, defending, or withdrawing, it is crucial to the success of the endeavor. Artillery consumes the most tonnage, but a mechanized infantry division can use up to 3,500 tons of ammunition a day when it is on the offensive. Motorized and armored forces also use vast amounts of petroleum, especially when they are on the offensive. An armored division can use up to 600,000 gallons of fuel a day, twice the amount sold by the average service station in a month. In intense combat, motorized formations will have many problems due to accidents, wear, and enemy action. In an offensive, a mechanized infantry division can consume up to 50 tons of spare parts, up to 75 tons of food and medical supplies, and 108,000 gallons of water a day.[1]

IRAQ'S LOGISTICAL CAPABILITIES

During the Iran-Iraq War, the Soviet Union, France, Italy, Germany, Great Britain, Brazil, and the United States all sold Iraq weapons, providing it with some of the finest arms in the world.[2] By 1990, Iraq was making some of its own artillery pieces and ammunition for export. The actual amount of ammunition it had when it invaded Kuwait is unknown, but it probably had a year's supply. Since Iraq had its own petroleum supplies, this item could probably have lasted indefinitely if its storage and production facilities remained intact. Data on spare parts are also unavailable, but a U.S. automobile maker stated that Iraq usually bought enough parts to last a year as a part of any car or truck purchase. Finally, while Iraq had limited food reserves and a limited production capability, it announced that the military would have top priority for food supplies. This decision, combined with food deliveries from Jordan, probably would have sustained the Army for more than a year. Thus, given these capabilities and supplies, Iraq probably could have endured the U.N. embargo for more than a year with no significant reduction in its military capability.

Iraq had four means of transporting military forces and supplies into the Kuwaiti Theater of Operations (KTO): roads; a railway; pipelines; and by air. At least three highways, and possibly a fourth, and a single rail line connected central Iraq with Basra. The railroad was well suited for transporting tanks and other large pieces of hardware, while the highways were better for moving supplies. Basra had oil refining facilities and terminals on the Iraqi strategic pipeline and the Iraq-Saudi Arabia (IPSA) pipeline. Three airfields near Basra allowed Iraq to rapidly move high priority cargo or passengers into the KTO.

In the KTO the principal transportation route between Kuwait and Iraq was a four to six lane highway running between Basra and Al Jahrah, where it split, with one route following the coast to Saudi Arabia and another running southwest toward the junction of the Iraq-Saudi Arabia-Kuwait tri-border. A two lane route ran from Basra to Umm Qasr, then followed the coastline to Al Jahrah, where it intersected with the main highway. An improved dirt road ran adjacent to the IPSA pipeline into southern Iraq, near the tri-border area. The four major highways and rail line running from central Iraq into the KTO converged at Az Zubayr, south of Basra, and the area was serviced by airfields at Safwan, Ash Shaibah, and Jalibah. The IPSA pipeline road, the coastal highway, and the Al Basrah-Al Jahrah highway also converged near Az Zubayr. Kuwait also had three airfields: Ali Al Salem, Kuwait International Airport, and Al Jaber, near the Saudi border. Since Kuwait had no railroads, all Iraqi supplies had to come by air, road, or coastal waterway.

THE COALITION'S LOGISTICAL CAPABILITIES

The Coalition had unlimited supplies of almost all needed items. There were ammunition stockpiles in Europe and America. Saudi Arabia had the largest oil reserves and production capacities in the world. There was enough food, but there was a potential shortage of water, as almost all potable water came from Gulf desalinization plants. Although they provided enough water for the Saudis and Coalition forces, their loss would have been a critical blow, and water purification equipment was shipped to provide a contingency.[3]

While the Coalition had enough supplies, their location was a problem. Since almost all supplies, except water, petroleum, and some food had to be shipped from Europe, Asia, or the United States, the Coalition was very dependent on transportation. Not having enough aircraft and ships for the troop deployment and to build up and sustain the required 60 days of supplies, the U.S. Transportation Command contracted with civilian businesses to support the operation.[4] Supplies were shipped from Germany, America, the Netherlands, Italy, and other nations.

The Saudi Arabian transportation infrastructure was also a problem. It had only four roads connecting northern Saudi Arabia with Riyadh and the coastal ports and no railway, which meant that all heavy armored equipment had to be transported by large heavy equipment transporters in order to minimize wear. Thus, truck transport and pipelines were the primary transportation means within Saudi Arabia, and the Coalition had to improve the transportation network and supplement it with military and civilian resources from Europe, America, and elsewhere.

IRAQI LOGISTICS OPERATIONS

Iraqi logistics doctrine, reflecting both Soviet and British influence, used a "push" system, whereby supplies were managed by the General Headquarters (GHQ), and when a need arose, it staffed the supply and transportation requests and then monitored the delivery of the supplies to forward depots.[5] These GHQ depots were probably located south and west of Basra, and since Basra was a base of operations for most of the Iran-Iraq war, there probably were several ammunition depots there.

Supplies from forward GHQ depots were then distributed to corps that lacked supply depots. Specific information on depot locations is not available, but it was likely that Iraq used warehouses in Kuwait City and Al Jahrah. In fact, given the civilian infrastructure in Kuwait City, with hospitals, service stations, and an airfield, it is likely that Iraq used the city as a corps support area. A second depot was probably located with the Republican Guard along Kuwait's northern border. Given the large numbers of supply depots the Coalition found along Highway 8 (on the south bank of the Euphrates, near Jalibah airfield), it was likely that another was located there.[6]

The British system was seen in supply distribution below the corps level, in which units subordinate to each headquarters requested supplies. Known as a "pull" system, it is flexible in that supplies can sent directly from a corps to a brigade or battalion, bypassing intermediate headquarters. Up to six days' supply was maintained in a corps area of operations, with three days at corps and three days at the weapons system, brigade, and division. From the corps level upward, transport was probably controlled by GHQ, and divisions had a transportation battalion and brigades a transportation company for resupply operations.[7]

The transportation network is often a major weakness of a logistics system, the rule being the fewer the routes, the more vulnerable the system. Iraq had only three or four highways and a single rail line to transport bulk cargo into the KTO. From Basra to the KTO, including southern Iraq, there were only three highways, but engineers also improved at least 500 kilometers of dirt tracks and roads.[8] However, since corps depots were 100 to 200 kilometers from front line troops, the roads linking the depots to the troops were highly vulnerable to air interdiction.

COALITION LOGISTICS OPERATIONS

The Coalition used a "pull" logistics system in that units requisitioned required supplies from higher headquarters and each headquarters maintained a standing list of requests from its subordinate units so that when a crisis developed, it could immediately begin shipping supplies. In America, the Military Traffic Management Command provided the transportation needed to sustain deployed forces, while military transportation resources were controlled by the U.S. Transportation Command. The Military Airlift Command transported troops, equipment, and supplies to Dhahran and Riyadh on military and contracted civilian aircraft. Strategic resupply was provided by the 1st Corps Support Command, which was subordinated to Third U.S. Army, under Schwarzkopf's command.[9] Except for food, fuel, and water, each nation supported its own forces, while port facilities were operated by local contractors under U.S. supervision. Each nation provided its own combat rations and the Saudis made fresh food (vegetables, dairy products, and other items) available to Coalition forces. Saudi Arabia also provided fuel and water, while the U.S. Central Command (CENTCOM) established logistics bases across northern Saudi Arabia to resupply combat divisions.

On January 17, 1991, in preparation for the offensive, VII Corps, along with its logistics base, began moving from Hafr al Batin 150 miles westward to get into position for its February 24th assault. Each U.S. combat division had a division support command consisting of main and forward support battalions for each combat brigade. Each of the armored divisions needed 290-300 trucks to haul its ammunition, fuel, water, and supplies, so that 3,500–4,000 trucks were required to support the operation from logistics bases forward. At least that many trucks were needed to keep supplies going from the ports to the logistics bases. Combat units consumed approximately 5,000,000 gallons of fuel, 1,300,000 gallons of water, 708 tons of food, 34,000 tons of ammunition, and 804 tons of medical and miscellaneous supplies daily.[10] Schwarzkopf said of this logistics effort:

> ... I can't recall any time in the annals of military history when this number of forces have moved over this distance to put themselves in a position to be able to attack. But what's more important – and I think it's very, very important that I make this point – and that's the logistics bases. Not only did we move the troops out there, but we literally moved thousands and thousands of tons of fuel, of ammunition, of spare parts, of water and of food, out here into this area, because we wanted to have enough supplies on hand so that if we launched this and if we got into a slugfest battle, which we very easily could have gotten into, we'd have enough supplies to last for 60 days. So it was an absolutely gigantic accomplishment, and I can't give credit enough to the logisticians and transporters who were able to pull this off ... [11]

LOGISTICS INTERDICTION

A discussion of Iraqi plans to interdict Coalition logistics is problematic, since its Air Force was quickly neutralized and it lost the ability to interdict the Coalition's rear areas. Had the Coalition's air campaign not been so successful so quickly, and had the Iraqi Air Force been able to conduct interdiction missions, then the situation would have been much more difficult. Likewise, it was this air victory that prevented Iraq from posing any threat to the Suez Canal, a critical choke point in the Coalition's logistical chain.

During the first week of February, the Coalition began attacking Iraq's supply routes, and by 11th, had reduced them to 30 percent of their prewar capacity. When most bridges across the Euphrates River were destroyed the Iraqis used low capacity temporary bridging. They showed great ingenuity in this respect, and it was because of this that the Coalition's bridge campaign was not completely successful. Likewise, strikes on Iraqi supply routes did not completely cut them. Rather, Iraq reduced the size of convoys using them from 200 vehicles to about 20–30 vehicles. However, once the emphasis of the air campaign was switched to the KTO, air power was very successful in halting the delivery of supplies within theater. Most Iraqi POWs were hungry and dehydrated and some said they had not been fed in over a week. One had been living on grass and rainwater.[12] The bombing campaign had completely wrecked the Iraqi distribution system because Coalition forces overran significant stockpiles of food and ammunition in Kuwait and Iraq, indicating that supplies were available, but Iraq could not get them to its soldiers.

LESSONS LEARNED

Clearly, disrupting the logistics system played a role in destroying the Iraqi Army, but that role was somewhat indirect. Had the war lasted longer than 100 hours, the Army would have had to curtail its activities due to shortages. Disrupting Iraq's strategic highway and rail network enabled the Coalition to destroy huge amounts of Iraq's military hardware. As the army tried to withdraw, it was trapped and Coalition ground and air power destroyed the remaining equipment at will. The massive destruction on the "highway of death" between Kuwait and Iraq was the most notable example of the Iraqi predicament.

In the Gulf War, the Coalition deployed forces and supplies from all over the world and successfully defeated the world's fourth largest army. Two factors permitted this enormous logistical feat: technology and complete freedom of movement. Technology such as fast sea lift, jet transport, and computerized movement control were developed after World War II. Also, the Coalition, unlike the

Allies of fifty years ago, were operating with complete freedom of movement on the ground, sea, and air. Had it been denied this freedom, either by terrorist act or conventional military action, the outcome of the conflict could have been altered. However, the Coalition's navies were prepared to counter all threats to Coalition shipping. The picture is less bright in merchant shipping. While there have been significant efforts to preposition supplies as contingencies, the war demonstrated that a sustained war effort must be supported by sea, since the tonnage exceeds greatly the available air capability. The Gulf War logistics chain made great use of a variety of commercial bottoms from many nations. These may not always be available in the future, and the decline of Western merchant navies may someday prove to be the weak link in attempts to sustain a war effort in the world's more remote reaches.

NOTES

1. Joseph Galloway, "The Point of the Spear," *U.S. News and World Report* (March 11, 1991): 41; and Charles Lane, et. al., "The Killing Ground," *Newsweek* (January 28, 1991): 30.
2. Joshua Hammer with Karen Breslau, "The German Connection," *Newsweek* (February 4, 1991): 57; and Stockholm International Peace Research Institute, "Who Sold What to Iraq?," *For Your Eyes Only* (March 4, 1991): 260–8.
3. Ibid.; and Joyce R. Starr, "High Cost of a Soldier's Thirst," *Jane's Defence Weekly* (October 6, 1990): 652.
4. "Desert Storm Subsides," *Army Logistician* (May-June 1991): 1.
5. Department of the Army, *The Iraqi Army* (Handbook 100–91) (Washington, DC: Department of the Army, 1991), p. 173.
6. Ibid., p. 175; and Galloway, p. 33.
7. *The Iraqi Army*, pp. 176–177.
8. Stephen V. Cole (ed.), "Gulf Crisis: Notes and Observations," *For Your Eyes Only* (October 29, 1990): 251–3.
9. Ian Kemp and Joris Janssen Lok, "The Armies in the Desert," *Jane's Defence Weekly* (February 23, 1991): 255.
10. "Chancellor Lauds Logistics," *Army Logistician* (May-June 1991): 1; and Galloway, p. 41.
11. General Norman H. Schwarzkopf Briefing, 28 February 1991.
12. Charles Lane, "Do Rude Surprises Lie Ahead?" *Newsweek* (March 4, 1991): 32; and Brian Duffy, et. al., "The 100–Hour War," *U.S. News and World Report* (March 11, 1991): 18.

12: Terrorism and Ecoterrorism Lessons
by
Bruce W. Watson

Anti-Terrorist Measures

As the Coalition deployed its forces, its members expected an immediate outbreak of terrorism by unprofessional terrorists responding to Iraqi pleas for help. Saddam had called for a holy war shortly after the Coalition began deploying troops in August 1990, and repeated this plea in a broadcast on January 20, 1991.

The West reacted by bolstering its antiterrorist defenses and by isolating Iraq from terrorist support. In the United States, national monuments, airports, public areas, government offices, and military facilities were afforded greater security, and blockades were even placed around the notoriously insecure National Naval Medical Center in Bethesda, Maryland. In Europe, those military forces that had not been sent to the Middle East viewed terrorism, not the Soviet Union, as the major threat. Security in European countries was similarly stepped up in public facilities, especially airports, and embassies. In France, the gendarmerie and the French territorial National Guard conducted operation *Vigipirate*, which provided special protection of all possible terrorist targets. Iraqi nationals in more than 30 nations were placed under close surveillance and were even jailed, and cooperation among U.S. and European antiterrorist forces was unprecedented. Forty ships from NATO's Standing Force Channel and On Call Force Mediterranean were deployed to the Mediterranean on duties that were specifically intended to counter the terrorist threat. The Coalition also enjoyed the cooperation of Libya as well as neutrality from Iran. All controlled the terrorist groups under their influence, and Egypt, Iran, and Syria pressured Libya to forego activities.[1]

While the result has been proclaimed as a victory against terrorism, terrorist incidents did occur, although none were the dramatic, spectacular incidents that Saddam had wanted. There were more than 160 attacks recorded worldwide from January 17th until March 6, 1991, and since there were only 456 incidents in 1990, 160 was far higher than the norm of 20 per month. However, it was difficult to determine which incidents were in response to the war. Several acts in Israeli-occupied territory following the killing and wounding of many Palestinians by Israelis during riots in Jerusalem on October 8, 1990, could be discounted since they would have occurred regardless of the war. But the motives behind other incidents were less easy to determine. There was such a marked increase in the number of incidents that we can reasonably conclude that at least some were committed by Iraq or by unprofessional and professional terrorists who were either sympathetic to Iraq or espoused other causes.

UNPROFESSIONAL PRO-IRAQI TERRORISM

Terrorist acts by amateurs sympathetic to Iraq were expected to begin soon after Coalition troops began arriving in Saudi Arabia. Lacking professionalism, these people acted emotionally with little planning, and while they could achieve spectacular results, it was far more likely that their achievements would be relatively minor. Iraq was linked to two incidents. The first, an attempted bombing of a U.S. facility by an Iraqi citizen, occurred in Manilla, the Philippines, on January 19, 1991. The bomb, two dozen sticks of dynamite, detonated while the terrorist was transporting it to the facility, blowing him up. A similar effort, involving the same amount of dynamite and targeted against the U.S. ambassador's home in Jakarta, also failed.[2]

The U.S. State Department said that five people were killed and about 50 were wounded in all the terrorist incidents, which also had caused property damage. It added that the groups were not communicating with each other and that there was no master plan being directed by a single group or person. It concluded that many were expressing solidarity with Baghdad but were not operating under Iraqi direction.[3]

Professional Pro-Iraqi Terrorism

Terrorist acts might also be waged by professional terrorist organizations sympathetic to Iraq. They would try to perform high-visibility acts such as killing prominent dignitaries, bombing aircraft such as the bombing of Pan Am flight 103 over Scotland in 1988, or high visibility massacres such as that which occurred in Rome's airport in 1985. These professional acts are complex and involve months of planning. A suitable target must be chosen. Extensive surveillance must be conducted to determine the target's habits and vulnerabilities. The act must then be planned, the destructive means (bombing, shooting, etc.) must be determined and the actual terrorist team must be chosen. A logistical network to support the team must be established and put in place. Arms, explosives, equipment, false documents, transportation, "legends" (false histories), safe houses, and many other items must be acquired, and hundreds of details must be attended to. Thus, such dramatic professional terrorist acts were not expected to occur on short notice. Rather, they would be expected months or even years after the war's end. It is likely that Middle Eastern terrorist organizations would commit such acts, but because of the time needed to plan and prepare, it was premature to conclude that the terrorists had forsaken action because they did not act before the war ended. However, the Coalition did take several actions that may have convinced these groups to forego such plans.

Since the Coalition was partially composed of Arab nations the war was something other than a classic Islamic versus Western "imperialistic" confrontation. Balancing this, however, was the fact that U.S., British, French, and other non-Islamic forces had been deployed to Saudi Arabia, which could be interpreted as an intrusion of infidels into the Islamic world. However, Western and Arab diplomatic measures effectively reduced the terrorist organizations' bases of support.

In the period from August onward, Coalition diplomacy worked to reinforce Iran's belief that it was in its best interests to remain neutral. Iran did not have the ability to defeat a huge Coalition force in Saudi Arabia, and conversely, its regional influence increased considerably with Iraq's defeat in the Gulf War and with the Iraqi Shiite and Kurd revolts in the immediate post ceasefire period. These factors meant that it was simply in Iran's best interest to restrain terrorist operations by Hizballah and other Iranian-supported terrorist organizations.

Diplomacy was also successful in limiting support by Libya. Progress toward this goal was revealed in early-November, when Abu Abbas stated that Libya had expelled 145 of his followers and had closed four training camps. He appealed to Qadhafi to reopen them, but Arab sources stated that the United States had asked Morocco's King Hassan and Egypt's Mubarak to pressure Libya to expel the terrorists. Thus, Arab terrorists were deprived of two major supporters, which seriously upset their operations.

Dissention among different terrorist groups also contributed to their inability to act and weakened them considerably. On September 7th, Arafat's PLO force ousted Abu Nidal Organization terrorists from Palestinian refugee areas in southern Lebanon after fierce gun battles killed 30 people and wounded at least 85.[4] Arafat was the only major terrorist leader to ally himself closely with Saddam, and this proved to be a grave miscalculation that led to a lowering of PLO morale and possibly affected its operations.

AMATEUR AND PROFESSIONAL TERRORISM SUPPORTING OTHER CAUSES

A third threat was from amateur and professional terrorists who espoused other causes and committed acts out of sympathy for Iraq or to keep attention focused on themselves. The problem was to determine which were responses to the war. For example, the Irish Republican Army fired three mortar shells from a van parked in Whitehall on February 7, 1991. Two landed outside the Foreign Office, while a third hit the garden of 10 Downing Street, barely 50 feet from where Prime Minister John Major was about to convene a Cabinet meeting. It blew out windows and did extensive damage. Likewise, explosives were found on a storage tank near a U.S. naval base in Norfolk, Virginia. Both incidents were initially believed to be the work of pro-Iraqi terrorists, but the IRA soon revealed that its act was part of its anti-British campaign rather than support for Iraq, and that planning for it had begun prior to the start of the Gulf crisis. It was probably intended to remind people, whose attention was fixed on the Gulf War, that it was still in business. The Norfolk incident appears to have been an attempt at insurance fraud.

These acts show how difficult it was for analysts to examine the 160 incidents that occurred in order to determine which were due to the war. Besides the Philippines and Indonesian incidents discussed above, there were grenade and rocket attacks against Western embassies in Yemen and bombings in Athens, resulting in property damage and the loss of five lives. Some groups declared their support for Baghdad. The most active were Turkey's Dev Sol, November 17 in Greece, and the Tupac Amaru Revolutionary Movement in Peru. In Adana, Turkey in February 1991, a U.S. civilian, Bobbie Mozelle, was shot by Dev Sol agents as he left home for work at the air base at Incirlik, where air strikes were launched against Iraq. Claiming responsibility for the crime, Dev Sol denounced the "bloody games of U.S. imperialism." It also carried out over a dozen bombings of Coalition members' buildings and vehicles. The Revolutionary Organization 17 November, a Greek terrorist group, also conducted a series of bombings, and in Peru, Tupac Amaru conducted terrorist acts.[5] Their real motive may have been to keep attention on themselves, rather than to show support for Iraq.

Terrorism by Iraq

The final threat was from Iraq, which was expected to use chemical warfare on the battlefield, and to commit other "extra-military activities" that would threaten the lives of non-combatants. The Coalition decided early on that such acts would not deter it from carrying out its mission. Iraq did not launch a major biological or chemical warfare offensive in the war. However, it performed four actions that are best classified as terrorism: using captured civilians as human shields, causing a massive oil spill in the Gulf, conducting Scud attacks on Israel, and burning Kuwaiti oil wells.

Using Civilians as Human Shields

Iraq's invasion occurred so rapidly that many foreigners were unable to escape. Saddam was quick to use them as human shields, to be deployed to military bases and targets in order to deter possible Coalition attacks upon them. In doing this, he had two objectives: to prevent attacks on his forces; and to break up the alliance against him.

Iraq had begun collecting foreigners by August 6th, and on the

18th, Saddam declared the blockade to be an act of war and announced that the hostages would suffer the same food shortages as Iraqis. However, as hostages were moved to military sites, Saddam sensed the international pressure and during his televised meeting with British hostages on the 23rd, said that they were not hostages, but their presence was required to prevent war. This backfired because it prompted the United Nations to pass even stiffer resolutions. Saddam responded on the 28th by saying that all women and children could leave, but then made this a political issue by delaying their departure. The issue dragged on until all hostages were allowed to leave. The Coalition had thwarted Saddam by continually asserting that his actions were heinous, thereby bringing great international pressure to bear.

Saddam tried to weaken the Coalition by releasing hostages to people who came to plead for their release. While most of those making such visits were not authorized by their governments to do so, such visits still represented a symbolic break in the Coalition's solidarity. Washington and London thwarted this ploy by emphasizing that bargaining with the lives of civilians was immoral and that all of them should be allowed to leave rather than a selected few who were freed during such visits. In the end, this resolute Coalition diplomatic posture managed to effect their release.

The Persian Gulf Oil Spill

The Coalition expected that Iraq would use all means at its disposal, including ecological warfare, in fighting the war. On January 23rd and 24th, it resorted to such tactics when it opened the valves to the pumps at Kuwait's supertanker loading dock, Sea Island Terminal, located ten miles off the Kuwaiti coast, and began discharging about 120,000 barrels of oil a day into the Gulf. Iraq also began releasing oil from five oil-filled Kuwaiti tankers at Al-Ahmadi and then set the oil slick afire. It may have hoped that releasing the oil would force a halt to Coalition military operations, thereby giving its military infrastructure a respite in which they could recover from the bombing. The Coalition assessed the situation and reacted. By January 30th, U.S. Air Force F-111 aircraft had stopped the oil flow by pinpoint bombing on the manifolds. Meanwhile, President Bush formed a group with members from the National Oceanographic and Atmospheric Administration, U.S.

Coast Guard, and Environmental Protection Agency, to assist in dealing with the oil spill.

There were varied estimates as to the amount of oil spilt and its effects. The U.S. Defense Department reported on January 30th, that the spill covered an area of 1,200 square miles, and estimates of the total amount of oil spilt ran up to 294 million gallons. While subsequent, more accurate estimates were much lower, other factors made this an ecological oil disaster of unprecedented proportions. Because the Gulf was shallow, there was relatively less water to dilute the oil than there had been in most earlier spills. Second, since the spill was in Iraqi-occupied territory, ecologists did not have immediate access to it and could not take prompt action. Thus, the oil spread and the slick decomposed. Third, the Gulf empties itself very slowly – even the most conservative estimate was three to five years to flush it out, in contrast to twenty-eight days for Prince William Sound, site of the *Exxon Valdez* accident.[6]

Releasing oil into the Gulf provided Iraq with no military or diplomatic benefit. As it spread, the slick was increasingly difficult to ignite, and even if afire, it would not have impeded Coalition amphibious landings along the coast. Diplomatically, the damage that was caused brought almost total condemnation.

Scud Attacks on Israel and Saudi Arabia
The Iraqi use of Scud missiles qualified as terrorism for two reasons. First, Scud was an older, very inaccurate missile that was of limited military value because it could not be used with confidence to destroy enemy installations. Rather, its use involved firing it in hopes of incurring the greatest damage possible. Secondly, Iraq fired them at civilian centers in Israeli and Saudi cities, acts that had no military meaning, but qualified as significant terrorism. (Appendix C presents a listing of the Scud attacks.)

The Coalition believed that Iraq would use its Scuds when the war began. It was uncertain if these missiles would have chemical warheads, but even if they did, the attacks would be bearable, because to launch a devastating chemical attack, Iraq would have to launch a barrage of Scuds and detonate them in the air to create the chemical blanket needed to kill large numbers of people. This was clearly beyond its capability, and if it used chemical warheads, it could at best hope to create isolated pockets of toxic atmosphere that might claim a few lives, but would not cause huge numbers of deaths that would reflect an effective chemical attack.[7] As expected, Iraq conducted Scud attacks against both Israeli and Saudi territory, but the problem was greater because Coalition intelligence had grossly underestimated the number of Scud launchers. The aim of striking Israel was to draw it into the war, banking on Israel's stated national security policy to retaliate for aggression. The first attack prompted an immediate public outcry for retaliation. However, to do so meant overflying Jordan to reach Iraqi targets, which would have brought Jordan into the war on Iraq's side and would have destroyed the Coalition. The war then would assume the character of an Arab-Israeli conflict, causing many Coalition Arab states, Syria, Egypt, Saudi Arabia, and the Persian Gulf Emirates among them, to possibly to withdraw from it. Also, as Schwarzkopf said, there was nothing that Israel could do that the Coalition was not doing to destroy the Scud capability.[8] The United States acted swiftly. Pressuring Israel not to retaliate, it quickly sent Patriot missiles to Israel, thereby providing for its defense. This prevented Israel's entry into the war and effectively thwarted Saddam's aims of destroying the Coalition and widening the war.

Using Scuds against Saudi territory was diplomatically less volatile but militarily more destructive. Most were intercepted, but on the night of February 25th, one hit a U.S. barracks in Dhahran, killing 27 U.S. soldiers and wounding 98 more. While the strike had virtually no military effect, it did account for a substantial part of the total loss of American lives in the war.

Burning Kuwaiti Oil Wells

While the Coalition realized that Iraq had the capability to destroy or set Kuwaiti oil wells afire, this was not allowed to interfere with the war effort. However, the worst-case scenario resulted. All 950 Kuwaiti oil wells were either sabotaged or set afire by retreating Iraqi forces, who also mined the approaches to many in the closing days of the war. The fires consumed as much as five million barrels a day, with devastating results. Fires spewed toxic smoke so thick that at noon Coalition forces advancing on Kuwait City had to use flashlights to see their maps. Smoke consisting of toxic particles and sulfurous gases threatened crops and water supplies as far away as Pakistan.[9]

The response was prompt. U.S. and British firefighters were

called in and work was begun. As of June 11th, 157 wells had been capped and 25,000 barrels of oil were being pumped daily, in contrast to 1,500,000 per day before the invasion.[10]

LESSONS LEARNED

There are several lessons concerning terrorism and the war. First, in the past, terrorism has thrived on the unresolved Arab-Israeli dispute, a conflict so dominant that it prevented the West from effectively influencing state supporters of terrorism. The war did not fall within this Arab-Israeli context, and Arab nations such as Syria that had supported terrorism in the past, joined the Coalition. This provided enough leeway for Coalition diplomacy to effectively contain terrorism during the war.

Whether this success will continue in the postwar period is problematic. Western democracies can deter or at least limit terrorism if they initially show determination and subsequently maintain the resolve not to be influenced by it. The unwavering positions of President Bush and Prime Ministers Thatcher and Major during the war doomed Iraqi terrorist and ecoterrorist acts to failure. Thus the Coalition managed to escape the problem of human shields and did not allow Iraq's ecoterrorist advantage to deter it from fighting the war. In this respect, resolve, effectively influencing the public through the media, and a clear-cut policy may limit the value of terrorism in the future.

Another lesson is that Israel can be influenced in its anti-terrorist policy. Its unequivocal retaliatory policy toward terrorism was reversed because of U.S. protection and diplomatic pressure. On the positive side, this could portend other Israeli concessions in postwar negotiations. Conversely, since Israel agreed not to retaliate once, it might be forced to forego retaliation again when provoked in the future.

The final lesson is that unprecedented international antiterrorist cooperation and the antiterrorist measures that were taken during the war may have also limited the number of terrorist acts substantially. Since Western antiterrorist organizations traditionally do not reveal their operations, we may never know how many terrorist acts they prevented. The scattered pieces of information that are available indicate that antiterrorist measures were unprecedented and we can conclude that they had an effect on the number of incidents that occurred. Having said this, we must also note that, while these measures may have had an effect, they were defensive. Far greater progress was made offensively, through diplomatic means. Here the aim was to limit state support for terrorism by convincing states that it was in their best interests to act alternatively. Without such support, the terrorist organizations were much more limited in what they could do. All of this reemphasizes a lesson that was already known: the ultimate solution to terrorism lies in diplomacy, not in antiterrorist defenses, and only through the aggressive search for diplomatic solutions to contemporary dilemmas can we hope to make substantial inroads.

NOTES

1. "Americans Afraid," *The Times* (London), January 28, 1991; and Scott Armstrong, "Unity in War Seen as Defeat for Terrorism," *Christian Science Monitor*, March 7, 1991.
2. Tom Masland, Rod Nordland, Daniel Pedersen, and Bob Cohn, "A Tide of Terrorism," *Time* (February 18, 1991): 35.
3. George Lardner Jr. "State Department Notes Increase in Terrorist Acts," *The Washington Post*, February 12, 1991, p. A15.
4. *The New York Times*, September 8, 1991, sec. I, p. 7.
5. Masland, p. 35; "World Notes: Britain, A Stab at the Heart," *Time*, February 18, 1991, p. 53; and George Lardner Jr. "State Department Notes Increase in Terrorist Acts," *The Washington Post*, February 12, 1991, p. A15.
6. "Apocalypse Row," *The Economist* (January 12, 1991): 63; "Environment: Dead Sea in the Making," *Time* (February 11, 1991): 40–41; Department of Defense Briefing, January 30, 1990; and "Saddam's Ecoterror," p. 39. These estimates varied widely, one cited 200 years for the Gulf versus a few days for Prince William Sound (see: "Saddam's Ecoterror," p. 38).
7. "David Frost Interview with General Norman Schwarzkopf," televised in Washington, DC on April 3, 1991, by the Public Broadcasting System.
8. Ibid.
9. Eric Schmitt, "The Environment: Fouled Region is Casualty of War," *The New York Times*, March 3, 1991, p. 19.
10. *The Daily Telegraph*, June 12, 1991.

PART V
THE CONSEQUENCES OF WAR

13: The Effects of the War on Other Nations
by
Bruce W. Watson, Bruce W. Watson, Jr., David Dunphy, Richard DeJong, Brian Gagne, Michael Kirsch, and Yong Pak

Today's world's interrelated nature means that wars can have far reaching effects, involving nations that do not even take part in them. While the Gulf War affected many non-participants, this chapter addresses only those that were affected most significantly. Regionally, it affected Israel, Jordan, Iran, and Libya, while for Germany and Japan, it influenced their relations with other powers.

ISRAEL – BRUCE W. WATSON AND MICHAEL KIRSCH

Effects on Israeli Foreign Policy – Bruce W. Watson
The war drew attention to two key aspects of Israeli policy. The first was expansionism, the very territory that Israel occupied. The crisis occurred at a time when the Soviet Union had unlocked the doors to hundreds of thousands of Soviet Jews who wished to emigrate. Their passage to Israel and settlement in the Occupied Territories inflamed the Palestinians who saw this as their land being taken from them. In addition, the Palestinian *Intifada* of civil upset and disorder had at times met with such severe Israeli response that it often prompted calls for Israel's censure in the United Nations.[1]

The second aspect was the U.S. connection. Americans for years had viewed Israel as their most loyal and only democratic ally in the Middle East. This influenced U.S. foreign policy so that America provided considerable financial aid and supported Israel in any relevant international issue. It is questionable who gained most from this relationship, but it certainly contributed to U.S. alienation from many Arab nations. In the Gulf War, it was in both their interests to keep Iraq's invasion of Kuwait and the Occupied Territories issue separated.[2] In an attempt to excuse the invasion, sometime after the event, and to split the Coalition, Iraq tried to link the two themes.

America's Coalition role began to affect its Israeli policy in August 1990. Believing that Saddam would use its Israeli policy to discredit it, Washington tried moderation. Israel and Washington agreed to work for a "credible" Arab-Israeli peace process as an alternative to Saddam's violent approach on September 5th, and on the 15th, the United States postponed its campaign to repeal a U.N. resolution equating Zionism to racism.

While the new U.S. policy caused misgivings in Israel, defense matters caused even greater concern. Besides sending forces, the United States wished to bolster Saudi defenses, and on the 18th, Secretary Cheney told Israeli Defense Minister Moshe Arens that a $1 billion Israeli defense request would be viewed sympathetically if Israel did not block a $20 billion arms sale to Saudi Arabia. On the 26th, Secretary Baker tried to assuage Israel by saying that any Iraqi attack would prompt a vigorous U.S. response, but on October 1st, when Bush said that resolving the Gulf crisis could pave the way for an Arab-Israeli settlement, both Israel and the U.S. Jewish community objected.

On October 8th, Israeli police opened fire on a Palestinian mob that had been throwing rocks, killing 21 and wounding a great many. Many of the riots and serious incidents of the Palestinian *Intifada* had attracted international attention, but the remarkable and horrific killing and wounding created by this event brought immediate international condemnation. Washington, Israel's greatest supporter, was in the difficult position of needing to keep the Coalition's Muslim members, most of whom were technically still at war with Israel, in the alliance. Criticism and condemnation from the highest level and in international fora did not persuade Israel to admit fault and led Washington and London to make unprecedentedly severe censurous remarks about Israeli policies toward their Palestinian population. This enabled the Coalition to hold together.

On December 6th, the United States helped draft a resolution calling for an international peace conference on the Middle East. While its help was meant to limit the damage to Israel, anything short of a U.S. veto would be a further erosion of U.S. support. America delayed a vote on both this resolution, and on another that criticized Israel for the Jerusalem clashes. But when Israel deported four Palestinians on the 16th, Washington agreed not to veto a resolution criticizing it, and when soldiers wounded 18 Palestinians during a strike protesting the expulsion of Palestinians, it joined in adopting a resolution criticizing the deportations and referring to "Palestinian territories" occupied by Israel. The violence and the nadir in U.S.-Israeli relations both continued, but after the war started, Iraqi Scud attacks brought defense concerns to the top of Israel's agenda.

Effects on Israeli Defense Policy – Michael Kirsch
The Coalition anticipated that Iraq might use of Scud missiles against Israel and took measures to minimize their effects. Iraq fired 40 Scuds at Israel, causing destruction and forcing Israel to revise its existing policy of retribution to all attacks on the State and its citizens. The first strike, seven Scuds fired at Tel Aviv and Haifa on January 18th, caused injuries and damage. Bush and Baker then spent hours convincing Shamir to not retaliate for fear that this might break up the Coalition and widen the war, but after they had his reserved assurance that he would at least not retaliate immediately, a second attack, four Scuds that landed in Tel Aviv, occurred on the 19th. (Appendix C lists these Scud attacks.) Israel and the United States then agreed on deploying Patriot missiles to Israel and the missiles and personnel were flown in, marking the first time that U.S. combat forces were stationed in Israel.[3]

The Scuds caused a major disruption in Israel. The chemical warfare threat meant that the entire population had to be protected. Gas masks were distributed, citizens prepared gas proof rooms and moved into them whenever there was an alarm, this being a major disruptive effect to normal life. Schools were closed, and the nation's business activity suffered. There were 15 subsequent Scud attacks, involving 29 missiles. By the end, Scuds had killed four people, injured at least 289, and left 4,000 homeless. None had hit anything of a military nature; the Scud attacks were a new form of international terrorism. The Israeli government's restraint whilst the country was under attack was applauded internationally, and the criticism of Israel before the outbreak of hostilities was forgotten.[4]

LESSONS LEARNED

Current Israeli policy is confronted with a dilemma, since Washington is committed to a conference on the Palestinian issue. In the end, Saddam may have achieved the goal he had pursued opportunistically, in that the Occupied Territories issue may get high-level international attention.

JORDAN – BRIAN GAGNE

The war created one of the worst crises in King Hussein's 37–year reign. Palestinian support for Iraq forced him to try and balance domestic wishes with international policy. Siding with the Coalition could mean his overthrow and supporting Iraq might mean a cut in Western aid and even another war with Israel. In this dilemma, he tried to remain neutral as he sought a means to avert war. His policy pleased no one, but was pursued because there was no alternative. Once war occurred, Jordan remained neutral as Iraq attacked Israel with Scud missiles.

The pressure on Jordan began when the U.N. Security Council imposed a trade embargo on Iraq, because its port of Aqaba on the Red Sea and its borders could be used to supply Iraq. While most of the population, the Palestinians in Jordan, avidly supported Iraq, the Coalition told the King that it expected him to close Aqaba to all Iraqi cargo, and thenceforth until the war began, he was under intense pressure. Domestic pressure came from pro-Iraqi and pro-Western groups; the pro-Iraqi Palestinians blamed the crisis on the Saudis and Kuwaitis, and pro-Western Jordanians encouraged the King to distance himself from Iraq. When the King tried to please both by condemning Iraq while allowing trade with Iraq to continue, he created more problems. Intelligence reported that Jordan was violating the sanctions by sending supplies to Iraq and was passing intelligence from reconnaissance by Jordanian RF-5 fighters collected along its Saudi and Israeli borders to Iraq. When these acts became public, Jordan was pressured to comply with the sanctions.[5]

Trying to solve this dilemma, the King worked for peace. On October 4th, he presented a peace plan to Iraq, but could not gain its approval. On the 7th, he and PLO leader Yasser Arafat devised a plan, but this failed because Iraq refused to withdraw from Kuwait. Discouraged but persistent, on the 13th, he presented a Jordanian-Moroccan-Algerian plan to Iraqi Foreign Minister Tariq Aziz, but it was soon rejected by the Coalition because it did not require a full Iraqi withdrawal from Kuwait. Addressing his Parliament on November 17th, he attacked the "blatant and shameless hypocrisy of nations involved in the military buildup in Saudi Arabia," implying that it was hypocritical for them to uphold international law in the Gulf while ignoring the Palestinian problem. He asked that Coalition forces withdraw and that Arab nations join the effort to solve the crisis peacefully. However, his cause was dealt a severe blow on the 29th, when the U.N. Security Council authorized the use of force if Iraq did not withdraw. In mid-December, he tried to open a dialogue between Egypt, Saudi Arabia, and Iraq. When Egypt and Saudi Arabia refused until Saddam showed a willingness to leave Kuwait, he suggested a Middle East conference to address both the Gulf crisis and the Arab-Israeli dispute. However, this plan foundered because the United States rejected any linkage between the two and continued to demand that Iraq withdraw from Kuwait. As the January 15th deadline approached without any sign of peace, Jordan mobilized most of its 80,000 troops, which assumed defensive positions along the Israeli-Jordanian border.[6]

LESSONS LEARNED

The war brought nothing but problems to Jordan. Hussein was faced with a "no-win" situation from the start, and it took time for the Coalition to fully realize his dilemma. His pro-Iraqi stance weakened his relations with the West, and Jordan emerged from the war with significant economic problems and luke-warm Western support. Thus, Jordan, more than any other Arab nation, must be concerned that the proposed Middle East conference achieve some progress concerning the Palestinian issue.

Iran – David Dunphy and Yong Pak

On August 15th, Saddam tried to gain Iran's support when he said he would release all war prisoners and return almost all the land taken during the Iran-Iraq War. However, having just fought a long and very costly war with Iraq, Iran was not obliged to come to Iraq's defense. Since this dislike of Iraq was offset by a contempt for Kuwait, which had helped to finance Iraq in the Iran-Iraq War, and a deep hatred of the United States, Iran remained neutral in the Gulf War.

Iran's diplomacy and considerable luck allowed it to emerge from the war with substantial diplomatic and material benefits, including the return of Iranian soldiers and territory and the diplomatic rewards resulting from voting for the U.N. resolution condemning Iraq's invasion. On September 5th, France's Societe Generale agreed to provide $1.8 billion to rebuild three Iranian petrochemical plants, on the 7th, London agreed to renew diplomatic relations and shortly thereafter, Saudi Arabia agreed to reconsider restrictions on the number of Iranians allowed to travel to Mecca. In a bid to further improve its relations, Iran played peacemaker by presenting ideas to end the war on February 4th that involved withdrawals of Iraqi forces from Kuwait and Coalition forces from the Middle East and establishing an Arab peacekeeping force along the Kuwait-Iraq border.[7] Although Washington deemphasized this plan, both the USSR and the U.N. Secretary General embraced it.

While improving relations with the West, Iran also appeared as an Islamic leader. Condemning Iraq's invasion and declaring itself neutral, it still let trucks with 150 tons of medicine, food, and other supplies proceed to Iraq, thereby helping Iraq at the margins of the crisis.

Economically, profits from the higher fuel prices caused by the war meant a monthly increase of $500 million for the first few months of the conflict. Iran's moderation also might improve its relations with the West, and if such amity were achieved, it might obtain loans needed to improve its economy. Politically, the war was also of value. President Ali Akbar Hashemi Rafsanjani could answer his radical opponents who claimed that the United States was a paper tiger. The Coalition's massive buildup discredited that notion and strengthened the power of moderate Irani political elements. Militarily, two changes in the balance of power made Iran a major regional power. Iraq's devastating defeat in the war and the U.N. proscriptions against developing nuclear, chemical, and biological weapons meant that Iraq, Iran's only real regional competitor, has been weakened greatly. Secondly, Iran received at least 115 Iraqi combat aircraft during the war. If it decided to place them in its Air Force, this would make it an armed force of considerable power.

Lessons Learned

Iran benefitted considerably and emerged at war's end with greater regional power and international prestige. The war brought considerable benefits and no disadvantages. It is significant that Iran realized this and intended to use its new power. In February, it said that excluding it from postwar talks on the Gulf would mean genuine security could not be achieved, a sign that it intended to become a regional leader.

Libya – Richard DeJong

Since Libya was not aligned with Iraq or the Coalition, it was not compelled to enter the war. Its role was to seek a peaceful solution, probably in an attempt to improve its relations with the Western nations. On August 5th, Libya and the PLO proposed a plan whereby Kuwait would cede Bubiyan and Warba Islands in the Gulf and the Rumaila oil fields and would pay large indemnities in return for an Iraqi withdrawal. The plan failed at an Arab League summit on August 10th. On the 20th, Qadhafi condemned the invasion and Iraq's using foreigners as human shields, and stated that if a U.N. naval blockade were created, he would send Libyan forces. On September 2nd, he revealed a Libyan-Jordanian-Sudanese plan. U.N. forces would replace Iraqi troops in Kuwait, all foreign troops in Saudi Arabia would be replaced by Arab or Moslem forces, and the embargo against Iraq would be lifted. Kuwait would cede Bubiyan and Warba Islands. This proposal also foundered, but when he announced it, he also said that he would defy the U.N. embargo by sending food to Iraq, and he authorized Iraqi ships to dock at Libyan ports to take on free food and fuel. Washington then said that Libya, South Africa, and

Yemen were shipping military materiel and substances for producing chemical weapons to Iraq.

Qaddafi again demonstrated moderation when he expelled 145
of Abu Abbas' terrorists in November, after Washington asked
President Mubarak and Morocco's King Hassan to press him to
eject them. He also was involved in several plans to end the crisis.
He met the leaders of Egypt, Syria, and Sudan on January 3, 1991
to consider ways to prevent war. Another peace attempt was a
Libyan-Yemeni-Algerian proposal on the 14th that stated if Iraq
began withdrawing from Kuwait before the January 15th deadline,
the three would pressure the United Nations to refrain from attacking Iraq, and would also begin a new drive to resolve the Palestinian
question. This proposal also failed. Libya proposed a cease fire on
the 24th, but the Security Council voted against it and Saddam
still refused to withdraw from Kuwait.

LESSONS LEARNED

Qadhafi emerged from the war with no substantial gains. He failed
to surpass King Hussein as the Arab emissary of peace, and made
only nominal gains vis-a-vis his relations with the West.

JAPAN AND GERMANY – BRUCE W. WATSON, JR.

The war created problems for Japanese and German relations with
the United States. Many in both nations opposed sending forces to
the Gulf, as this would violate the constitutional controls placed on
their armed forces after the end of World War II, while others
admitted their nations' reliance on Middle East oil, but questioned
getting into a war that did not seem to affect their immediate
interests. Meanwhile, Washington, seeking financing for the
Coalition, was critical of German and Japanese reservations to
provide aid. It viewed both as world powers that would suffer unless
Saddam were stopped, and while it would fight for their interests,
it fully expected that they would pay for such help. Thus, the
war contributed to U.S. anti-Japanese feeling, while Germany's
assistance was seen as barely adequate.

Japan's first consideration was whether it should even become
involved in a Gulf war. On August 23rd, it offered its first aid; loans
and grants to Arab nations suffering from the blockade's effects.
Egypt's President Mubarak conceded that this would help but said

that it would by no means cover all the costs that these nations faced. On the 30th, Japan offered more aid, but Washington was critical because this involved loans and grants to Egypt, Turkey, and Jordan instead of direct aid to the Coalition. As a result of this pressure and a personal request from Bush to Prime Minister Kaiufu, Japan pledged $1 billion. Even this was criticized by many U.S. Congressmen who said that a $1 billion pledge against the entire war cost was an insult. On September 14th, Japan pledged another $3 billion, but said that $600 million of it was to be used for humanitarian aid.

Several Japanese leaders also sought an expanded role in the war. The cabinet initiated a bill that would allow Japanese to serve as noncombatants, while military leaders openly supported sending troops to the Gulf. This was not popular with the public, 60% of whom voiced their disapproval in an opinion poll.

On December 11th, Japanese leaders said that support for the Coalition was ebbing. Japan had given only $200 million of its promised $4 billion, and this was the first inkling that it might repudiate its war pledges. However, on January 14th, Foreign Minister Taro Nakayama gave Bush assurances of Japanese support, and on the 24th, faced with a growing sense of guilt and U.S. pressure, Japan pledged another $9 billion.[8]

The war also created problems for Germany. Its constitution prevented it from sending forces to the Gulf, while German firms had helped Iraq to develop a chemical warfare arsenal. Thus, it appeared that Germany had helped create Iraq's chemical threat and was now shirking its duties by letting others do its fighting for it. Chancellor Helmut Kohl proposed sending minesweepers to the Gulf, but was opposed by Foreign Minister Hans-Dietrich Genscher, who said the 1949 Constitution forbid this. Meanwhile, seven industrialists were arrested for supplying Iraq with items needed to make poison gas. On September 7th, Germany said that it probably would not agree to directly financing the Coalition's war effort because this might violate laws barring military activity, but proposed helping nations affected by the economic sanctions. Kohl subsequently pledged aid and began to work for constitutional changes that would allow deploying troops to the Gulf. Bonn subsequently pledged assistance to Israel and nations suffering under the sanctions, and economic aid to the Coalition itself (see Appendix A). Additionally, it sent planes and missiles to defend

Turkey and ships to the Mediterranean to bolster the defenses there as U.S. naval power was redeployed southward. These deployments were strictly under NATO auspices and had nothing to do with the Coalition.[9]

LESSONS LEARNED

In summary, neither Japan nor Germany was convinced of the war's necessity and bridled under U.S. pressure for assistance, and the war strained their relations with the United States and Great Britain. In another context, the war was seen as other nations fighting for German and Japanese interests. After the war, both tried to amend their constitutions with regard to their armed forces to preclude such dilemmas in the future, but these proposals met with strong domestic opposition.

NOTES

1. "The Old Sore," *The Economist* (January 19, 1991): 23.

2. "The Other Local Superpower," *The Economist* (January 12, 1991).

3. "Israel and the Shaky Equation," *The Guardian*, January 19,1991. p. 26; "Israel Under Attack," *The Times* (London), January 19, 1991; and "Scud Wars," *The Times* (London), January 23, 1991.

4. Michael Sheridan, "The Israelis Brace for More Attacks," *The Independent on Sunday*, January 20, 1991, p. 3; "Keeping Out," *Economist* (January 26, 1991): 21; and Richard Owen, "Israel counts on a Peace Dividend," *The Times* (London), January 30, 1991.

5. William E. Smith, "The Beleaguered Messenger," *Time* (August 27, 1990): 28; "Heads You Win, Tails I Lose," *The Economist* (September 1, 1990): 39.

6. Richard Beeston, "Hussein Abandons Linkage with Palestine", *The Times* (London), February 23, 1991, p. 3; "Jordan in the Middle," *The Economist* (January 26, 1991): 23; R. Owen, "Failure by PLO to Open Front," *The Times* (London), February 1, 1991, p. 3; and Omar-al-Hassan, "Arafat Eclipsed as He Leads His People into Wilderness," *The Times* (London), January 30, 1991, p. 2.

7. Gerald Butt, "Teheran Hosts Talks on Ways to End War," *The Daily Telegraph*, February 1, 1991; "Could Peace Break Out," *The Economist* (February 9, 1991): 27; and Jeffrey Bartholet, "Iran's New Gulf Game," *Newsweek* (March 25, 1991): 22–23.

8. "They'll Remember Their Friends," *The Economist* (February 2, 1991): 13; and "The Lone Superpower," *The Independent on Sunday*, January 20, 1991, p. 18.

9. Richard Owen, "Genscher Tries to Mend Rift Caused by Iraq Weapons Deal," *The Times* (London), January 25, 1991; Norman Stone, "War Brings Out the Mouse in the Continent's Wealthy Giant," *The Sunday Times* (London), January 27, 1991; Ian Murray, "Germany Gives 2.9 Billion Pounds More to Stem Criticism of Its Role," *The Times* (London), January 30, 1991, p. 4; and Baron Hermann von Richthofen, "Where We Stand – Germany's Case," *The Sunday Times* (London), February 3, 1991.

14: Cardinal John J. O'Connor on the 'Just War' Controversy
by
Bruce W. Watson

No nation involved in the Gulf War welcomed it, and all, to a greater or lesser extent, debated its necessity. Debating war is not exclusively a 20th century phenomenon and the discussion of a "just war" is not a new one. The issue is not even limited to the West, as in the Islamic world, a jihad, or holy war must also meet exacting criteria. Saddam went to great lengths to justify his call for a jihad during the Gulf War (see chapter 3).

The British, French, and other Coalition members had reservations about the justness of the Gulf War.[1] There was impressive consideration of the issue in the British press and the issue was discussed thoroughly.[2] Thus, to them, giving detailed attention only to the U.S. controversy over the war's justness might appear as myopic. Still, the issue stands as a lesson because it can affect the U.S. ability as the world's single superpower, with a role as international policeman, to sustain a future war effort.

Experiencing the defeat in Vietnam and considering it an unjust war, many Americans are still very sensitive to the U.S. use of military power. Short and decisively successful as the war was, it still triggered antiwar demonstrations and discussion of the just war issue. Had the war lasted longer or had Coalition casualties been higher, it is a virtual certainty that the antiwar movement would have gathered momentum. Since this issue was further defined during the Gulf War and will reappear the next time the United States faces the prospect of war, it should be considered to determine the lessons that were learned.

THE CHOICE OF CARDINAL JOHN O'CONNOR

There are several reasons why this chapter cites almost exclusively the views of Cardinal John O'Connor of the Catholic Archdiocese of New York. He has a broad ecumenical background, which included serving two tours of duty as a Navy chaplain in Vietnam, and serving as the senior chaplain of the U.S. Naval Academy and later as the Chief of Chaplains of the U.S. Navy. After retiring, he served as Bishop of the Military Ordinate where he supported all military and State Department Catholics stationed overseas. These experiences prompted him to consider profoundly the issue of war and all major religious and secular positions on the subject. Second, he has an enviable academic and literary background. He wrote *A Chaplain Looks at Vietnam*, which in my opinion is the best political defense of the U.S. involvement in the Vietnam War that has ever been published.[3] He also holds a doctoral degree in political theory from Georgetown University, has an extensive background in clinical psychology, and could easily have pursued a highly successful career in academia after retiring from the Navy. Finally, the debate of the justness of the Gulf War reached its highest articulation in New York, and the Cardinal posited several arguments that have advanced our understanding of the issue. Specifically, proceeding from the established positions concerning a just war, he considered them in light of the devastating power of contemporary weapons – both the so-called "smart weapons" and the weapons of mass destruction.

THE TRADITIONAL VIEWS ON A JUST WAR

One of the earliest discussions on just war was provided in the fourth century by St. Augustine who tried to reconcile the need to kill in war with Christian concepts of brotherhood. St. Thomas Aquinas considered this issue in the thirteenth century and it was raised again in the seventeenth century by Spanish theologians who hoped to limit rather than justify the war-making power of the emerging nation-states. In the twentieth century as modern weapons enabled combatants to wreak havoc on defenseless civilians, many just war concepts were adopted into international law. Our understanding has evolved from these contributions. In brief, a just war considers both a war's purpose and the means by which it is waged. It must be declared for a just cause by a legitimate authority, must be fought for the right intentions in a correct manner, and only as a last resort. Wars of aggression, such as India's war against Pakistan in 1971, are always immoral. However, besides defensive wars which are relatively easy to justify, wars may be waged on behalf of the helpless or against grave threats to the international order. Finally, a war must have a reasonable degree of success in that if waged, the chances must be good that the "just aims" of the combatant will be achieved. In short, a just war must benefit mankind.

Under these concepts, a goal such as access to cheap oil is not acceptable. Likewise, justifying the Gulf War on the basis of last resort is questionable, since it could be argued that the Coalition did not wait long enough to allow economic sanctions to have their full impact. Conversely, Iraq's invasion of Kuwait could be reasonably interpreted as an unjust war of aggression, and Iraq's treatment of the Kuwaitis was so brutal that the war could be justly waged on behalf of that helpless population.

CARDINAL O'CONNOR'S CONTRIBUTION

If given the opportunity, I am sure that the Cardinal would present his case in a much more complete form than will be presented here. Based on a series of homilies given in January and February 1991, the following demonstrates a progression in his thinking that first considers the necessity of war and then discusses the entire issue of just war. Together, they provide an evolution that might not have been achieved had the entire issue been considered in retrospect. Additionally, they reflect the passion of the moment, which might also be tempered over time. Thus, they amount to a moral position that interprets the war and advances our understanding, thereby providing a basis for discussion in possible future American wars.

Before January 17th, the Cardinal's discussions focused on three factors: inevitability, unpredictability, and winning ability. Addressing the war's inevitability, he said:

.... the human race has casually accepted war as the only serious road to peace. It's as though we were all members of the chorus or actors in a Greek tragedy. Our destiny is inevitable. We describe it and act it out as fatalistically as Oedipus kills his own father and marries his own mother.

How can this be? How can war be inevitable to men and women of hope? Every war is a failure, no matter who "wins." Every war is a failure of human reason. Every war is a failure to believe that war is *not* inevitable, that peace is possible. Friedrich Nietzsche said: "The world no longer believes, because believers no longer sing."

.... What I am saying, therefore, is quite different from suggesting for a moment that our national leaders are the guilty parties. I *am* suggesting that many of *us*, much of the entire human race, have simply come to accept war as we have accepted violence in our streets, raping and maiming of the vulnerable and helpless, brutality and crime as unavoidable realities of life.

.... In other words, we have come to accept war itself as though it were completely beyond our control, and that is the real sadness. We have come to accept war as people without faith. We have come to accept war as the essential condition of peace.[4]

He drew three conclusions. First, war was not inevitable. "Humanity can not resign itself to the scourge of war." "Believe war is inevitable and it will become inevitable." Thus, we must believe that peace is possible, and in this respect, there was nothing magical about January 15, 1991, the deadline that the United Nations gave Iraq to withdraw from Kuwait. Rather, one could be discouraged that the date passed without results, but could still work to maintain peace. Second, "moral authority *can* contribute to make dialogue, reason and law prevail in the end; ... " "Is it *right* – morally right – to go to war? This question can only be answered after one examines the requirements of the so-called just war, then asks if these requirements have been met." Thus, not all wars are permissible. Rather only that war that has been assessed against existing standards of just war, and one that is a last resort, to be used when all else has failed and there is no alternative. This begs consideration of the embargo then in effect against Iraq. Had the world assessed its effects accurately? Would it fail, or would it eventually force Saddam to succumb? Third, "disastrous and unforeseeable consequences must be averted."[5] Here he is concerned with war's unpredictability. A war that initially qualifies as a just war can become one that does not. Also, since many modern weapons had never been used in combat before, they could add a degree of unpredictability that could affect the war.

We can fulfill our responsibilities in assessing whether a war should be fought by determining whether it qualifies as a just war. Here O'Connor expanded on the established definition of a just war, noting that it must meet several criteria, the most complex of which may be "proportionality:"

... war can be justified only in response to unjust aggression and only as a last resort. All peaceful alternatives must be exhausted.

Next, war is permissible only to confront "a real and certain danger," that is, to protect innocent life, to preserve conditions necessary for decent human existence, and to secure basic human rights.

War must offer probability of success, so that the last state may not be worse than the first. No war can be entered into for frivolous reasons. Further, a nation must accord with the principle of proportionality. The damage to be inflicted must be proportionate to the good to be achieved.

Proportionality is critical both in terms of going to war and in terms of how a war is fought. What is called "total war" is condemned. *No one* can claim the right to destroy civilization by waging the kind of total war that could be waged today, with no weapons barred.

The principle difficult to separate from proportionality is called discrimination. To wage war against innocent civilians is immoral. Any response to unjust aggression must be directed against the unjust aggressors, not on those caught up in a war not of their own making. Certainly obliteration bombing is a gross violation of the principle of discrimination.[6]

After the war began on January 17, 1991, O'Connor focused on two aspects. The first concerned how the war was conducted, cautioning that the destruction must be limited:

.... now that war is underway, *only* those means which accord with the criteria of "just war" teaching will be used. The first of these is that under absolutely no circumstances, with no justification can any nation or any people attack the innocent deliberately and directly. We know, tragically, that often there is a fallout in war and the innocent suffer and can be killed. But never, never would there be justification for direct bombing, direct killing of civilians as was done over Germany during World War II.[7]

The second aspect concerned the U.S. public. Observing that most Americans participated in an outburst of patriotism and a minority gathered together in a peace movement, O'Connor took a position that was destined to please no one. It is a worthy contribution to the entire antiwar issue and demands our attention. He began with a word of caution to both sides. To the patriotic, he had several words of caution:

I worry a great deal about the war in the Middle East, about what it is doing to the people of Iraq and what it is doing to us. I worry that the press has been virtually excluded. I worry that we may learn after the fact that countless numbers of innocent people have been killed or maimed, or left homeless or helpless.

.... But I worry that war itself has not yet seemed to chasten us, to sober us, to force us to ask not whether God is on our side, but whether we are on His. Have we seen any serious signs of self-discipline here at home while our troops are subject to the potential discipline of death in the Middle East? Have we in any way reduced our commitment to the material, the sensual? Have we even *begun* to ask questions about ourselves as a society? Will our direction change if we "win" the war? Do we believe it unthinkable that we could "lose" the war? Or have we, indeed, asked ourselves what we mean by winning or losing?[8]

Also critical of many in the peace movement, he cited Pope John Paul II's view that, "It should be noted that freedom of conscience does not confer a right to indiscriminate recourse to conscientious objection," and said that this obviously implied "the right to reasonable, intelligent thought-through recourse to conscientious objection." However, such objection must be responsible: " ... I may personally insist that $2 + 2 = 5$. But that doesn't make $2 + 2 = 5$. Nobody is going to give me an opportunity to handle money if I think $2 + 2 = 5$."[9] Rather, there is a discipline that must be imposed in the process:

Every individual has the grave duty to form his or her own conscience in the light of objective truth ... When conscience that conforms to the objective moral law and divine law is tossed out the window, and we become a law unto ourselves, we can generate chaos.

.... No individual conscience can *create* truth; it can only seek truth. Conscience must be conformed to the truth and not vice versa. Conscience can not be established on false propaganda. The same is the case with nations. And in mentioning this, we might well remind ourselves of the grave responsibility every nation has to tell its people the truth.[10]

Lessons Learned

Through the ages, man has considered war and has developed the concept of just war. O'Connor attempted to provide order to U.S. consideration of the Gulf War, thereby developing the parameters for future discussion should war again occur. For two reasons, these guidelines are extremely valuable. First, there is a strong U.S. antiwar tradition that can definitely affect America's ability to prosecute a war. Whether such efforts would be positive or inimical to mankind can only be determined in a moral context. Second, many see war as "inevitable" and blithely support a conflict without ever considering whether it is either necessary or justified. To them, the Cardinal's guidelines are equally relevant. Whether in the future we will consider what he said is problematic. I am pessimistic and fear that should war occur again, then the same ill-based, emotional sides will be drawn in the ensuing controversy. Still, the guidelines have been provided and are worthy of our attention as a lesson of this war that can be of value in the future.

Notes

1. See, For example, Robin Gedye, "100,000 Protest in Germany," *The Daily Telegraph*, January 18, 1991; "Peace Rallies," *Times* (London), January 20, 1991; and Clifford Longley, "An Anguished Catholic Treads a Careful Line," *Times* (London), February 21, 1991, p. 14.

2. See, for example, the excellent piece, "Reflections on the Morality Not Just of War, But of Peace," by Cardinal Archbishop of Westminster Basil Hume that appeared in *The London Times* on January 28, 1991. It inspired several insightful comments in the February 2nd edition of that paper. *The Daily Telegraph* also printed an editorial on February 25, 1991 that made several excellent points.

3. See: John J. O'Connor, *A Chaplain Looks at Vietnam* (Cleveland and New York: The World Publishing Company, 1968). If this excellent work has a flaw, it is when the Cardinal discusses the battlefield. Here, where he has seen too much blood and destruction, his words appear comparatively less objective than his incisive discussions concerning the political and moral purposes of the U.S. involvement in the war.

4. John Cardinal O'Connor in *Homily*, January 18, 1991, pp. 2–3.

5. Ibid., p. 2.

6. Ibid., p. 5.

7. John Cardinal O'Connor, *Homily*, January 20, 1991, p. 2.

8. Cardinal John J. O'Connor, "From My Viewpoint: Lest We Forget ..." *Catholic New York*, January 24, 1991.

9. John Cardinal O'Connor, *World Day of Peace*, January 27, 1991.

10. Ibid., pp. 2, 4.

15: The Issue of Media Access to Information
by
Bruce W. Watson

The issue of media access to combat information is a lesson of the Gulf War, since it could affect future U.S. warfighting ability and it appears to be more volatile in America than it is in other nations. In Great Britain, while the media persist in reporting government scandals and insensitively intrude into the Royal Family's matters, they appear more willing to accept the government's withholding of war information. For example, in the Falklands War of 1982, the government controlled the means of communication and thus exerted such influence as to delay reporting early British losses because this news might have had an adverse impact on the war effort. Other nations appear to hold similar views, and in the Gulf War, Israel, Jordan, Saudi Arabia, and Iraq all imposed severe controls without provoking significant outcries from their journalists.

In America, the issue dates back to the Vietnam War, which was a crisis in the military-media relationship. In the media's view, the military actively restricted information in order to influence reporting, and through this, public opinion. To the military, reporters were the enemy and were considered so biased against the U.S. cause that they were tantamount to traitors. Relations between the two were at their worst at war's end. This problem continued in Grenada, where reporters were not allowed to accompany combat forces and were given no assistance in getting to the island. While in one sense, this was a reaction to the perceived wrongs committed by the press in Vietnam, it was also a message to cooler heads that the existing relationship could not continue. The answer was to create a press pool consisting of reporters that the military would convey to a conflict. It would report on combat events, and its news would be shared by all.

Administrative and political factors made the first use of the pool, in the Panama intervention in December 1989, a failure. There were four administrative problems: there was inadequate planning, inadequate support, the pool was simply too large to move easily, and there were great delays in disseminating pool reports. Since these problems were unforeseen, one would expect that they would be corrected. However, a far different situation existed concerning Cheney's decision on when to call out the pool. To prevent news leaks, he delayed until 7:30 p.m., after the end of the evening's news broadcasts. This meant that the pool could not arrive in Panama until hours after the invasion began. Unlike unforeseen administrative problems, this was a deliberate restriction of press access that showed distrust and meant that the media issue was still a problem. In commenting on access during Panama, I proposed two solutions: assigning full-time reporters to field commands so that they would be in place when a war began; or sequestering the pool so that it could be deployed quietly before hostilities commenced without endangering security.[1] Neither they nor other ideas were instituted, and the situation remained unchanged at the start of the Gulf War.

THE PROVISIONS FOR THE U.S. MEDIA IN THE GULF WAR

By August 8th, Washington was actively seeking Saudi visas for U.S. journalists. On the 10th, the Saudis told Cheney that they were being processed, but in the interim, a media pool would be accepted if the America provided transportation. The press pool was activated and arrived in Saudi Arabia on the 13th.[2]

Support to the media was multifaceted. Press accommodations were provided at Dhahran, and press conferences supplemented pool reporting from the field. Morning (EST) CENTCOM briefings from Saudi Arabia were updated by Pentagon briefings held almost every afternoon, key U.S. figures held press conferences to provide further access, and the Pentagon provided continuous support. Events moved along at a brisk pace and televised reporting was so organized that Kurt Vonnegut was not too far from the mark when he said it was tantamount to a television mini-series.[3] The apparent pro-military tenor of media reporting was disrupted when the ground offensive began on February 24th and for security reasons, Cheney suspended the scheduled daily briefings until further notice. Such actions were vital to the success of the Coalition's offensive, which its leaders believed would be a difficult enterprise. (Most strategists state that an army on the offensive should have a two-to-one advantage over the defense. Coalition forces were at a disadvantage, since the ratio was three-to-two in favor of the defending Iraqis. Also, while the Coalition had control of the air and might have softened up the Iraqis through constant air sorties, the Iraqi Army had combat experience. Third, the Coalition's strategy of launching a feint along the eastern front while moving major forces westward and providing for their support was ambitious, bold and ingenious, and if revealed, could have meant disaster and a lengthy, bloody conflict). Subsequent events occurred rapidly. Possibly because the U.S. Marines made such remarkable progress on the eastern front, the Pentagon insisted on only a short news blackout and soon resumed briefings on the war. Disgruntled reporters claimed that since the French, British, and Arabs were much more open about the war and were getting all the publicity, the government had reversed its policy.[4]

Influencing the Media

Many nations, including Iraq, Jordan, Israel, and the United States, tried to influence the media. Iraqi controls were the most oppressive. The state-controlled Iraqi media, through false news reports, led the Iraqis to believe that they were winning, and did not publicly inform them that they lost the war. Similar control was placed on foreign reporting in that all reporters' movements were controlled, so that they saw only what Iraq wanted reported. This affected CNN's Peter Arnett's reporting and reached a climax when he reported on the Coalition's bombing of Amiriya bunker, as the camera showed the civilian dead being taken from the complex. The Coalition had struck Amiriya because it believed it was a military facility and did not know it was being used as a shelter. CNN stressed the civilian dead rather than the building's military importance, and this so influenced Western public opinion that it was a turning point in the war; henceforth, the Pentagon controlled the bombing. Schwarzkopf depicted the reporting of this incident as "aiding and abetting the enemy" because it implied that he was "deliberately lying to the American people that [he was] targeting civilians."[5]

Jordan's controls were similar to Iraq's. Its media reported consistently that Iraqi forces were winning, but when the Coalition won, it finally revealed the devastating Iraqi defeat. Israel's strong controls were most evident in the reporting of Scud missile attacks. Media access to the locations of impacting Scuds was allowed only after the government had determined a response, and reports stressed the public's concern and depicted a government having difficulty coping with public demands for a military response. This complemented nicely Israel's requests for the provision of American arms and thereby coincided with the nation's national goals.

The U.S. Defense Department ground rules imposed on the media protected combat forces while imposing moderate controls that did not amount to a gross violation of freedom of the press. However, the military did commit violations by overly restricting the media's freedom of movement and by exceeding the ground rules. Pool spaces were given only to television networks, wire services, some radio groups, and a few magazines and newspapers, and there were unnecessary problems in the system. Pool reports were cleared by the censors and then were later held up in order to force word changes such as "giddy pilots" to "proud pilots," or "fighter-bomber" to "fighter." Some delayed reports were so stale that they were unusable, and others, such as bombing Iraq's nuclear capability, which had already been reported by the French and discussed by Schwarzkopf, were withheld. There also were problems at the lowest combat levels. Press officers warned reporters who asked hard questions that they were 'anti-military' and that their requests for interviews with senior military commanders and visits to the field were in jeopardy. Many reporters deliberately circumvented the abuses by hiding out with combat units and were hidden by officers and troops, but were arrested and detained by Military Police when found.[6]

The dispute was further defined by Pete Williams and *The Washington Post's* Michael Getler. Williams claimed that the system was not censorship, because the media, not the military, made the final decision to broadcast or publish. Concerning abuses by field press officers, he said that escorts should not "throw themselves in front of a camera" when they disagree with an interview, and that they had to be taught their jobs, so that reporters "won't feel their interview subjects are intimidated." He concluded, "there are clearly some things we could have done better." He also discussed transmission delays and said "we must do better at getting stories back to the press center."[7]

Giving the opposing view, Getler cited four elements in the Pentagon's plan to control the press: "censorship by delay," possible because the military controlled news transmission and decided which stories were sent and how quickly; "death by briefing," where the military, not the press, was the source of information, and determined what, when, and how news should be released; "blacking out the ugly parts", specifically the first hours of the offensive that potentially are the ugliest look at warfare; and "leak-proof pools," in that only pool members went to front, and the military controlled the means of communicating their stories back to the rear. He was unfair in his "blacking out the ugly parts," in that during the first hours of a war, the fog of war comes down very quickly and it is some time before higher headquarters have a reasonable idea of precisely what is happening on the ground. It was therefore difficult for them to provide the media any form of coherent picture. Conversely, he identified a significant problem in his "death by briefing."[8] Governing this entire issue was Schwarz-kopf, who stated that in Vietnam the military lied to the press frequently and that he did not intend to repeat that crime. He said, "... when we went into this thing, I was bound and determined that we were going to tell it like it was, absolutely tell it like it was."[9] This meant that at times information was withheld until its truth could be substantiated, but that when it was released, it was correct. In retrospect, he achieved his goal as there were very few factual errors in the briefings, and we must view Getler's criticism in light of the General's personal standards which precluded abuses on the command level. Conversely, seeing Schwarzkopf or others clad in desert fatigues made it appear that they had just come from the operations center with the latest, most accurate and complete news possible within existing security requirements. However, when the military prepares a briefing, it places great emphasis on the intended audience. For example, the daily Joint Chiefs of Staff intelligence briefings must be less than three minutes long but must contain everything the Chiefs need to know about intelligence for the day. Teams of experts highly expert in compressing and deleting data spend hours sifting through thousands of reports on hundreds of topics so that only data that meet strict criteria are presented. The CENTCOM and Pentagon briefings that seemed so candid were prepared by just such people, and their question always was: did the public need this information?[10] This power put the military in the dual role of news subject and reporter, with a possible conflict of interest and certainly with considerable censorship power.

Conversely, Getler underrated the media's support of this situation. Television reporters never questioned the content or scope of the briefings with enough emphasis to prompt a public reaction, and the response from the press, while more rebellious, was muted. Television anchors even supported the briefings by referring to their experts to expand upon the material presented, and these experts never questioned the accuracy of the briefings.

From the above we can conclude that the military committed abuses and the media reacted by reporting news via both official and illicit means. However, two episodes will profoundly affect future military-media relations. The first and most significant involved the Bob Simons CBS News crew that went to the Kuwaiti border on February 7th, in violation of existing ground rules. Captured, taken to Basra and then to Baghdad, they were kept in isolation, beaten, and interrogated. Pressure on Iraq, including President Mikhail Gorbachev's personal intercession, prompted their release. The second incident was similar. On March 5th, about three dozen journalists from several nations were reported missing near Basra. The U.S. military expressed its concern, said it was doing everything it could, but that the issue would not be pursued with Iraq because "it wasn't part of the war." Did this mean that the military would protect those journalists who were under its control but would not afford protection to those who were not? Williams' argument, that since the military was responsible for newsmen it should control their movements, presented an "either-or" situation that is not valid.[11] Just because the military is not responsible for reporters not under its protection does not mean that it cannot work for the release of reporters who are captured by the enemy. Such a blanket rule means that the military should not be concerned about the people held hostage by Iraq in the Autumn of 1990 or the Kuwaitis taken hostage during the war. A far more reasonable argument is that the military will be concerned with what the government says it should be concerned with, and that a decent government will concern itself with citizens who happen to be reporters, regardless of whether it had authorized their presence in a particular place at a particular time.

Conclusions

One still marvels at the news coverage of the war, in that its scope, depth, and length were overwhelming. Yet one wonders about other aspects of the war that went largely unreported. Where was the coverage of the wounded, prisoner-of-war camps, and ground combat? Reporters state that they were denied access to these stories. The result was a packaged, clean war, where smart weapons surgically destroyed bridges, and military equipment and installations. We were overawed with these precision weapons, and the whole thing appeared so clean and precise that one could forget that people were dying. With only a few exceptions, the public was not privy to the "dirty" part of the war where people bled, were in pain, and died. Estimates on the Iraqis killed ran up to 100,000, but these remained in the abstract, since the blood of battle was seldom shown. One might attempt to justify this control because the press was a powerful factor in the war. Saddam was known to follow the foreign press closely, and Iraq was quick to use occurrences such as the air strike on Amiriya for propaganda purposes. Indeed, the controls may well have been a factor in the Coalition's sensational success. By conveying a space age, sanitary, surgical war, the public's sense of euphoria was maintained and this may not have been possible if the more humanly destructive aspects were revealed. And there is every reason to believe that news hungary reporters would have dwelled on such information if they could have gotten it. Thus one might conclude that the government did what it had to do in controlling access. We might then state that ours is an imperfect world and concessions must be made. However, to do so is wrong because it ignores the current U.S. view on war which requires considerable information to determine if a war is just (see chapter 14).

Lessons Learned

After the war's first day, military and political spokesmen consistently made every effort to damp down public euphoria and to warn that there might be serious setbacks. Few heeded this advice, and the war went so splendidly that when it was over, the public's view was that of a post-sports competition elation that "our side won." This causes one to consider America's next war. Will it be more difficult? America can hardly expect to be as fortunate concerning losses in future conflicts. Will it go into it naively, with a "we did it in the Gulf and we'll do it here" attitude? The first lesson, then, is that General Colin Powell correctly observed that "we have put Vietnam behind us." But what has replaced it? Does America realize fully the inhumanity of war and that it must be only a last resort? Or does it think that war can be fought surgically and decisively where right is on its side and it suffers amazingly few losses? Will America carry this with it to its next conflict? If so, to what degree is the media responsible because of the way it portrayed the war? The media often are cited as a factor in the defeat in Vietnam because they brought the blood and horror into American living rooms night after night. In future years, will that same media be criticized for not having fully conveyed the horrors of this war, thereby establishing unsound U.S. attitudes for the next conflict? These questions deserve our consideration.

The second lesson is that the military still believes that the media are a danger that must be controlled. One can argue that the media have earned this reputation, and left free, will act irresponsibly. Protecting those in combat must always be the highest priority and measures including censorship must be taken to ensure their safety. But the military must realize that abuses often result from such great power. In the Gulf, abuses were averted by Schwarzkopf's high moral ideals and his resolve to "tell it like it was." Thus, it is a minor thing when an officer insisted that a reporter change "giddy pilots" to "proud pilots" to make the Air Force look good. However, it also reflects that although Schwarzkopf's integrity precluded problems in this war, an institutional problem remains, and excessive control over the press can lead to abuses. Here, the Bob Simons incident was crucial because the military can assert justifiably that unescorted newsmen were in danger. Peter Bluff, who was with Simons, said of his capture, "It was the corner ... I probably won't look around the corner so readily again which disappoints me because that's the fascination of what we do."[12] It is possible that in a larger sense, it is a corner for the entire news media, one that they will be more hesitant to look around in the future. If so, then this has ominous implications.

The final lesson is that the press pool contributes to existing animosity. To the media the military prohibits access to the combat front, but then allows access via a pool situation where it can control the transmission of information. In this sense, the pool becomes a liability to the media rather than a service. The solution is that a pool should exist to help rather than hinder the press. It should help reporters get to the conflict and should be used for so-called "media opportunities", such as interviews with key figures. Elsewhere the media should enjoy greater freedom, should be allowed to the front, and as conditions permit, should be afforded protection by military forces. Responsibility for their lives rests with themselves and their organizations. If captured, they should be afforded the same consideration as other Americans held hostage.

The initial result of this could be heavy casualties among reporters as the media learns to be more prudent in gathering news. What also will result will be a restoration of power to the media. This is a risk, because their irresponsible actions in Vietnam could presage similar behavior and cost more lives in the future, since the search for news at any price is the primary motivator of the amoral contemporary U.S. journalist. The record shows that while there have been a few instances where the press has withheld news because it was in the public's interest to do so, there have been many more where news has been released that endangered people's lives and was inimical to just causes.

However, this is not for the U.S. military to decide through censoring information. To do so creates more dangers that it prevents. Should the time come, and it may well come, when the media's actions become irresponsible, then it is the public's duty to bring such abuses to the government's attention and the President's and the Congress' duty to take appropriate action. In this respect, the Gulf War is instructive. In February 1991 polls, 83 percent of Americans felt that the media were not doing a responsible job of covering the war, 80 percent supported the Pentagon's restrictions on journalists, and 60 percent wanted even more control. Though the correctness of the public's desire for military control of the media is questionable, the polls reveal an attitude tantamount to a rebellion against unbridled, irresponsible journalism. The public wants a more responsible press. It remains for Americans to identify the appropriate mechanisms to assure such responsibility.

NOTES

1. Bruce W. Watson, "Assessing Press Access to Information," in *Operation JUST CAUSE*, edited by Bruce W. Watson and Peter G. Tsouras (Boulder, CO: Westview Press, 1991), pp. 133–145, 149.

2. Statement of Pete Williams, Assistant Secretary of Defense for Public Affairs before the Committee on Governmental Affairs, United States Senate, February 20, 1991.

3. Speech by Kurt Vonnegut to the student body of Virginia Tech, Blacksburg, Virginia, March 3, 1991.

4. British reporting was actually much more prompt during these hours, but the criticism persisted there as well. See, for example, "Threat to Journalists in Move to Stop Independent Coverage," *The Times* (London), February 26, 1991; and John Keegan, "Hollow Voices in an Empty Box," *The Daily Telegraph*, March 2, 1991.

5. "David Frost Interview with General Norman Schwarzkopf," April 3, 1991, Public Broadcasting System; "Barbara Walters' Interview with General Norman Schwarzkopf," *20/20*, ABC, March 22, 1991.

6. Malcolm W. Browne, "The Military vs. the Press," *The New York Times Magazine*, March 3, 1991; and Christopher Walker, "Strong-Arm Tactics Used to Curb War Reporting," *The Times* (London), February 8, 1991.

7. Pete Williams, "Let's Face It, This Was the Best War Coverage We've Ever Had," *The Washington Post*, March 17, 1991, pp. D1, D4.

8. Michael Getler, "Do Americans Really Want to Censure War Coverage This Way?" *The Washington Post*, March 17, 1991, p. D4. See also: "Good News Only," *The Economist* (January 19, 1991): 26.

9. "Barbara Walters' Interview."

10. Based on personal observation, but the press made similar observations. See, for example, Con Coughlin, "How the War Is Told," *The Daily Telegraph*, February 5, 1991, p. 17; and Stephen Robinson, "The Pentagon Stars in a Late Side Show," *The Daily Telegraph*, February 5, 1991, p. 17.

11. Howard Kurtz, "Fate of 3 Dozen Journalists Unknown," *The Washington Post*, March 7, 1991, p. A27; and Williams, p. D4.

12. "Free at Last" segment of *Sixty Minutes* televised on March 3, 1991.

PART VI
CONCLUSIONS

16: Lessons Learned and Looking to the Future
by
Bruce W. Watson

On June 8, 1991, the United States held a victory day parade in Washington, DC, and a similar, although smaller, parade was held in London on June 21, 1991. The troops were welcomed home and commended for their deeds, as both nations looked to the future. However, many are still attempting to grasp the war's significance.

What was this war, and what lessons does it provide? It helps to begin by putting it in perspective. In comparison to history's earlier conflicts, the war was rather small in that it was not a very long one, lasting only weeks instead of months or years, and it was not an extremely violent one. Likewise, culturally, the results of this war will not be substantial. It is doubtful that it will spawn an F. Scott Fitzgerald, Ernest Hemingway, or even a Leon Uris. Artistically, no Guernicas appear in sight, and musically, "Voices that Care" and "I'm Proud to Be an American" are hardly comparable to the 1812 Overture.

No, the war's contribution lies elsewhere. Its significance is in its profound political, economic, scientific-technical, and military impact, which makes it of the greatest importance to us all. If we can fathom its significance and the lessons it offers, then we can learn and profit from the experience.

POLITICAL LESSONS

The war's significance to international relations is that it is the first violent manifestation of the post-Cold War era. Its relevance is in the fact that it occurred at all. From 1946 until 1987, the world was bipolarized and peace was maintained through an overriding

Soviet-American rivalry. Harrowing and nerve-racking at times, it nonetheless was a peace; its several wars were contained with limited violence for fear that escalation would drive the world into armageddon. However, that balance was broken with the rapprochement and the emergence of America as the world's only superpower. Unless the United States is willing to assume the role of world's policeman, and there is much evidence to indicate that it is not, then that overriding control is gone. The Gulf War would not have occurred even a few years earlier when Iraq was the client of an aggressive Soviet Union that might have come to its defense, and it harkens back to the pre-1946 period of combat alliances, mobilizations, field maneuvers, and large battles. In doing so, it is a harbinger of the future. War is back and the future 41 years may be much more violent than the last. Likewise, some of the Gulf War's aspects – human hostages, the terrorism of the Scud missile attacks, and the ecoterrorism of the oil spills and oil fires, may presage equally nasty acts in future wars. Also, the high tech war waged by the Coalition showed the high degree that collateral damage can be reduced. Thus, military high tech makes wars more surgical and, for this reason, perhaps more likely in the future.

Another lesson is that wars with limited military aims do not necessarily solve the root political problems that brought them about. Thus, the Gulf War objective of liberating Kuwait was achieved, but it has not removed the underlying source of the aggression, Saddam himself, and has served to accentuate other significant political problems, such as the plight of the Kurds in Iraq and the lack of democracy in Kuwait.

On a more specific note, the war affirmed many of Clausewitz's postulations. War is indeed an extension of politics on a more violent level, and when a nation's actions are so outrageous, they invite war. Also, a nation's diplomacy must be based on military power. If too ambitious and without adequate military support, as Iraq's was, then it will likely suffer reverses.

Turning to the effects on specific nations, the war reaffirmed the existence of the Anglo-American relationship and its benefit to the world. The latter offers the power and a firm commitment to freedom, the former centuries of experience and possibly a firmer grasp on the world's pulse. (At a minimum, the British certainly have a greater sense of perspective. I remember calling Mr. Bruce George, M.P. at 4 a.m. on February 24, 1991, to tell him that the ground offensive had begun. He was away and I left a message with Parliament's answering service that the war had begun. The operator replied, "Oh it has, has it?" When I asked if Mr. George had left a forwarding number, her reply was, "Young man, do you have any idea what time it is?" Nothing like 800 years of history to put a war in perspective.) For the British, this war puts two successive wars in their plus column, which certainly helps to balance the reduction in global status brought about by the loss of an empire. While Britain seems intent on strengthening the ties to and of Continental Europe, the Anglo-American relationship remains healthy.

Equally important, the war emphasized to Great Britain that she remains a world leader, that conviction and strength of purpose are just as important as one's military inventory on the world's stage.

For France, the war brought closer relations with America and Britain but also highlighted her need for decisiveness and her previous self-imposed isolation. Both need attention if she is to play a leading role in the emerging Europe. For the European Community the lesson was that there is much to be done in respect to both political and military cohesion. For Italy, the lesson was that there are international and regional roles for her to play and that she is capable militarily of having greater influence. For Germany, the lesson is that the pall of World War II remains. Its chemical warfare assistance to Iraq recalled the darkest deeds of Nazi Germany. Additionally, it exacerbated existing difficulties with America by not participating more actively in the Coalition. For Israel, the war highlighted the problems with the Occupied Territories and that the United States found it could be much more effective if it could resolve the Arab-Israeli problem. Israel should expect greater pressure from America to resolve its differences with the Arabs. For the Arab nations in the Coalition, the war demonstrated yet again just how disunited the Arab world is.

Great attention should be paid to collective security agreements and to coalition warfare strategy. To many nations that are developing nuclear warfare technology, the lesson is that there are limits and that many nations – the United States, Great Britain, and others – may not tolerate the existence of such arsenals. Finally, for the world's leading economic powers, the lesson is that Great Britain and the United States expect them to participate actively in defending their interests. The war did little but deepen the ongoing U.S.-Japanese animosity. In the future, Germany, Japan, Korea, and other economic powers should expect pressure to develop the power to defend their interests.

MILITARY LESSONS

There are both general and specific military lessons to be gleaned from the war. The air campaign virtually won the war in that it so devastated Iraq that the ground campaign was over in hours. This means that we must reconsider the conventional wisdom that air power is not enough to win wars. It may be that we will conclude that air power is sufficient to win some confrontations.

The ground campaign reaffirmed what strategists since Sun Tzu have stressed concerning the importance of good strategy, daring, good discipline, and training. Those trained and led well performed well; those who were not, did not.

In the maritime scene, the war reaffirmed the belief that blockades are of limited military value and often are not sufficient to force a nation to submit within a reasonable amount of time. Additionally, mine warfare remains as a very great naval problem. Mines are now so sophisticated that great sums are needed for systems to defeat them effectively. Finally, there is still a great need for battleships; missiles have not replaced their massive destructiveness.

Concerning specific military lessons, the use of electronic warfare (EW) in the war was unprecedented, and proved that EW investment had been well worth the money. EW contributed greatly, and the war showed that EW could be successfully integrated into many weapon systems. Likewise, the war showed that the spending in high tech weapons had been worthwhile. JSTARS was an overwhelming success, Stealth proved its worth, the Stand-off Land Attack Missile (SLAM) and precision guided munitions were tremendously successful, as was Tomahawk, although it was found that Tomahawk needs identifiable terrain on its approach route if it is to hit its target. Night vision devices were a great success, reaffirming what the U.S. military had learned in Panama. A second lesson is that while EW and high tech are highly significant militarily, they are very expensive. There will be pressure in the 1990s to perfect even more advanced systems, but future U.S. defense cutbacks will limit this progress and Great Britain and France will find it even more difficult to finance developing such systems.

Turning to command and control, the U.S. military's current unified and specified command system is a successful approach in that it worked well in Panama and Kuwait. The war showed that a unified command can be expanded successfully into a multinational Coalition. Logistics was a success story, reaffirming the common beliefs concerning protecting one's lines of communication and attacking one's opponent's supply structure. A lesson of the war was that in multi-national warfare, it is best if one nation controls logistics and supports all other participants.

There were many intelligence problems, and, while the following emphasizes U.S. intelligence, it assumes that, while others have said little about their intelligence performance, there were inputs from British, French, and other intelligence groups to Coalition intelligence and that these did not resolve the following problems. Operational/tactical intelligence centers, particularly the military service intelligence organizations, performed well. Here the major complaints were that the intelligence was not delivered quickly enough, and that larger intelligence groups are needed. Turning to national intelligence organizations, the National Security Agency appears to have done well in providing timely signals intelligence on all command levels. The performance of Central Intelligence Agency and Defense Intelligence Agency appears to have been less adequate. The Coalition never located Saddam, the number of Scud launchers was severely underestimated, striking the Amiriya bunker was an embarrassment, bomb damage assessment was abysmal, and while chemical warfare was expected Iraq never deployed such weapons. The Bush administration may be quite unhappy with U.S. intelligence performance. While publicly he resigned, Judge Webster may have been asked to leave CIA. He subsequently said that perhaps the Agency should place greater stress on intelligence accuracy. It seems certain that the White House will now emphasize intelligence quality instead of guarding against intelligence abuses. If past patterns prevail, then there will be a slackening of controls, a resulting spate of intelligence abuses, and another round of scandals and investigations, possibly before the turn of the century. The lesson of the war, then, is that America still has not found the ideal balance between control and performance when it comes to managing its intelligence community.

The final military lesson pertains to the U.S. military. The war taught the United States that, in spite of all the noble efforts, a wasteful, pernicious, destructive competition continues among the U.S. military branches. In this war, the Air Force prevailed, and General Schwarzkopf's strategy reduced the role of thousands of Marines afloat to posing a threat that was never realized. There are defense cuts looming, and each service intends to use its performance in this war to attack the others. The summary reports that have been issued by each overemphasize its accomplishments while ignoring the contributions of other services. And this may be only the start. The destructiveness of the Armed Forces' infighting that occurred from 1946 to 1950 that resulted in the "revolt of the admirals" may be repeated in the 1990s. This can be prevented if the four services take a united approach, saying that some types of military power are relevant in some wars, and others in others. Air power was very relevant in the Gulf War, but ground forces, Marines, or sea power would be of the greatest importance in other types of wars. Thus preparedness means a balanced military, one that has sufficient land, sea, air, and amphibious power to counter all threats. Having said this, one must add that it is very idealistic and probably will not work.

In other issues, the war also provided lessons. Concerning international terrorism, it taught that the answer is through diplomacy, not counterterrorism. While the latter impedes terrorism, the former can resolve it. Thus, the tempo of terrorism in 1992–1994 is contingent on the success of the ongoing Bush-Baker Middle East diplomacy. Concerning the just war issue, some progress was made, but a problem remains. On the one hand, there are people in all nations who are readily willing to go to war without ever considering a war's justness. An equal problem is the antiwar movement which sees all wars as wrong, when in reality, at times force is justified and must be used. Such exclusive positions leave little room for rational thought. The controversy continues, and given the strength of antiwar sentiment in America, could impact adversely on a U.S. effort in future wars. Finally, the war taught us that the issue of media access to information remains as a festering sore. In New York, reporters refused to take part in a victory celebration in June 1991, not wanting to celebrate the victory of a war that they claim they were not allowed to report. At least in America, unless significant measures are taken, the military must expect press hostility in the next war.

Finally, this chapter keeps referring to the next war. The next war will surely come, but we may postpone it a while if we can heed the lessons of this one.

APPENDICES

A: Financial and Non-Military Support for the Coalition
by
Bruce George, MP, and Joe Sanderson

Australia: medical/surgical team.

Belgium: One billion Belgian francs for British and French military operations. NBC equipment for Turkey, medical equipment, air and ground transport to support US, UK, France and the Netherlands. 2,800 hospital beds, 50 medical personnel.

Bulgaria: 1 unit of army engineers.

Canada: medical/surgical team.

Czechoslovakia: 400 medical personnel.

Denmark: 9 million krona to UK, 5.5 million krona for humanitarian assistance, 25 million krona of the EC's financial assistance. NBC equipment to Turkey, medical equipment and staff to Turkey and Saudi Arabia, C-130s for transport, Danish ships in Gulf to act as supply ships.

Finland: $11.2 million in humanitarian and economic aid.

Germany: $8.9 billion in military aid; $1.4 billion in aid to Egypt, Jordan and Turkey; $826 million emergency aid to Israel; $77 million in loans to US, UK, and Italy. Field medical facilities. Provided road, rail, air, and sea transport for Allied forces from Germany to Gulf.

Hungary: Medical personnel.

Italy: $160 million in aid to nations worst affected by sanctions. U.S. authorized use of Italian military bases, merchant ships used to transport US troops and equipment.

Japan: $10.74 billion ($9.429 billion paid, $1.37 billion pledged).

Kuwait: $16.006 billion ($11.099 billion paid, $4.907 billion pledged).

Luxembourg: $2 million to WEU partners, $3.3 million to EC to help Turkey, Jordan, Egypt, and Bangladesh, $7 million to the WEU, $5 million to US.

Netherlands: $4 million refugee relief, $48 million bilateral aid. 50,000 NBC suits given to Turkey. 2 units of Patriot missiles, 2 Hawk squadrons sent to Turkey.

New Zealand: Medical/surgical team.

Norway: Field hospital in Saudi Arabia, fuel for US ships in Gulf embargo.
Philippines: Medical personnel.
Poland: Military field hospital.
Portugal: Allowed US use of Azores and bases in Portugal for transporting forces.
Romania: Medical team with CW defense specialists.
Saudi Arabia: $16,839 billion ($11.593 billion paid, $5.246 billion pledged).
Sierra Leone: 30 medical personnel.
Singapore: Medical team.
South Korea: $385 million ($163 million paid, $222 million pledged).
Spain: Facilities and logistical support to US forces.
Sweden: $20 million in humanitarian and economic aid. Field hospital and medical personnel.
Turkey: Closed down Iraqi pipelines, borders to Iraq. Allowed US aircraft to use Incirlik Air Base for air strikes.
United Arab Emirates: $4 billion ($4.087 billion paid).

B: The U.N. Security Council Resolutions Concerning the Gulf War
by
Bruce W. Watson and Bruce W. Watson, Jr.

August 2, 1990 – Resolution 660 condemned Iraq's invasion of Kuwait and demanded that Iraq withdraw from Kuwait and begin negotiations. The vote was 14–0, with Yemen not voting.

August 6, 1990 – Resolution 661 imposed an embargo on all trade with Iraq except for medicine and humanitarian food supplies. The vote was 13–0, with Cuba and Yemen abstaining.

August 9, 1990 – Resolution 662, passed unanimously, declared that Iraq's annexation of Kuwait had no legal validity.

August 18, 1990 – Resolution 664, passed unanimously, demanded that Iraq permit all foreigners to leave Kuwait and rescind its order closing the diplomatic missions in Kuwait.

August 25, 1990 – Resolution 665 authorized imposition of a naval blockade on Iraq and Kuwait to ensure compliance with sanctions. The vote was 13–0, with Cuba and Yemen abstaining.

September 13, 1990 – Resolution 666 authorized humanitarian food shipments distributed exclusively by international aid agencies. The vote was 13–2, with Cuba and Yemen voting against it.

September 16, 1990 – Resolution 667, passed unanimously, condemned Iraqi raids on French and other diplomatic premises in Kuwait.

September 24, 1990 – Resolution 669, passed unanimously, asked the United Nations sanctions committee for recommendations on economic assistance to other nations affected by the embargo.

September 25, 1990 – Resolution 670 called on all member states to restrict flights to Iraq to merely those on humanitarian or medical missions, and called on states to detain Iraqi-flagged ships that had been breaking sanctions when they entered port. The vote was 14–1, Cuba against.

October 29, 1990 – Resolution 674 demanded Iraq desist from taking hostages and oppressing Kuwait, asked states to document evidence of this, and urged the Secretary-General to undertake peace efforts. The vote was 13–0; Cuba and Yemen abstained.

November 28, 1990 – Resolution 677 asked the Secretary-General to keep safe a smuggled copy of Kuwait's pre-invasion population register to prevent Iraqi repopulation. The vote was 14–1, Cuba against.

November 29, 1990 – Resolution 678 approved use of all necessary means to drive Iraq from Kuwait after January 15, 1991. The vote was 12–2.

C: Iraqi Scud Launches During the Gulf War[1]
by
Bruce W. Watson

Day	Against		Results
	Israel	*Saudi Arabia*	
Jan 18	7	0	Landed in Tel Aviv and Haifa, 7 injured.
Jan 19	4	0	Landed in/near Tel Aviv.
Jan 20	0	2	Destroyed by Patriot missiles.
Jan 21	0	7	6 destroyed by Patriots, one fell in water.
Jan 22	1	7	1 landed on apartment house in Israel, 3 dead 96 injured; 7 intercepted over Saudi.
Jan 23	1	4	All intercepted.
Jan 25	8	2	Most of those launched at Israel intercepted at low altitude, with 1 dead, 65 injured, widespread damage; all Scuds aimed at Saudi Arabia intercepted.
Jan 26	4	1	All destroyed by Patriots.
Jan 28	1	1	Scud aimed at Israel fell in Palestinian village in West Bank. No damage reported in Saudi Arabia.
Jan 31	1	0	Scud aimed at Israel fell in West Bank.
Feb 2	1	0	Destroyed by Patriot.
Feb 3	1	1	Scud against Saudi Arabia intercepted, Scud against Israel fell in remote area.
Feb 8	0	1	Destroyed by Patriot missile.
Feb 9	1	0	17 injured in Tel Aviv.
Feb 11	1	1	Scud against Israel destroyed by Patriot, no damage reported in Saudi Arabia.
Feb 12	1	0	Destroyed by Patriot.
Feb 14	0	4	Two fell in northern Saudi Arabia, some casualties.
Feb 16	4	1	No damage in Saudi Arabia; light in Israel.

Feb 19	1	0	No details given.
Feb 21	0	3	Aimed at King Khalid Military City, no details.
Feb 22	0	4	No injuries or damage reported.
Feb 23	1	2	No injuries reported in Israel.
Feb 24	0	3	No injuries or damage reported.
Feb 25	2	1	One landed on U.S. Barracks in Dhahran, 28 U.S. dead and 100 U.S. injured. No injuries or damage reported in Israel.
Feb 26	0	1	No damage reported.
TOTAL	40	46	

[1] General Merrill McPeak, Chief of Staff, U.S. Air Force, *The Air Campaign: Part of the Combined Arms Operation* (Washington, DC: Department of the Air Force, 1991), briefing graphic 16. There is considerable disparity among sources as to the total number of Scuds that were fired. One reported that 2 Scuds were fired at Bahrain. General McPeak's figures were developed from a variety of Coalition sources and are considered the most reliable.

D: Air Forces
by
Rod Alonso and Bruce W. Watson

AIR ORDERS OF BATTLE

I. COALITION AIR ORDERS OF BATTLE[1]

A. Coalition Combat aircraft strength by aircraft type:

Type	Number	Type	Number
A-4	18	F-14	100
A-6E	110	F-15	42
A-7E	24	F-15C	120
A-10	144	F-15E	48
AV-8B	60	F-16	261
B-52G	45	F-111E/F	82
Buccaneer	12	F-111	18
CF-18	24	F-117	42
EA-6B	42	F/A-18	190
E-2C	30	Jaguar	68
F-4G	48	Mirage	68
F-5	97	RF-4C	24
		Tornado	103

Total 1,820 combat aircraft

B. Coalition Combat aircraft by nation:

Nation	Number	Type	Total
Bahrain	12	F-5	
	12	F-16	24
Canada	24	CF-18	24
France	24	Jaguar	
	18	Mirage	42
Italy	10	Tornado	10
Kuwait	18	A-4	18
Oman	20	Jaguar	20
Qatar	12	Mirage	12
Saudi Arabia	48	Tornado	
	85	F-5	
	42	F-15	175

United Arab Emirates	50	Mirage	50
United Kingdom	45	Tornado	
	12	Buccaneer	
	12	Jaguar	69
United States (fixed wing)			1,376
Air Force	120	F-15C	
	48	F-15E	
	249	F-16	
	82	F-111E/F	
	18	F-111	
	144	A-10	
	42	F-117	
	48	F-4G	
	24	RF-4C	
	45	B-52G	(820)
Navy	90	A-6E	
	24	A-7E	
	100	F-14	
	106	F/A-18 (USMC)	
	30	EA-6B	
	30	E-2C	(380)
Marine Corps	20	A-6E	
	84	F/A-18	
	60	AV-8B	
	12	EA-6B	(176)
Totals	Non-U.S.		444
	U.S.		1,376
	Total Coalition combat aircraft		1,820

Concerning non-combat aircraft and air defense support, besides the United States Air Force and the Royal Air Force, the following nations provided support aircraft or air defense aircraft or systems: Argentina provided 2 transport aircraft; Belgium deployed 18 Mirage-5 fighter bombers to Turkey, and provided 4 transport aircraft; Canada provided air defense and transport aircraft; France provided 10 support aircraft, 2 Crotale missile batteries to Saudi Arabia and 1 Crotale battery to Qatar; Germany sent 18 Alphajets and 11 Hawk and Roland air defense units to Turkey; Italy sent 6 F-104s to Turkey; New Zealand provided an undetermined number of aircraft; and Spain provided 3 C-130 transports and 1 KC-130 tanker. The German, Belgian, and Italian deployments to Turkey were part of NATO ACE Mobile Force (Air), and were not under CENTCOM control.

II. IRAQI AIR ORDER OF BATTLE:[2]

There is considerable disagreement concerning Iraq's aircraft inventory. This table is based on International Institute for Strategic Studies, *The Military Balance, 1990–1991* (London: Brassey's, 1990), and other sources:

Bombers: 8 Tu-22s, 4 Tu-16, and 4 H-6 (Chinese Tu-16)

Fighters/FGA/Reconnaissance: 30 J-6 (Chinese MiG-19), 40 J-7 (Chinese MiG-21), 30 MiG-29, 32 MiG-25, 90 MiG-23, 155 MiG-21, 64 Mirage EQ5/-2000, 30 Mirage F-1, 30 Su-7, 70 Su-20, 16 Su-24, and 60 Su-25.

Airborne Early Warning: 2 Il-76

Tankers: 1 Il-76

Transports: 10 An-2, 10 An-12, 6 An-24, 2 An-26, and 19 Il-76.

Training: 35 AS-202, 88 EMB-312, 50 L-29, 40 L-39, 16 MB-233, 16 Mirage F1, 50 PC-7, 30 PC-9/Su-7B, 2 Tu-22, and 10 Yak-11.

AIRCRAFT LOSSES

III. COALITION:

Date	Aircraft	Nation/Cause
Jan. 17	F/A-18A	U.S., by SAM, possibly SA-2.
	A-4KU	Kuwaiti, hit by AAA fire
	Jaguar A	French, hit by A-7s over Al Jaber
Jan. 18	A-6E	U.S., possibly from Roland missile
	A-6E	U.S., near Abadan
	F-15E	U.S., by AAA fire
	Tornado	British, hit by SAM
	Tornado	Italian, shot down
	Tornado	British, over NE Kuwait, probably by AAA fire
	Tornado	Saudi, probably by AAA fire
	OV-10A	U.S., by SAM at Ras-al-Mishab
	F-4G	U.S., crashed in Saudi Arabia
Jan. 20	F-15E	U.S., by AAA fire near NW border with Iraq
	F-16	U.S., West of Talil, by AAA fire
	F-16	U.S., Southeast of Baghdad, by SAM

	A-6E	U.S., returned to carrier, total loss.
	Tornado	British, while attacking
	Tornado	British, non-combat loss
	UH-60	U.S., non-combat loss in medevac mission.
Jan. 21	F-14A	U.S., by SAM over Wadi Amif
	AH-64	U.S., non-combat loss
Jan. 22	Tornado	British, by AAA while attacking airfield
	AH-1	U.S., Cobra, non-combat loss
Jan. 23	F-16	U.S., by AAA over Kuwait
	AV-8B	U.S., training accident
	AH-64	U.S., non-combat loss
Jan. 24	Tornado	British, over Basrah
Jan. 26	F/A-18C	U.S., non-combat loss
Jan. 28	AV-8B	U.S., by AAA over Faylakah Island
	AH-1S	U.S., non-combat loss
Jan. 29	U.S.	U.S., no details
Jan. 31	AC-130H	U.S., crashed in Persian Gulf, 14 killed.
Feb. 2	A-6E	U.S., by AAA over Kuwait City
	A-10	U.S., by short-range SAM
	AH-1J	U.S., crashed while returning from mission. Crew killed, non-combat loss
Feb. 3	UH-1N	U.S., non-combat loss
	B-52G	U.S., non-combat loss, crashed nearing Diego Garcia
Feb. 5	F/A-18C	U.S., crashed in Gulf returning to carrier
Feb. 7	F-18	U.S., combat loss
	UH-1H	U.S., non-combat loss
Feb. 10	AV-8B	U.S., by AAA over southern Kuwait
Feb. 13	F-5E	Saudi, hit by AAA over SW Iraq
Feb. 14	EF-111A	U.S., crashed in Saudi Arabia after battle damage
	Tornado	British, hit by SAMs or AAA
	F-5E	Saudi, hit by AAA over Iraqi front line
Feb. 15	A-6E	U.S., crashed in Saudi Arabia after battle damage.
	2 A-10	U.S., SAMs while attacking Republican Guards.
Feb. 16	F-16C	U.S., non-combat loss
	UH-1	U.S., non-combat loss
Feb. 18	F-16	U.S., north of Saudi border, pilot rescued.
Feb. 19	A-10	U.S., combat loss
	OA-10	U.S., by AAA over Kuwait

Feb. 21	OH-58	U.S., lost in combat
	SH-60	U.S., non-combat loss
	CH-46	U.S., non-combat loss
	F-16	U.S., non-combat loss
	UH-60	U.S., crashed on medeivac mission.
Feb. 23	AV-8B	U.S., by AAA near Ali al Salem airfield.
	CH-46	U.S., non-combat loss
Feb. 25	AV-8B	U.S., by AAA southeast of Kuwait City
	OV-10D	U.S., by AAA fire
	AH-64	U.S., no details provided
Feb. 27	OV-1D	U.S., combat loss

IV. IRAQ:

The U.S. Navy states that the following Iraqi aircraft were destroyed on the dates indicated (these figures do not include helicopters):

MiG-21	4 January 17 (2), February 6 (2)
MiG-23	8 January 26 (3), January 27 (4), January 29 (1)
MiG-25	2 January 17 (1), January 19 (1)
MiG-29	6 January 17 (4), January 19 (2)
Mirage F-1	9 January 17 (3), January 19 (2), January 24 (2), January 27 (2)
Su-22	5 February 7 (3), March 20 (1), March 22 (1)
Su-25	2 February 6 (2)
Tu-16	3 January 24 (3)

The U.S. Air Force provides a more complete listing and states the following as Iraqi aircraft losses in the Gulf War:

Cause	Aircraft Lost
Lost in air-to-air engagements	35
Lost in air-to-ground attacks	55
Destroyed by Coalition ground forces	31
Destroyed in Shelters (estimated)	141[3]
Crashed flying to Iran	6
Combat aircraft flown to Iran	115
Civil/military transports flown to Iran	33
Total confirmed destroyed	127
Total estimated destroyed	141
Total flown to Iran	148
TOTAL	416

SPECIFIC BRITISH ROYAL AIR FORCE AND U.S. AIR FORCE
DEPLOYMENTS

V. BRITISH ROYAL AIR FORCE DEPLOYMENTS

Aircraft No/type	Role	Squadrons Represented (from which aircraft/ crews were drawn)
18 Tornado F3	air defense	5, 11, 23, 25, 29, 43
45 Tornado GR1	attack	9, 14, 15, 16, 17, 20, 27, 31, 617
6 Tornado GR1A	reconnaissance	2, 13
12 Jaguar GR1A	attack/recce	6, 41, 54, 226 OCU
12 Buccaneer	Pavespike	12, 208, 237 OCU
19 Puma	helicopter ops	33, 230
17 Chinook	helicopter ops	7, 18
4 Nimrod MR	Maritime	42, 120, 201, 206
17 Victor,	refueling	55
Tristar, and	refueling	216
VC10K	refueling	101
7 C130	air transport	24, 30, 47, 70
1 HS 125	air transport	32

RAF Regiment

Muharraq:	58 Light Armoured Squadron	66 Squadron (Rapier)
	4 Wing Headquarters	33 Wing Headquarters
Tabuk:	51 Light Armoured Squadron	26 Squadron (Rapier)
	6 Wing Headquarters	
Dhahran	51 Light Armoured Squadron	20 Squadron (Rapier)
	34 Sqn Light Armoured Sqn	4 Wing Headquarters
SH Force:	1 Light Armoured Squadron	

RAF Reserve Units in Theater (at various locations):
4626 Aeromedical Evacuation Squadron, Royal Auxiliary Air Force
   (RAF Hullavington)
4624 Movements Squadron, Royal Auxiliary Air Force
   (RAF Brize Norton)
No 7006 Flt RAFVR (Intelligence) RAF High Wycombe
No 7644 Flt RAFVR (Public Relations) RAF Uxbridge

1 Aeromedical Evacuation Squadron (RAF Lyneham)
2 Parachute Squadron RAF Regiment (RAF Hullavington)
Mobile Met Unit
RAF War Hospital (with units from the RAF Hospitals at Halton and
    Ely).

Total personnel: At the peak of hostilities, some 5,500 Royal Air Force
personnel including reservists were deployed to the Gulf in support of RAF
operations.

VI. U.S. AIR FORCE DEPLOYMENTS[4]

A. Active U.S. Air Force Units

Tactical Fighter Wings (TFWs): 1TFW, Langley AFB, Virginia; 4TFW,
Seymour Johnson AFB, North Carolina; 10TFW, RAF Alconbury, United
Kingdom; 20TFW, RAF Upper Heyford, United Kingdom; 23TFW,
England AFB, Louisiana; 33TFW, Eglin AFB, Florida; 35TFW, George
AFB, California; 36TFW, Bitburg AB, Germany; 37TFW, Tonopah,
Nebraska; 48TFW, RAF Lakenheath, United Kingdom; 50TFW, Hahn
AB, Germany; 52TFW, Spangdahlem AB, Germany; 347TFW, Moody
AFB, Georgia; 354TFW, Myrtle Beach AFB, South Carolina; 363TFW,
Mountain Home AFB, Idaho; 388TFW, Hill AFB, Utah; and 401TFW,
Torrejon AB, Spain.

Tactical Airlift Wings (TAWs): 314TAW Little Rock AFB, Arkansas;
317TAW, Pope AFB, North Carolina; and 435TAW, Rhein-Main AB,
Germany.

Military Airlift Wings (MAWs): 60MAW, Travis AFB, California;
62MAW, McChord AFB, Washington; 63MAW, Norton AFB, California;
436MAW, Dover AFB, Delaware, 437MAW, Charleston AFB, South
Carolina; and 438MAW, McGuire AFB, New Jersey.

Miscellaneous Units: 17th Reconnaissance Wing (SAC), RAF Alconbury,
United Kingdom; 67th Tactical Reconnaissance Wing, Bergstrom AFB,
Texas; 552nd Airborne Warning & Control Wing, Tinker AFB, Okla-
homa; 507th Tactical Air Control Wing, Shaw AFB, South Carolina;
602th Tactical Air Control Wing, Davis-Monthan AFB, Arizona; 820th
RED HORSE Civil Engineering Squadron, Nellis AFB, Nevada; 823rd
RED HORSE Civil Engineering Squadron, Hurlburt Field, Florida; and
Special Operations Units.

Air Transportable Hospitals: MacDill AFB, Florida; Homestead AFB, Florida; Holloman AFB, New Mexico; Myrtle Beach AFB, South Carolina; Tyndall AFB, Florida; Davis-Monthan AFB, Arizona; Langley AFB, Virginia; Shaw AFB, South Carolina; Seymour Johnson AFB, North Carolina; and England AFB, Louisiana.

B. Air Force Reserve

Tactical Fighter Wings (TFWs): 301TFW, Carswell AFB, Texas; 419TFW, Hill AFB, Utah; 442TFW, Richards-Gebaur AFB, Missouri; 482TFW, Homestead AFB, Florida; and 917TFW, Barksdale AFB, Alabama.

Tactical Fighter Groups (TFGs): 507TFG, Tinker AFB, Oklahoma; 944TFG, Luke AFB, Arizona; 924TFG, Bergstrom AFB, Texas; and 926TFG, NAS New Orleans, Louisiana.

Tactical Air Groups (TAGs): 907TAG, Rickenbacker ANGB, Ohio; 908TAG, Maxwell AFB, Alabama; 910TAG, Youngstown MAP, Ohio; 911TAG, Greater Pittsburgh IAP, Pennsylvania; 913TAG, Willow Grove ARFF, Pennsylvania; 914TAG, Niagara Falls IAP, New York; 927TAG, Selfridge ANGB, Michigan; 928TAG, O'Hare ARFF, Illinois; and 934TAG, Minneapolis, Minnesota.

Air Refueling Groups (ARGs): 916ARG, Seymour Johnson AFB, North Carolina; and 940ARG, Mather AFB, California.

Miscellaneous Units: 919th Special Operations Group, Eglin AFB, Florida; and 932d Aeromedical Airlift Group, Scott AFB, Illinois.

Bomb Wings: 2BW, Barksdale AFB, Louisiana; 379th BW, Wurtsmith AFB, Michigan; and 42nd BW, Loring AFB, Maine.

C. Air National Guard (ANG) Units

Fighter Interceptor Groups (FIGs): 107FIG, Niagara Falls, New York; 119FIG, Fargo, North Dakota; 120FIG, Great Falls, Montana; 125FIG, Jacksonville, Florida; 142FIG, Portland, Oregon; 147FIG, Ellington ANGB, Texas; 58FIG, Burlington, Vermont; 177FIG, Atlantic City, New Jersey; and 191FIG, Selfridge ANGB, Michigan.

Fighter Interceptor Wings (FIWs): 102FIW, Otis ANGB, Massachusetts; and 44FIW, Fresno, California.

Tactical Fighter Groups (TFGs): 112TFG, Greater Pittsburgh IAP, Pennsylvania; 138TFG, Tulsa, Oklahoma; 150TFG, Kirkland AFB, New Mexico; 162TFG, Tucson, Arizona; 169TFG, McEntire ANGB, South Carolina; 178TFG, Springfield, Ohio; 180TFG, Toledo, Ohio; 181TFG, Terre Haute, Indiana; 185TFG, Sioux City, Iowa; and 188TFG, Fort Smith, Arkansas.

Tactical Fighter Wings (TFWs): 116TFW, Dobbins AFB, Georgia; 121TFW, Rickenbacker ANGB, Ohio; 122TFW, Fort Wayne, Indiana; 127TFW, Selfridge ANGB, Michigan; 131TFW, St. Louis, Missouri; 132TFW, Des Moines, Iowa; 140TFW, Buckley ANGB, Colorado; and 174TFW, Syracuse, New York.

Tactical Reconnaissance Wing (TRW): 117TRW, Birmingham, Alabama.

Tactical Reconnaissance Groups (TRGs): 152TRG, Reno, Nevada; 186TRG, Meridian, Mississippi; 109TAG, Schenectady, New York; 130TAG, Charleston, West Virginia; 135TAG, Baltimore, Maryland; 139TAG, St. Joseph, Missouri; 145TAG, Charlotte, North Carolina; 153TAG, Cheyenne, Wyoming; 164TAG, Memphis, Tennessee; 166TAG, Wilmington, Delaware; 167TAG, Martinsburg, West Virginia; and 179TAG, Mansfield, Ohio.

Tactical Airlift Group (TAG): 189TAG, Little Rock AFB, Arkansas.

Tactical Airlift Wings (TAWs): 118TAW, Nashville, Tennessee; 123TAW, Lousiville, Kentucky; 133TAW, Minneapolis, Minnesota; 136TAW, NAS Dallas, Texas; 137TAW, Oklahoma City, Oklahoma; and 146TAW, Channel Island ANGB, California.

Military Airlift Groups (MAGs): 105MAG, Newburgh, New York; and 172MAG, Jackson, Mississippi.

Air Refueling Groups (ARGs): 128ARG, General Mitchell IAP, Wisconsin; 134ARG, Knoxville, Tennessee; 151ARG, Salt Lake City, Utah; 157ARG, Pease AFB, New Hampshire; 160ARG, Rickenbacker ANGB, Ohio; 161ARG, Phoenix, Arizona; 170ARG, McGuire AFB, New Jersey; and 190ARG, Forbes Field, Kansas.

Air Refueling Wings (ARWs): 101ARW, Bangor, Maine; 126ARW, O'Hare ARFF, Illinois; 141ARW, Fairchild AFB, Washington; and 171ARW, Greater Pittsburgh IAP, Pennsylvania.

Miscellaneous Groups: 129th Air Rescue Group, NAS Moffett Field, California; 226th Combat Communications Group, Martin ANGS, Alabama; 281st Combat Communications Group, Coventry, Rhode Island; 224th Joint Chiefs of Staff Squadron, Brunswick, Georgia; and 290th Joint Chiefs of Staff Squadron, Tampa, Florida.

NOTE: Only partial SAC participation is identified; KC-135, KC-10 and other SAC units not identified.

VII. U.S. AIR FORCE COMBAT STATISTICS[5]

Type	Aircraft Number	Sorties	Remarks	Combat Mission Rate Capable Combat	Peace[6]
F-117A Stealth	40+	1,300	2,000 tons of bombs. 6,900 flight hours.	85.8%	81.8%
F-15E Strike Eagle	48	2,200	LANTIRN Pods, 2 F-15Es Lost	95.9%	87.9%
F-16 Fighting Falcon	249	13,500	72 LANTIRN (Nav pods only) capable F-16s	95.2%	90.2%
A-10A/OA-10A Thunderbolt II	144	8,100		95.7%	90.7%
F-111F	NA	4,000	FLIR System, 1500 armor kills, stopped Gulf oil spill	85%	77%
B-52 Stratofortress	NA	1,624	25,700 tons of munitions; 29% of all US bombs; 38% of all USAF bombs. Total over 72,000 weapons.	81%	79%
HC-130 Hercules	830	NA	PSYOPS, 15,000–lb bombs	NA	NA
(AC)Spectre (MC)Combat Talon II (EC)Compass Call	NA	NA	MH-53J Pave Low Pathfinder for Army Apache; Comms Jammer		
F-15 C/D Eagle	120	5,900	Made all AF fixed-wing air kills	94%	86%
EF-111 Raven	18	900	Jammed Iraqi Air Defense System	87.5%	NA

| F-4G Wild Weasel | 48 | 2,500 | SAM Killer with HARM | 87% | NA |

VIII. U.S. AIR FORCE SUPPORT AIRCRAFT STATISTICS[7]

Aircraft Type	Number Deployed	Sorties Flown	Flight Hours	Mission	Remarks
C-130 Hercules	145+	46,500	75,000	Theater Airlift	8/2/90–4/2/91 moved 209,000+ troops, 300,000+ tons of cargo. Over 500 sorties daily in ground offensive.
C-5A/B	NA	NA	NA	Strateg. Airlift	90% of force assigned to war.
C-141 Starlifter	NA	NA	NA	Strateg. Airlift	80% of force assigned to war.
KC-135[8] Strato-tanker	256	4,967	19,089	Aerial Refueler	Desert Shield: re-fueled 14,588 air-craft with 68.2 mil. gals. jet fuel.
KC-10 Extender tanker	46	15,434	59,943	Aerial Refueler	Desert Storm: re-fueled 15,434 air-craft with 110.2 mil. gals. jet fuel
E-3B/C Sentry Sentry	11	4 continuous continuous	NA	Airborne Surveil-lance and C³	1/17/91 to ceasefire: controlled over 3,000 sorties daily.
E-8A Joint STARS	2	54	535	Ground Surveil-lance	In developmental test and evaluation stages.
RC-135 Rivet Joint	NA	NA	NA	ELINT Collec-tion	

IX. U.S. MISSILES AND AERIAL WEAPONS USED IN THE GULF WAR[9]

U.S. Air Force

Weapon	Delivery	Guidance/Remarks
AGM-65D/G Maverick	F-16, A-10, F-15E	Imaging infrared radar-guided armor killer.
AIM-7E/F/M Sparrow	F-15C/D, F-14, F/A-18	Solid-state infrared homing missile that downed 23 Iraqi aircraft.

AIM-9L Sidewinder	F-111, F-15C/D, F-16, A-7, A-10	Passive radar-guided high speed anti-radiation missile. Downed 6 Iraqi a/c.
AGM-88A/B/C Harm	F-4G, EF-111A, B-52, F-15	Passive radar-guided high speed anti-radiation SAM killer.
GBU-10	F-117A	Paveway II 2,000–lb laser guided bomb.
GBU-12	F-111F	Precision-guided munition-destroyed over 150 armored vehicles nightly.
GBU-15V1/B	F-111F, F-15E, F-16D	Precision (electro-optically)-guided bomb (day attack) with TV camera.
GBU-25V2/B		Precision (electro-optically)-guided bomb (EOGB) (night attack) w/ IR sensor.
GBU-27	F-117A	2,000–lb. laser guided bomb. Hard target killer (aircraft shelters, strategic bunkers in Baghdad) with I2000 penetration case.
GBU-24	F-111F, F-15E	Used against chemical, biological, and nuclear targets, bridges, aircraft shelters, other strategic targets.
GLU-109/B		Guided by Paveway II LGB and possibly GBU-15 EOGB. 2,000–lb bomb that penetrates 28.8 feet reinforced concrete.
CBU-7/B	AV-8B	Combined effects munition (CEM) used in close air support.
CBU-52	B-52G	Used against troops and equipment.
BLU-97/B	B-52	
Mk-82	B-52G	2,000 pound bomb; (B-52G carries 51).
Mk-82		Demolition bomb with LGB adapted (kit).
M118		Demolition bomb with LGB adapted (kit).

| Bunker | probably | Custom built to order. Probably |
| Buster | F-117A | LGB-adapted to destroy hard targets. |

U.S. Navy/Marine Corps

Weapon	Delivery	Guidance/Remarks
Tomahawk	Missouri, Wisconsin,	TERCOM-aided inertial guidance.
TLAM-D	Spruance-, Virginia-,	264 TLAM-C (land attack), 27
TLAM-C	Ticonderoga-class	TLAM-D (combined bomblets
	ships. SSNs USS	effect) launched.
	Louisville, Pittsburgh	
Rockeye II		Cluster bombs, 4,473 expended.
MK-20		
HARM		Passive radar. 644 expended.
AGM-88A/B/C		SAM killer; high speed anti-radiation missile.
SLAM		7 expended.
WALLEYE		124 expended.
MK-82		2,000–lb bomb; 7,735 expended.
MK-82 (with laser kit)		2,000–lb bomb; 179 expended.
MK-83		6,980 expended.
MK-83 (with laser kit)		175 expended.
MK-84		863 expended.
MK-84 (with laser kit)		195 expended.

NOTES

[1] These figures were derived from *Jane's Defence Weekly*, *Armed Forces International*, and U.S. Defense Department News Briefings. Deployments not listed include the transfer of two NATO Airborne Early Warning Force (NAEWF) E-3A AWACS from Geilen Kirchen, Germany to Konya, Turkey. The Royal Saudi Air Force also contributed an unspecified number of E-3A AWACS to the Coalition Air Forces. The total U.S. combat aircraft total was actually higher because data are

not available for some aircraft, such as AC-130 gunships. The total Coalition aircraft is estimated to be almost 2,000.

[2] Department of Defense, *DOD News Briefing*, Washington, DC, March 21, 1991.

[3] In the future, the actual number of aircraft estimated to have been destroyed in shelters will probably increase markedly when an in depth analysis of all Iraqi airfields containing hardened aircraft shelters that were struck is completed.

[4] "The Forces of Desert," *Air Force Magazine* (March 1991): 40; Department of the Air Force, USAF CS Group, Washington, D.C., April 29, 1991; and SACEUR Statement before U.S. Senate Committee on Armed Services, March 7, 1991.

[5] Department of the Air Force, *White Paper: Air Force Performance in Desert Storm* (Washington, DC, 1991), pp. 2–6; and Michael A. Dornheim, "Trapez Gives F-117 Ability to Carry Variety of Weapons," *Aviation Week & Space Technology* (April 8, 1991): 72.

[6] Mission capable rate for peace and war is the number of aircraft that are actually capable of fulfilling their missions and are not suffering mechanical or other difficulties.

[7] *Air Force White Paper*, p. 14.

[8] Refueling sortie numbers and flight hours are broken out for Desert Shield and Desert Storm operations but are combined total for both the KC-135 and KC-10 which are not listed individually.

[9] Compiled from several sources, including *Air Force White Paper*; Department of the Navy, *Chief of Naval Operations Testimony to Congress* (Washington, DC, 1991); and *Department of Defense News Briefings*.

E: Ground Forces
by
Peter Tsouras, Elmo C. Wright, Jr., and Bruce W. Watson

I. COALITION GROUND ORDER OF BATTLE

Afghanistan	300 Mujahedeen troops (under Joint Forces Command)
Bahrain	3,500 troops (under Joint Forces Command)
Bangladesh	2,000 troops (under CENTCOM administrative command)
Czechoslovakia	350 men, comprising a chemical protection unit; 170 Army troops to Saudi Arabia (under CENTCOM administrative command).
Egypt	40,000 troops (including 4th Armored Division, 3rd Mechanized Division, and some special forces), 400 tanks (mainly M-60), 600 APCs, 300 artillery pieces (including 122mm howitzers and 155mm SP-M109, BM-21 rocket launchers) (under Joint Forces Command)
France	13,500 troops, 110 tanks (2,500 vehicles), 120 helicopters (see order of battle below)
Kuwait	7,000 troops (under Joint Forces Command)
Morocco	2,000 troops (under CENTCOM administrative command)
Oman	2,500 troops, 24 tanks (under Joint Forces Command)
Niger	400 troops (under CENTCOM administrative command)
Pakistan	10,000 troops (under Joint Forces Command)
Qatar	4,000 troops, 24 tanks (under Joint Forces Command)
Saudi Arabia	95,000 troops, 550 tanks (under Joint Forces Command)
Senegal	500 troops (under CENTCOM administrative command)
Syria	20,000 troops (under Joint Forces Command)
United Arab Emirates	4,000 troops (under Joint Forces Command)

United Kingdom   35,000 troops, consisting of 1st Armoured Division (4th and 7th Armoured Brigades), reinforced by artillery, engineer and air corps assets, three infantry battalions for POW handling, and a large logistics support organization (see order of battle below)

United States   532,000 troops, 2,000 tanks (see order of battle below)

II. UNITED STATES GROUND FORCES

A. U.S. ARMY

3RD U.S. ARMY (ARCENT) (Lieutenant General John Yeosock)

US XVIII CORPS (Lieutenant General Gary Luck)

1st Cavalry Division
1st Brigade: 2 tank, 1 mechanized infantry, 1 artillery battalions
2nd Brigade: 2 tank, 1 mechanized infantry, 1 artillery battalions
1st ("Tiger") Brigade, 2nd Armored Division: 2 Tank, 2 mechanized infantry, 1 artillery battalions
Division Troops: 1 MLRS battery, 1 air defense artillery, 1 engineer, 1 cavalry, 1 helicopter gunship battalions

24th Infantry Division (Mechanized) (Major General McCaffrey)
1st Brigade: 1 tank, 2 mechanized infantry, 1 artillery battalions
197th Separate Infantry Brigade (Mechanized Brigade): 1 tank, 2 mechanized infantry, 1 artillery battalions, 1 cavalry troop
Division Troops: 1 MLRS battery, 1 air defense artillery, 1 engineer, 1 cavalry, 1 helicopter gunship battalions

82nd Airborne Division
1st Brigade (325th Parachute Regiment): 3 airborne infantry battalions
2nd Brigade (504th Parachute Regiment): 3 airborne infantry battalions
3rd Brigade (505th Parachute Regiment): 3 airborne infantry battalions
Division Troops: 1 light tank, 1 air defense artillery, 3 105mm towed artillery, 1 engineer, 1 reconnaissance, 1 helicopter gunship, 1 transport helicopter battalions

101st Air Assault Division (Major General Peay)
1st Brigade (187th Air Assault Regiment): 3 airmobile infantry battalions
2nd Brigade (327th Air Assault Regiment): 3 airmobile infantry battalions

2nd Brigade (502nd Air Assault Regiment): 3 airmobile infantry battalions
Division Troops: 1 air defense artillery, 3 105mm towed artillery, 1 engineer, 1 helicopter gunship, 3 transport helicopter battalions

Corps Troops
3rd Armored Cavalry Regiment: 3 armored cavalry squadrons, 1 air cavalry squadron, 1 artillery battalion
12th Aviation Brigade: 5 helicopter battalions (gunships and transport)
18th Corps Aviation Brigade: 3 helicopter battalions (gunships and transport)
18th Field Artillery Brigade: 4 artillery battalions

III Corps Artillery (attached to XVIII Corps)
7th Field Artillery Brigade: 4 artillery battalions
212th Field Artillery Brigade: 4 artillery battalions
214th Field Artillery Brigade: 4 artillery battalions

11th Air Defense Artillery Group: 3 to 5 air defense artillery battalions

36th Engineering Group

U.S. VII CORPS (Lieutenant General Fred Franks)

3rd Armored Division
6 tank, 5 mechanized infantry, 1 engineer, 1 air defense artillery, 3 artillery, 1 cavalry, 2 helicopter gunship, 2 transport helicopter battalions, 1 MLRS battery
350 M1A1, 330 M2/M3, 72 M109, 8 MLRS

1st Armored Division
1st Infantry Division (Mechanized)
6 tank, 4 mechanized infantry, 1 engineer, 1 air defense artillery, 3 artillery, 1 cavalry, 2 helicopter gunship, 1 transport helicopter battalions
350 M1A1, 280 M2/M3, 72 M109, 8 MLRS

2nd Armored Cavalry Regiment
Corps Troops
3 armored cavalry, 1 air cavalry squadrons, 1 artillery battalion
125 M1A1, 115 M3, 24 M109, 25 + helicopters

1st Brigade, 2nd Armored Division (to reinforce 1st Mechanized Division): 2 tank, 1 (or 2) mechanized infantry, 1 artillery battalions
115 M1A1, 75 M2, 24 M109

3rd Brigade, 3rd Infantry Division (Mechanized): 1 tank, 2 mechanized
   infantry, 2 artillery battalions
56 M1A1, 150 M2/M3, 48 M109
3 Field Artillery Brigades (drawn from 17th, 41st, 42nd, 72nd, and 210th),
   about 4 artillery battalions each: mix of M109 155mm MLRS, M110
   8–inch, and LANCE

19th or 130th Engineer Brigade

B. U.S. MARINE CORPS

1ST MARINE EXPEDITIONARY FORCE (MARCENT) (Lieutenant
General Walter Boomer)

1st Marine Division (Expeditionary Force)
1st Marine Expeditionary Brigade
7th Marine Expeditionary Brigade
4th Marine Expeditionary Brigade (Afloat)
13th Marine Expeditionary Unit (Battalion) (Afloat)
1st Marine Tank Battalion (M60A3)
2nd Marine Tank Battalion (M1A1)

2nd Division (Expeditionary Force)
5th Marine Brigade
6th Marine Brigade
4th Marine Tank Battalion (M60A3)
8th Marine Tank Battalion (M60A3)

III. UNITED KINGDOM GROUND FORCES

Overall Commander Lieutenant General Peter de la Billiere
1st Armoured Division Major General Smith (initially under the operational
control of the 1st MEF, but then switched to VII Corps)
   16th/5th The Queen's Royal Lancers (armored reconnaissance regiment with 48 Scimitar Combat Vehicle Reconnaissance (Tracked)
(CVR(T)) mounting Rarden 30mm gun, 16 Striker CVR(T) with Swingfire ATGW
   2nd, 26th, 40th Field Regiments Royal Artillery (RA) (each with 24
M109 self-propelled (SP) 155mm howitzers)

32nd Heavy Regiment RA (12 M110 8–inch SP howitzers)
39th Heavy Regiment RA (12 MLRS)
12th Air Defence Regiment RA (24 Rapier SAM systems)
23, 127 Batteries RA (each 8 M109s)
21 Battery Air Defence Battery RA (24 Javelin SAM systems)
21, 23, 39 Engineer Regiments Royal Engineers (RE) (field engineers equipped with the Combat Engineer Tractor (CET), and FV 432 APCs, some with Bar minelayer/Ranger mine projector systems, bridging and plant)
32 Armoured Engineer Regiment RE (armoured vehicles Royal Engineers (AVREs) with 165mm demolition charge projectors or 105mm gun with mine plough, both being based on Centurion tank, armoured vehicle launched bridges (AVLB) and CET)
3, 37 Field Squadrons RE
15, 45 Field Support Squadrons RE
4 Regiment Army Air Corps (12 Gazelle and 24 Lynx (armed with TOW) helicopters)

4th Armoured Brigade (Brigadier Hammerbeck)
14/20th King's Hussars (43 Challenger 1s)
1st Battalion The Royal Scots (45 Warriors)
3rd Battalion The Royal Regiment of Fusiliers (45 Warriors)

7th Armoured Brigade (Brigadier Cordingly)
The Royal Scots Dragoon Guards (57 Challenger 1s)
Queen's Royal Irish Hussars (57 Challenger 1s)
1st Battalion The Staffordshire Regiment (45 Warriors)

NOTES

1. Armored reconnaissance was augmented by elements of 1st The Queen's Dragoon Guards and 9/12 Lancers.
2. Armor was augmented by elements of The Life Guards, 17th/21st Lancers, and 2nd Royal Tank Regiment.
3. Infantry was augmented by elements of 1st Battalion Grenadier Guards and 1st Battalion Queen's Own Highlanders.
4. After the ground campaign had been launched, three additional infantry battalions – 1st Battalion Coldstream Guards, 1st Battalion The Royal Highland Fusiliers, and 1st Battalion The King's Own Scottish Borderers – were sent to the Gulf, primarily for POW handling.
5. The following supporting elements were also present:
   Royal Artillery – observation post battery
   Royal Engineers – topographic squadron, explosive ordnance disposal squadron (EOD), postal and courier regiment.

Royal Corps of Signals – two regiments plus seven additional squadrons, air support squadron, electronic warfare squadron, and additional troops.

Royal Corps of Transport – four transport regiments plus two additional squadrons, one tank transporter regiment, two ambulance squadrons (one from the Ghurka Transport Regiment), two movement control squadrons, one port squadron.

Royal Army Medical Corps – two armored field ambulances, one airmobile field ambulance, three field hospitals, one general hospital (Territorial Army).

Royal electrical and Mechanical Engineers – three armored and one aircraft field workshops.

Royal military Police – two provost companies.

Royal Pioneer Corps – one group and two companies.

IV. FRENCH GROUND FORCES

Overall Commander General Michel Roquejeoffre

6th Light Armored Division Daguet, Reinforced
1st Foreign Legion Armored Regiment (35 AMX-10RC)
1st Regiment de Spahis (35 AMX-10RC)
2nd Foreign Legion Infantry Regiment (VAB APCs)
21st Marine Infantry Regiment (VAB APCs)
68th Marine Artillery Regiment (four batteries of towed 155mm howitzers, one battery of Mistral SAMs)
6th Foreign Legion Engineer Regiment

From 4th Airmobile Division
5th Combat Helicopter Regiment (10 20mm gunships, 30 antitank helicopters with HOT antitank guided missiles)
1st Transport Helicopter Regiment
1st Infantry Regiment (airmobile)

From 9th Marine Division
2nd Marine Infantry Regiment (VAB APCs)
Detachment, 3rd Marine Infantry Regiment (269 men)
11th Marine Artillery Regiment (four batteries of towed 155mm howitzers)

From 10th Armored Division
4th Dragoon Regiment (40 AMX-30B2 main battle tanks)

V. IRAQI GROUND FORCES

At the end of the Iran-Iraq War the Iraqi Ground Forces consisted of just under one million men and were organized into seven corps consisting of a total of 4 armored, 3 mechanized and 40 infantry divisions, together with a number of special forces/commando brigades and two surface-to-surface missile brigades. Also included in the manpower total was the Republican Guard Force (RGF) of two armored, five mechanized, and one special forces divisions. It seems, however, that by the time the Gulf War began after the calling up of reservists had resulted in an increase in the Army's divisional strength, giving it a total up to 60.

REPUBLICAN GUARD FORCES

Hammurabi and Medina Armored Divisions, each with two armored and one mechanized brigades with possibly a special forces/commando brigade attached, totalled about 300 T-72 tanks, 200 BMP-1/2 IFVs, 36 152/155 SP guns, 18 130mm towed guns, 54 BM-21 mobile rocket launchers, and 36 120mm mortars.

Tawakalna Mechanized Division with one armored and two mechanized brigades with possibly a special forces/commando brigade attached, totalled about 220 T-72 tanks, 270 BMP-1/2 IFVs, 36 152/155 SP guns, 18 130mm towed guns, 54 BM-21 mobile rocket launchers, and 36 120mm mortars.

Special Forces Division with 2–3 special forces/commando brigades, each with 3 special forces battalions, a 12–gun artillery battalion, six 120mm mortar batteries, a reconnaissance company, an antitank company, an assault engineer company, a medical company, and a signal company.

IRAQI ARMY

Armored Division – two armored and one mechanized brigades, totalling some 245 T-72/T-62 tanks, 200 IFVs/APCs, 72 122/152mm self propelled guns, and 30 120mm mortars.

Mechanized Division – one armored and two mechanized brigades, totalling some 175 T-72/62 tanks, 280 IFVs/APCs, 72 122/152mm self propelled guns and 130mm towed guns, and 30 120mm mortars.

Infantry Divisions – three infantry brigades, with 35 T-54/55 tanks, 72 122/130mm towed guns, and 30 120mm mortars.

Additionally, each corps had an artillery brigade of some 54 towed and/or special purpose guns.

It should, however, be noted that most divisions were not up to full complement and that some may have been up to one-third below it.

VI. WAR LOSSES

COALITION

United States
148 killed
458 wounded

Great Britain
47 killed
43 wounded

France
2 killed
25 wounded

Egypt
14 killed
120 wounded

Kuwait

An unknown number, estimated to be between 500 and 1000, of civilians and some military were killed, and many injured, during the Iraqi occupation of Kuwait.

IRAQ

60,000 to 100,000 military personnel are estimated to have been killed or wounded in action.
2,000 to 3,000 civilians are estimated to have been killed, and from 5,000 to 7,700 injured.

F: Naval Forces
by
Bruce W. Watson

NAVAL ORDERS OF BATTLE

I. COALITION NAVAL ORDERS OF BATTLE[1]

(Dates are in month/day/year order)[2]

A. UNITED STATES
Aircraft Carriers
America (CV-66), 1/15–4/3/91
Eisenhower (CVN-69), 8/8–8/24/90
Independence (CV-42), 8/5–11/4/90
John F. Kennedy (CV-67), 9/14/90–3/12/91
Midway (CV-41), 11/2/90–3/14/91
Ranger (CV-61), 1/13–4/19/91
Saratoga (CV-60), 8/22–9/21/90; 10/23–12/9/90; 1/6–3/11/91
Theodore Roosevelt (CVN-71), 1/14–4/20/91

Submarines
Chicago (SSN-721), 2/7–3/7/91
Louisville (SSN-724), 1/18–1/30/91
Newport News (SSN-750), Mediterranean
Philadelphia (SSN-690), Mediterranean
Pittsburgh (SSN-720), Mediterranean

Battleships
Missouri (BB-63), 1/1–3/24/91
Wisconsin (BB-64), 8/18/90–3/13/91

Cruisers
Antietam (CG-54), 8/5–11/3/90
Biddle (CG-34), 8/22–9/21/90; 10/23–12/9/90; 1/9–3/13/91
Bunker Hill (CG-52), 10/28/90–3/10/91
England (CG-22), 7/31–11/3/90
Gates (CG-51), 9/14/90–3/12/91
Horne (CG-30), 1/24–4/20/91
Jouett (CG-29), 8/5–11/4/90

Leyte Gulf (CG-55), 1/14/91–TBD
Mississippi (CGN-40), 9/14/90–3/12/91
Mobile Bay (CG-53), 10/30/90–3/14/91
Normandy (CG-60), 1/15–4/3/91
Philippine Sea (CG-58), 8/22–9/21/90; 10/25–12/9/90; 1/6–2/9/91
Princeton (CG-59), 1/13–4/29/91 (hit mine 2/18/91)
R.K. Turner (CG-20), 1/14–4/20/91
San Jacinto (CG-56), 9/14/90–3/12/91
South Carolina (CGN-37), 10/23–12/11/90
Ticonderoga (CG-47), 8/8–8/24/90
Valley Forge (CG-50), 1/13–4/19/91
Virginia (CGN-38), 1/15–4/3/91
Worden (CG-18), 10/28/90–2/15/91

Destroyers
Caron (DD-970), 1/14/91–TBD
Fife (DD-991), 10/30/90–3/14/91
Goldsborough (DDG-20), 8/5–11/4/90
Hewitt (DD-966), 11/2/90–3/14/91
H.W. Hill (DD-986), 1/13–3/12/91
John Rodgers (DD-983), 8/19–8/24/90; 1/15–4/3/91
Kidd (DDG-993), 2/1/91–TBD
Leftwich (DD-984), 12/4/90–3/8/91
MacDonough (DDG-39), 10/17/90–2/24/91
Moosbrugger (DD-980), 10/3–11/27/90; 12/21/90–3/12/91
O'Brien (DD-975), 8/13–12/9/90
Oldendorf (DD-972), 11/2/90–3/14/91
P.F. Foster (DD-964), 1/13–4/19/91
Pratt (DDG-44), 1/15–4/3/91
Preble (DDG-46), 1/15–3/12/91
D.R. Ray (DD-971), 6/9–9/18/90
Sampson (DDG-10), 8/24–9/21/90; 11/1–12/16/90
Scott (DDG-995), 8/8–8/24/90
Spruance (DD-963), 2/8–3/11/91
Tattnall (DDG-19), 8/19–8/24/90

Frigates
Barbey (FF-1088), 7/31–11/3/90
R.G. Bradley (FFG-49), 7/28–11/12/90
Brewton (FF-1086), 8/5–11/4/90
Curts (FFG-38), 11/2/90–3/14/91
Ford (FFG-54), 1/26–3/24/91
John L. Hall ((FFG-32), 8/8–8/24/90

Halyburton (FFG-40), 1/18–4/9/91
Francis Hammond (FF-1067), 1/23–4/21/91
Hawes (FFG-53), 1/14/91–TBD
Jarrett (FFG-33), 1/24–4/20/91
McInerney (FFG-8), 2/5–6/12/91
Montgomery (FF-1082), 8/24/90–1/9/91
Nicholas (FFG-47), 10/17/90–2/24/91
Paul (FF-1080)
Reasoner (FF-1063), 8/5–11/4/90
Reid (FFG-30), 4/27–9/9/90
S.B. Roberts (FFG-58), 9/5/90–3/12/91
Shields (FF-1066), 10/30/90–2/15/91
Taylor (FFG-50), 7/28–11/12/90
T.C. Hart(FF-1092), 8/24–12/11/90; 1/15–3/11/91
Vandergrift (FFG-48), 4/27–9/9/90
Vreeland (FF-1068), 1/18/91–TBD

Amphibious Ships
Anchorage (LSD-36), 1/12/91–TBD
Barbour County (LST-1195), 1/12/91–TBD
Blue Ridge (LCC-19), 8/28/90–TBD
Cayuga (LST-1186), 9/5–11/8/90; 1/12–3/13/91
Denver (LPD-9), 1/12/91–TBD
Dubuque (LPD-8), 9/9–10/13/90
Durham LKA-114, 9/5–11/8/90; 1/12–3/13/91
Fort McHenry (LSD-43), 9/5–11/8/90; 1/12–3/13/91
Frederick (LST-1184), 1/12/91–TBD
Germantown (LSD-42), 1/12/91–TBD
Guam (LPH-9), 9/8/90–3/23/91
Gunston Hall (LSD-44), 9/3/90–3/23/91
Iwo Jima (LPH-7), 9/8/90–3/23/91
Juneau (LPD-10), 1/12/91–TBD
La Moure County (LST-1194), 9/8/90–3/14/91
Manitowac (LST-1180), 9/8/90–3/23/91
Mobile (LKA-115), 1/12/91–TBD
Mount Vernon (LSD-39), 1/12/91–TBD
Nassau (LHA-4), 9/6/90–3/23/91
New Orleans (LPH-11), 1/12/91–TBD
Ogden (LPD-5), 9/5–11/8/90, 1/12–3/13/91
Okinawa (LPH-3), 9/5–11/8/90, 1/12–3/13/91
Pensacola (LSD-38), 9/6/90–3/14/91
Peoria (LST-1183), 1/12/91–TBD
Portland (LSD-37), 9/3/90–3/23/91

Raleigh (LPD-1), 9/8/90–3/14/91
Saginaw (LST-1188) 9/6/90–3/23/91
San Bernadino (LST-1189) 9/9/90–10/13/91
Schenectady (LST 1185), 9/9–10/10/90
Shreveport (LPD-12), 9/3/90–3/23/91
Spartanburg County (LST-1192) 9/3/90–3/23/91
Tarawa (LHA-1), 1/12/91–TBD
Trenton (LPD-14) 9/3/90–3/23/91
Tripoli (LPH-10), 1/12/91–TBD (hit mine 2/18/91)
Vancouver (LPD-2), 1/12/91–TBD

Mine Warfare Ships
Adroit (MSO-509), 9/90–TBD
Avenger (MCM-1), 9/90–TBD
Impervious (MSO-449), 9/90–TBD
Leader (MSO-490), 9/90–TBD

Auxiliaries
A.J. Higgins (TAO-190), 9/9/90–TBD
Acadia (AD-42), 10/18/90–3/12/91
Algol (TAKR-287), 10/24/90–4/20/91
Altair (TAKR-291), 9/90–3/26/91
Beaufort (ATS-2), 1/29/91–TBD
Bellatrix (TAKR-288), 9/90–3/26/91
Cape Cod (AD-43), 2/26/91–TBD
Capella (TAKR-293), 9/90–4/91
Chauvenet (TAGS-29), 9/90–TBD
Cimmaron (AO-177), 8/5–11/4/90
Comfort (TAH-19), 8/30/90–3/23/91
Concord (AFS-5), 9/18–9/25/90
Curtiss (TAVB-4), 9/10/90–4/9/91
Denebola (TAKR-289), 10/17/90–3/5/91
Detroit (AOE-4), 8/24–9/21/90, 11–7–12/16/90, 1/6–3/6/91
Flint (AE-32), 8/5–11/4/90
Haleakala (AE-25), 2/9–3/14/91
Hassayampa (TAO-145), 9/8/90–3/14/91
J. Humphreys (TAO-188), 1/15–4/23/91
Jason (AR-8), 1/12–4/4/91
Kalamazoo (AOR-6), 1/15–3/30/91
Kansas City (AOR-3), 1/13–4/19/91
Kilauea (TAE-26), 9/3/90–3/8/91
Kiska (AE-35), 11/2/90–3/14/91
LaSalle (AGF-3), Homeport

Mars (AFS-1), 12/21/90–3/22/91
McKee (AS-41), 3/3/91–TBD
Mercury (TAKR-10), 10/10/90–3/18/91
Mercy (TAH-20), 9/15/90–3/21/91
Mount Hood (AE-29), 2/1–3/13/91
Neosha (TAO-143), 8/8–8/23/90
Niagara Falls (AFS-3), 1/15/91–TBD
Nitro (AE-32), 1/16–4/10/91
Opportune (ARS-41), 11/26/90–3/31/91 (Med)
Passumpsic (TAO-107), 1/24–3/25/91
Platte (AO-186), 1/14–4/13/91
Pollux (TAKR-290), 10/90–3/91
Ponchatoula (TAO-148), 1/12–3/16/91
Puget Sound (AD-38), 2/18/91–TBD
Regulus (TAKR-292), 10/90–3/91
Sacramento (AOE-1), 1/1–3/24/91
San Jose (AFS-7), 9/24/90–3/13/91
San Diego (AFS-6), 1/14–4/6/91
Santa Barbara (AE-28), 1/15/91–TBD
Savannah (AOE-4), 10/8–10/13/90
Seattle (AOE-3), 9/14/90–3/11/91
Shasta (AE-33), 1/13–4/29/91
Sirius (TAFS-8), 11/17–11/23/90; 2/10–4/3/91
Spica (TAFS-9), 10/11/90–3/14/91
Suribachi (AE-21), 8/8–8/22/90; 1/15–4/3/91
Sylvania (AFS-2), 10/8–10/13/90; 1/12–2/17/91
Vulcan (AR-5), 1/23–2/15/91
W.S. Diehl (TAO-193), 10/30/90–3/13/91
White Plains (AFS-4), 8/17–10/15/90
Wright (TAVB-3), 9/90–TBD
Yellowstone (AD-41), 9/25–10/13/90; 1/8–2/27/91

Aircraft Squadrons

HC-11	DET 4	11/2/90–3/14/91
	DET 7	1/1–3/24/91
	DET 8	1/13–4/19/91
	DET 11	8/5–11/4/90
HC-1	DET 6	8/28–TBD
HC-6	DET 1	1/15–TBD
	DET 4	10/8–10/13/90;1/12–2/17/91
	DET 5	1/15–3/13/91
	DET 7	11/17–11/23/90;2/10–4/3/91
HC-8	DET 1	10/8–10/13/90

	DET 2	8/24–9/21/90;11/7–12/16/90;1/6–3/6/01
	DET 5	9/14/90–3/11/91
	DET 4	1/14–4/6/91
HM-14	DET 1	**ABU DHABI**

HS-11, SH-3H, *America*, 1/15–4/3/91
HS-12, SH-3H, *Midway*, 11/2/90–3/14/91
HS-14, SH-3H, *Ranger*, 1/13–4/19/91
HS-3, SH-3H, *Saratoga*, 8/22–9/21/90;10/23–12/9/90;1/6–3/11/91
HS-5, SH-3H, *Eisenhower*, 8/8–8/24/90
HS-7, SH-3H, *John F. Kennedy*, 9/14/90–3/12/91
HS-8, SH-3H, *Independence*, 8/4–11/4/90
HS-9, SH-3H, *Theodore Roosevelt*, 1/14–4/20/91

HSL-32	DET 7	8/24–12/11/90;1/15–3/11/91
HSL-33	DET 7	4/27–9/9/91
	DET 9	8/5–11/4/90
HSL-34	DET 1	8/22–9/21/90;10/23–12/9/90;1/9–3/13/91
	DET 5	2/1/91–TBD
HSL-35	DET 7	7/31–11/3/90
HSL-36	DET 8	1/18/91–TBD
HSL-37	DET 6	11/2/90–3/14/91
HSL-42	DET 1	9/14/90–3/12/91
	DET 3	1/14/91–TBD
	DET 6	10/3–11/27/90;12/21/90–3/12/91
	DET 7	7/28–11/12/90
	DET 8	2/5–6/12/91
	DET 9	7/28–11/12/90
HSL-43	DET 8	4/27–9/9/91
HSL-44	DET 5	1/14–4/20/91
	DET 6	1/18–4/9/91
	DET 7	1/15–4/3/91
	DET 8	10/17/90–2/14/91
	DET 9	9/14/90–3/12/91
HSL-46	DET 7	8/22–9/21/90;10/25–12/9/90;1/6–2/9/91
HSL-48	DET 1	2/8–3/11/91
	DET 2	1/14–4/19/91
	DET 3	1/14–TBD

VA-115, A-6E, *Midway*, 11/2/90–3/14/91
VA-145, A-6E, *Ranger*, 1/13–4/19/91
VA-155, A-6E, *Ranger*, 1/13–4/19/91
VA-185, A-6E and KA-6D, *Midway*, 11/2/90–3/14/91
VA-196, A-6E and KA-6D, *Independence*, 8/5–11/4/90
VA-34, A-6E and KA-6D, *Eisenhower*, 8/8–8/24/90
VA-35, A-6E and KA-6D, *Saratoga*, 10/23–12/9/90;1/6–3/11/91

VA-36, A-6E, *Theodore Roosevelt*, 1/14–4/20/91
VA-46, A-7E, *John F. Kennedy*, 9/14/90–3/12/91
VA-65, A-6E, *Theodore Roosevelt*, 1/14–4/20/91
VA-72, A-7E, *John F. Kennedy*, 9/14/90–3/12/91
VA-75, A-6E and KA-6D, *John F. Kennedy*, 9/14/90–3/12/91
VA-85, A-6E and KA-6D, *America*, 1/15–4/3/91
VAQ-130, EA-6B, *John F. Kennedy*, 9/14/90–3/12/91
VAQ-131, EA-6B, *Ranger*, 1/13–4/19/91
VAQ-132, EA-6B, *Saratoga*, 10/23–12/9/90;1/6–3/11/91
VAQ-136, EA-6B, *Midway*, 11/2/90–3/14/91
VAQ-137, EA-6B, *America*, 1/15–4/3/91
VAQ-139, EA-6B, *Independence*, 8/5–11/4/90
VAQ-140, EA-6B, *Eisenhower*, 8/8–8/24/90
VAQ-141, EA-6B, *Theodore Roosevelt*, 1/14–4/20/91
VAW-113, E-2C, *Independence*, 8/5–11/4/90
VAW-115, E-2C, *Midway*, 11/2/90–3/14/91
VAW-116, E-2C, *Ranger*, 1/13–4/19/91
VAW-121, E-2C, *Eisenhower*, 8/8–8/24/90
VAW-123, E-2C, *America*, 1/15–4/3/91
VAW-124, E-2C, *Theodore Roosevelt*, 1/14–4/20/91
VAW-125, E-2C, *Saratoga*, 10/23–12/9/90;1/6–3/11/91
VAW-126, E-2C, *John F. Kennedy*, 9/14/90–3/12/91
VF-1, F-14A, *Ranger*, 1/13–4/19/91
VF-102, F-14A, *America*, 1/15–4/3/91
VF-103, FA-14A and others, *Saratoga*, 10/23–12/9/90;1/6–3/11/91
VF-14, F-14A, *John F. Kennedy*, 9/14/90–3/12/91
VF-142, F-14A, *Eisenhower*, 8/8–8/24/90
VF-143, F-14A, *Eisenhower*, 8/8–8/24/90
VF-154, F-14A, *Independence*, 8/5–11/4/90
VF-2, F-14A, *Ranger*, 1/13–4/19/90
VF-21, F-14A, *Independence*, 8/5–11/4/90
VF-32, F-14A, *John F. Kennedy*, 9/14/90–3/12/91
VF-33, F-14A, *America*, 1/15–4/3/91
VF-41, F-14A, *Theodore Roosevelt*, 1/14–4/20/91
VF-74; F-14As and others, *Saratoga*, 1/15–4/3/91
VF-84, F-14A, *Theodore Roosevelt*, 1/14–4/20/91
VFA-113, F/A-18A, *Independence*, 8/5–11/4/90
VFA-15, F/A-18A, *Theodore Roosevelt*, 1/14–4/20/91
VFA-131, F/A-18, *Eisenhower*, 8/8–8/24/90
VFA-136, F/A-18, *Eisenhower*, 8/8–8/24/90
VFA-151; F/A-18A, *Midway*, 11/2/90–3/14/91
VFA-192; F/A-18, *Midway*, 11/2/90–3/14/91
VFA-195; F/A-18, *Midway*, 11/2/90–3/14/91

VFA-25, F/A-18C, *Independence*, 8/5–11/4/90
VFA-81, F/A-18C, *Saratoga*, 10/23–12/9/90;1/6–3/11/91
VFA-82, F/A-18C, *America*, 1/15–4/3/91
VFA-83, F/A-18C, *Saratoga*, 10/23–12/9/90;1/6–3/11/91
VFA-86, F/A-18C, *America*, 1/15–4/3/91
VFA-87, F/A-18A, *Theodore Roosevelt*, 1/14–4/20/91
VP-19   8/28/90–2/2/91
VP-23   10/2–11/10/90
VP-4   11/10/90–3/10/91
VP-40   2/6–3/10/91
VP-46   1/26–3/10/91
VP-8   12/5/90–3/10/91
VP-91   2/9–2/23/91
VPMAU   2/12–2/24/91
VPU-1   1/25–3/10/91
VPU-2   9/12/90–3/10/91
VRC-50 (FUJAIRAH)Provided detachments for duration
VS-22, S-3B, *John F. Kennedy*, 9/14/90–3/12/91
VS-24, S-3A, *Theodore Roosevelt*, 1/14–4/20/91
VS-30, S-3B, *Saratoga*, 10/23–12/9/90; 1/6–3/11/91
VS-31, S-3B, *Eisenhower*, 8/8–8/24/90
VS-32, S-3B, *America*, 1/15–4/3/91
VS-37, S-3A, *Independence*, 8/5–11/4/90
VS-38, S-3A, *Ranger*, 1/13–4/19/91
VRC-30   1/13–4/19/91
VRC-40   1/14–4/20/91
VP-11   11/10–12/9/90
VQ-1   8/8/90–3/10/91
VQ-2   12/6/90–3/10/91

Other Participating U.S. Navy Units
COMNAVSPECWARCOM   8/12–9/29/90
COMNAVSPECWARGRU ONE   8/12/90–TBD
COMSPECBOATRON ONE   8/12/90–4/3/91
SPECBOATU TWELVE   8/12/90–4/3/91
SPECBOATU THIRTEEN   8/12/90–4/3/91
SPECBOATU ELEVEN   8/12/90–4/3/91
SEAL TEAM THREE   8/12/90–4/3/91
SEAL TEAM ONE   8/12/90–3/12/91
SEAL TEAM FIVE   8/12/90–TBD
SDV TEAM ONE   1/15–4/3/91
COMNAVSPECWARU TWO   8/9/90–4/2/91
SEAL TEAM TWO   8/9/90–3/2/91

SEAL TEAM FOUR	8/9/90–3/2/91
SEAL TEAM EIGHT	8/9/90–4/17/91
COMSPECBOATRON TWO	8/9/90–3/2/91
SPECBOATU TWENTY	8/13/90–TBD
NAVSPECWARUNIT TWO	1/20–3/16/91

U.S. Navy Staffs
Note: There were six carrier battle groups, two battleship action groups, and as many as thirteen submarines deployed for the war. Carriers battle groups normally have cruisers, destroyers, and frigates (CGs, DDG/Dds, FFG/FFs) for escorts, as well as an oiler for fuel. A commander of a cruiser-destroyer group (CCDG) is a rear admiral. The CCDG is divided into destroyer squadrons, commanded by captains, designated as commander, destroyer squadron, or CDS. There are also commanders of cruiser groups (CCGs), CPGs, and CPRs. The following are the staffs that participated in the war. If known, the dates that they participated, and their compositions have also been provided:

C7F; 8/28/90–TBD
CCDG-12; 1/14/91–TBD
CCDG-2; 1/15–4/3/91; *Ticonderoga* (CG-47), *Scott* (DDG-995), *Tattnall* (DDG-19), *John Rodgers* (DD-983), *John L. Hall* (FFG-32), *Paul* (FF-1080), *Suribachi* (AE-21). Operated with *Eisenhower*.
CCDG-1; 8/5–11/4/90; *Jouett* (CG-29), *Antietam* (CG-54), *Goldsborough* (DDG-20), *Brewton* (FFG-1086), *Reasoner* (FF-1063), *Cimarron* (AO-177), and *Flint* (AE-21). Operated with *Independence*.
CCDG-3; January through at least April 1991; *Horne* (CG-30), *Kidd* (DD-993), *Jarrett* (FFG-33), *McInerney* (FFG-8), *Sacramento* (AOE-1). Operated with *Missouri* (BB-63).
CCDG-5; 1/24–4/24/91; *Valley Forge* (CG-50), *Princeton* (CG-59) (hit mine, 2/18/91), *Horne* ((CG-30), *Harry W. Hill* (DD-986), *Paul F. Foster* (DD-964), *Jarret* (FFG-33), *Francis Hammond* (FF-1067), *Kansas City* (AOR-3), *Shasta* (AE-33). Operated with *Ranger*.
CCDG-8; 10/23–12/9/90; 1/6–3/11/91; *South Carolina* (CGN-37), *Biddle* (CG-34), *Thomas C. Hart* (FF-1092), and *Detroit* (AOE-4). Operated with *Saratoga*.
CCG-2; 1/15–4/22/91
CCG-5; 11/2/90–3/14/91
CCG-6; 10/23–12/9/90; 1/6–3/11/91
CCG-7; 1/13–4/19/91
CCG-8; 1/14–4/20/91; *Leyte Gulf* (CG-55), *Richmond K. Turner* (CG-20), *Caron* (DD-970), *Hawes* (FFG-53), *Vreeland* (FF-1068), *Platte* (AO-186), *Santa Barbara* (AE-28). Operated with *Roosevelt*.
CDS-14; 1/15–4/391

CDS-15; 11/2/90–3/14/91; (*Mobile Bay* (CG-53), *Bunker Hill* (CG-52), *Fife* (DD-991), *Olendorf* (DD-972), *Hewitt* (DD-966) [augmentee], and *Curts*(FFG-38). Operated with *Midway*.

CDS-17; *Shields* (FF-1066); 10/29/902/15/91

CDS-22; 1/14/91–TBD; *Normandy* (CG-60), *Virginia* (CGN-38), *Preble* (DDG-46), *William V. Pratt* (DDG-44), *Halyburton* 9FFG-40), *Kalamazoo* (AOR-6), *Nitro* (AE-23). Operated with *America*.

CDS-23; 8/5–11/4/90

CDS-24; 10/23–12/9/90; 1/6–3/11/91; *Philippine Sea* (CG-58), *Sampson* (DDG-10), *Spruance* (DD-963), *Elmer Montgomery* (FF1082). Operated with *Saratoga*.

CDS-32; 10/23–12/9/90; 1/6–3/11/91

CDS-35; 2/1–4/20/91

CDS-36; 12/2/90–3/12/91; *Thomas S. Gates* (CG-51), *San Jacinto* (CG-56), *Mississippi* (CGN-40), *Moosebrugger* (DD-980), *Samuel B. Roberts* (FFG-58), and *Seattle* (AOE-3).

COMUSNAVCENT; 8/28/90–TBD

CPG-2; 9/6/90–3/24/91

CPG-3; 1/12/91–TBD

CPR-1; 1/12/91–TBD

CPR-5; 1/12–3/13/91; *Okinawa* (LPH-3), *Ogden* (LPD-5), *Durham* (LKA-114), *Fort McHenry* (LSD-43), *Cayuga* (LST-1186).

CPR-6; 9/8/90–3/24/91

CPR-9; *Tarawa* (LHA-1), *Tripoli* (LPH-10), *New Orleans* (LPH-11), *Vancouver* (LPD-2), *Denver* (LPD-9), *Juneau* (LPD-10), *Anchorage* (LSD-36), *Germantown* (LSD-42), *Mount Vernon* (LSD-39), *Mobile* (LKA-115), *Barbour County* (LST-1195), *Frederick* (LST-1184), *Peoria* (LST-1183).

CPR-12; *Nassau* (LHA-4), *Guam* (LPH-9), *Iwo Jima* (LPH-9), *Shreveport* (LPD-12), *Raleigh* (LPD-1), *Trenton* (LPD-14), *Pensacola* (LSD-38), *Port-land* (LSD-37), *Gunston Hall* (LSD-44), *Saginaw* (LSD-1138), *Spartanburg County* (LSD-1192), *Manitowoc* (LST-1180), *La Moure County* (LST-1194).

B. GREAT BRITAIN

Destroyers

HMS *York* (*Manchester*-class Type 42C); 6/4/90–10/30/90

HMS *Gloucester* (*Manchester*-class Type 42C); 9/15/90–3/14/91

HMS *Cardiff* (*Sheffield*-class Type 42); 10/17/90–2/23/91

HMS *Exeter* (*Sheffield*-class Type 42); 1/27/91–

HMS *Manchester* (*Manchester*-class Type 42C); 1/23/91–

Frigates
HMS *Jupiter* (*Leander*-class); 6/4/90–10/22/90
HMS *Battleaxe* (*Broadsword*-class Type 22 ASW); 6/4/90–10/22/90
HMS *Brazen* (*Broadsword*-class Type 22 ASW); 9/30/90–2/23/91
HMS *London* (*Boxer*-class Type 22 ASW); 9/30/90–3/14/91
HMS *Brave* (*Boxer*-class Type 22 ASW); 1/27/91–
HMS *Brilliant* (*Broadsword*-class Type 22 ASW); 1/27/91–

Hunt-class Minehunters
HMS *Cattistock*; 9/7/90–4/4/91
HMS *Atherstone*; 9/7/90–4/4/91
HMS *Hurworth*; 9/7/90–4/4/91
HMS *Dulverton*; 1/2/91–4/17/91
HMS *Ledbury*; 1/2/91–4/17/91
HMS *Bicester*; 3/7/91–
HMS *Brocklesby*; 3/7/91–
HMS *Brecon*; 3/7/91–

RFA Logistics Landing Ships
Sir Bedivere-class *Sir Tristram*; 10/7/90–4/10/91
Sir Bedivere-class *Sir Bedivere*; 10/10/90–4/11/91
Sir Galahad-class *Sir Galahad*; 10/19/90–
Sir Bedivere-class *Sir Percivale*; 10/19/90–4/9/91
Sir Bedivere-class *Sir Lancelot*

Ocean Survey Ships (employed as mine countermeasures headquarters and support ships)
HMS *Herald* (Improved *Hecla*-class); 9/7/90–3/20/91
HMS *Hecla* (*Hecla*-class); 2/3/91–

Replenishment Ships
RFA *Orangeleaf* (*Appleleaf*-class); 6/4/90–2/22/91
RFA *Olna* (*Olwen*-class); 8/30/90–3/26/91
RFA *Fort Grange* (*Fort*-class), with 2 Sea King 5 and 2 Sea King 4 helicopters; 8/30/90–
RFA *Resource* (*Resource*-class); 11/5/90–3/26/91
Aviation support ship RFA *Argus*, with 4 Sea King 4 helicopters; 11/7/90–3/26/91
Repair ship RFA *Diligence*; 10/90–11/90
RFA *Bayleaf* (*Appleleaf*-class); 1/27/91–

Naval Air Squadrons
815 Lynx on Type 42 destroyers and *Jupiter*
826 2 Sea King 5s on *Fort Grange*, 2 Sea King 5s on *Olna*, and HNethMS *Zuiderkruis*. Conducted minehunting and miscellaneous tasks.
829 Lynx on Type 22 frigates
845 Sea King 4 disembarked to support 1(BR) Division. Total of at least 12 SK4s.
846 4 Sea King 4s on *Argus* and 1 on *Fort Grange* for casualty evacuation and miscellaneous tasks, 2 on *Fort Grange* for mine searching and miscellaneous tasks. 846 NAS flew troops to Kuwait City to clear booby traps and mines before the Ambassador returned. It also transported Prime Minister Major on his visit to the Gulf.
848 Sea King 4 disembarked to support 1(BR) Division.
Sea Kings were equipped with self-defense suites, global positioning systems, and full night vision goggle capability. During hostilities, they were used for nighttime search and rescue, and for mine search, to recover bodies, for the embassy troop lift, and for casualty evacuation. The helicopters detailed ashore were used for Coalition troop movements, moving enemy prisoner of war guard forces, allied and enemy casualties, and logistics.

Lynx MK 3 helicopter operations:
Group W – 4 Lynx were modified for the Gulf.
Group X – 5 Lynx were modified and enhanced for the Gulf.
Group Y – 5 Lynx were modified and enhanced for Gulf.

FRANCE: 13 ships in Operation *Artimon* under WEU. These included aircraft carrier *Clemenceau*, missile-armed destroyers *Dupleix* and *Montcalm*, frigates *Commandant Bory*, *Commandant Ducuing*, *Doudart de Lagree*, and *Protet*, and supply ship *Var*. Missile destroyer *Du Chayla*, destroyers *Jeanne de Vienne* and *La Motte-Picquet*, corvette *Premier Maitre L'Her*, intelligence ship *Berry*, supply ships *Durance* and *Marne*, repair ship *Jules Verne*, tug *Buffle*, and hospital ships *Rance* and *Foudre* were also deployed.

ITALY: Small squadron under WEU. Ships participating included: destroyer *Audace*, frigates *Libeccio*, *Zeffiro*, *Orsa*, *Luppo* (January), and *Saggitario* (January), assault ship *San Marco*, and supply ships *Stromboli* and *Vesuvio*. Two corvettes were sent to eastern Mediterranean.

AUSTRALIA: Initial deployment: *Perry*-class frigates *Adelaide* and *Darwin*, replenishment ship *Success*. *Westralia* replaced *Success* in January 1991. *Adams*-class destroyer *Brisbane* and frigate *Sydney* replaced *Adelaide* and *Darwin*.

ARGENTINA: Destroyer *Almirante Brown* and frigate *Spiro*.

BELGIUM: 1 frigate (*Wielingen*, replaced by *Wandelaar*), 4 minehunters (including *Iris* and *Myosotis*) and auxiliary *Zinnia* under WEU command.

CANADA: Destroyers *Athabaskan* and *Terra Nova*, and oiler *Protecteur*.

DENMARK: Corvette *Olfert Fischer* in Gulf.

GERMANY: 19 ships deployed to Mediterranean to protect the entrance to the Suez Canal. Ships included minehunters *Malburg*, *Koblenz*, and *Wetzlar*, minesweepers *Laboe* and *Ueberherrn*, command ship *Werra*, and ammunition ship *Westerwald*. Five mine warfare ships sent for postwar mineclearing operations.

GREECE: Frigate *Limnos*, which was relieved by *Elli*. Three ships for military sealift.

KUWAIT: Craft *Istiqlal* and *Al Sanbouk*, and auxiliary *Sawahil*.

NETHERLANDS: 2 frigates (*Witte de With* and *Pieter Florisz*) and support ship *Zuiderkruis* under WEU. Frigates were replaced by *Philips van Almonde* and *Jacob van Heemskerck* in November 1990. Two minehunters sent to eastern Mediterranean. Three mine warfare ships sent to clear mines after the war.

NORWAY: Cutter *Andenes* in Persian Gulf to support Danish corvette *Olfert Fischer*.

POLAND: Hospital ship *Wodnik* and auxiliary *Piast*.

PORTUGAL: Logistic transport ship *Sao Miguel* under WEU.

SPAIN: Frigates *Santa Maria*, *Descubierta*, and *Cazadora* in Gulf under WEU. These were relieved by frigates *Numancia*, *Infanta Elena*, and *Cazadora*. One frigate sent to eastern Mediterranean.

II. IRAQI NAVAL ORDER OF BATTLE:[3]

1 Training frigate *Ibn Marjid* (formerly *Ibn Khaldum*)
5 Osa II missile attack boats (Soviet)
2 Osa I missile attack boats (Soviet)

3 SO-1 submarine chasers (Soviet)
6 P6 fast attack torpedo boats
5 Zhuk patrol boats (Soviet)
2 Poluchat I patrol boats (Soviet)
8 PO2 coastal patrol craft
2 Bogomol coastal patrol craft
9 PB 90 coastal patrol craft
6 Rotork Type 412 coastal patrol craft
6 Winchester hovercraft
2 T-43 minesweeper (Soviet)
3 Yevgenya minesweepers (Soviet)
4 Nestin minesweepers (Yugoslav)
3 Polnocny-C landing ships (Soviet)
3 Modified roll-on/roll-off cargo ships
1 Spasilac salvage ship *Aka* (Soviet)
1 Transport
1 Yacht *Qadissayah Saddam*
14 tugs and tenders

Ships Damaged or Destroyed

I. COALITION: none destroyed; USS *Tripoli* (LPH-10) and *Princeton* (CG-59) damaged by mines on February 18, 1991.

I. IRAQ:[4]

Jan. 22	1 T-43 minesweeper was disabled by A-6Es.
	1 patrol boat was disabled.
Jan. 23	1 *Al Qaddissayah*-class tanker was disabled by A-6Es.
	1 *Winchester*-class hovercraft was sunk by A-6Es.
	1 Zhuk patrol boat was sunk by A-6Es.
Jan. 24	1 Zhuk patrol boat was sunk by A-6Es.
	1 Spasilac salvage ship was sunk by A-6Es.
	1 minelayer was sunk by a Harpoon from a Saudi ship.
	1 minesweeper was sunk by a mine while evading an A-6E.
	4 ships were struck at Umm Qasr naval base.
Jan. 25	1 minelayer was hit while laying mines near sea oil terminal.
Jan. 26	1 patrol boat was hit in Kuwait harbor.
	1 TNC-45 craft was struck and left burning by A-6Es.
Jan. 27	1 ship was sunk by A-6Es.
Jan. 29	17 small boats were attacked; 4 sunk, 12 damaged.

	1 large patrol boat was sunk by Sea Skua from HMS *Cardiff*.
Jan. 30	8 attack boats were struck, 4 were sunk, 3 were damaged, including Osa missile boats. Landing craft were also possibly hit and damaged.
	1 T-43 hit by Sea Skua from HMS *Gloucester*, left burning.
	1 TNC-45 were hit by Sea Skua from HMS *Gloucester* and left burning.
	3 LSMs were sunk by Jaguars and A-6Es.
Feb. 1	1 patrol boat was left burning at Min-al-Bakr oil terminal by A-6E.
Feb. 2	1 missile boat was hit by 2 laser-guided bombs and a second was possibly hit, at Al Kalia naval facility. 3 patrol boats were struck; 1 destroyed, 2 damaged.
	1 patrol boat was destroyed by A-6Es in Kuwait harbor.
Feb. 8	1 training ship and a TNC-45 patrol boat were struck by A-6Es at Cor-al-Zubayr.
Feb. 9	1 Zhuk was damaged by a Rockeye from an A-6E near Faylakah Island.
Feb. 10	2 patrol boats were sunk by A-6Es in the northern Gulf.
Feb. 14	1 Osa missile boat was sunk in Kuwait Bay by A-6Es.
Feb. 20	1 gunboat bombed by S-3 aircraft.

[1] Ships deployed to the eastern Mediterranean Sea were under NATO auspices, and were not subordinated to CENTCOM.

[2] Office of the Chief of Naval Operations, *The United States Navy in "Desert Shield" "Desert Storm"* (Washington, DC: Department of the Navy, 1991.)

[3] Computed from A.D. Baker III, *Combat Fleets of the World 1990/1991*, edited by Bernard Prezelin, (Annapolis, MD: Naval Institute Press, 1990); and other sources.

[4] Iraq seized from Kuwait 5 Lurssen TNC45 and 1 Lurssen FPB57 fast attack craft, 5 Seagull, 15 Thorneycraft, 1 Halter Marine, and 7 Magnum Sedan patrol craft, 4 Loadmaster and 6 Vosper Singapore-type landing craft, 10 tugs and launches, and 3 Azmut customs launches. Some of these were reported destroyed by the Coalition, which explains why its claims of vessels damaged and destroyed exceeds the Iraqi naval inventory.

ABOUT THE CONTRIBUTORS

Authors and Senior Analysts

ROD ALONSO works for the Defense Intelligence Agency. A retired U.S. Air Force officer with 28 years of service who served three tours of combat duty in Vietnam, he has thirty years experience in intelligence, including tours in air intelligence, operational intelligence, and indications and warning. An expert on Soviet naval aviation and Third World air forces and a graduate of the Air, Command and Staff and Air War Colleges, he is currently completing his Master of Science degree in Strategic Intelligence at the Defense Intelligence College. During his career, Mr. Alonso has written hundreds of reports, studies, and examinations that established U.S. intelligence positions on the broadest range of intelligence issues.

B.L. CYR, JR. is a senior analyst at the U.S. Army's Intelligence Threat and Analysis Center in Washington, D.C. A Russian linguist and Soviet specialist, Mr. Cyr's experience includes seven years of active duty service in the U.S. Navy, and thirteen years in Naval Intelligence, where he was the U.S. Navy's top expert on the world's merchant fleets. Mr. Cyr's experience also includes several years experience at European Command in West Germany and frequent travel to the Soviet Union. The author of literally hundreds of political, sociological, and national defense studies, Mr. Cyr is currently preparing two works on national defense issues. His future plans include several more years of intelligence service and then a career in academia.

BRUCE GEORGE, MP (Labour) is senior opposition Member of the House of Commons Defence Select Committee, General Rapporteur of the Political Committee of the North Atlantic Assembly, and Editor of *Jane's NATO Handbook, 1991–1992*.

GERALD HOPPLE (1949–1991) was Associate Professor of Information Systems and Systems Engineering at George Mason University. Beginning in the mid-1970s, he has conducted significant research in indications and warning, forecasting, defense problem solving, command and control, and information systems engineering and was considered one of America's leading indications and warning systems experts. A senior consultant to the National Research Council of the National Academy of Sciences, he wrote 17 books and over 100 published articles on the above subjects, and served as the co-editor of the Series on Decision Support Systems.

DAVID C. ISBY is a Washington-based attorney and analyst on national security issues. He currently works as a senior staff member for BDM International, a consulting firm in McLean, Virginia. An expert on Southwest Asian affairs and the author of nine books and over 200 articles, he frequently appeared as an expert commentator on television and radio and in print in both Great Britain and the United States during the Gulf War. Mr. Isby has worked in the U.S. Congress as a legislative assistant, and has served as an editor of *Strategy and Tactics* magazine. He often appears on the *CBS Evening News* and the *MacNeil-Lehrer News Hour*.

TIMOTHY LISTER is a graduate of the universities of Pennsylvania and Oxford and works as a journalist for the BBC World Service.

RAIMONDO LURAGHI fought in World War II and then in the liberation war against Nazi Germany. He is Director of Graduate Studies in History of the Americas at the University of Genoa, where he also directs the Center for Defence Studies. He holds a full professorship at the Free University of Rome. President of the Italian Society for Military History, he represents Italy in the International Bureau for Comparative Military Historical Studies. The author of several books and articles on historical and strategic problems, his most recent effort is an analysis of the Mediterranean basin in *NATO After Forty Years*, published by the Center for NATO Studies of Kent State University.

JOEL H. NADEL is a military capabilities analyst specializing in logistics with the Department of the Army's Intelligence and Threat

Analysis Center in Washington D.C., a student of historical and current military art, and an officer in the Virginia Army National Guard. He received his undergraduate degrees from Wentworth Military Academy and Monmouth College, in Monmouth, Illinois. He was commissioned in the U.S. Army in 1978 and subsequently served in combined arms assignments in the United States, South Korea, and Germany prior to his release from active duty. He resides in Virginia with his wife, Myong Hi and son, Daniel.

JAMES PIRIOU is a Parliamentary Research Assistant in the House of Commons.

JOE SANDERSON is a Parliamentary Research Assistant in the House of Commons.

PETER TSOURAS is an analyst at the U.S. Army's Intelligence and Threat Analysis Center, Washington, DC. The author of several articles on naval and army matters, he has written extensively on national security matters, and coedited *Operation Just Cause: The U.S. Intervention in Grenada*. He is currently writing a comprehensive study of ground-based military power since World War II, and coedited *U.S. Army: A Dictionary* with Bruce Watson. He is also writing a study of German military strategy in World War II.

BRUCE W. WATSON served as a naval intelligence officer for twenty-two years. He is currently associated with the Defense Intelligence College, and serves as an adjunct professor at George Mason University, the University of Virginia, and the University of Maryland. He is a free-lance writer and consultant on defense matters. He has served as vice chairman and as chairman, Comparative Foreign Policy Section, International Studies Association, and is a professor emeritus at the Defense Intelligence College. The author of *Red Navy at Sea* and *The Changing Face of the World's Navies: 1945 to the Present* (Arms and Armour Press, 1991), he has coedited three books on the Soviet Navy, has written several articles on the subject, has written or co-edited seven other books on defense and national security matters, and is the editor-in-chief of the Garland Press encyclopedia series on military affairs.

BRUCE W. WATSON, JR. is associated with Virginia Polytechnic Institute and State University and will intern at the House of Commons during the Autumn of 1991. While his initial articles appear in this book, he has five years of experience in research, writing, and editing on national defense and intelligence subjects. He assisted significantly in the research for *Operation Just Cause* (Westview Press, 1990), *The Changing Face of the World's Navies: 1945 to the Present* (Arms and Armour Press, 1991), the entry on military intelligence for the 1990 edition of *Encyclopaedia Britannica*, and *The Soviet Naval Threat to Europe* (Westview Press, 1989). He also assisted significantly in the editing of the Garland Press encyclopedia series on military affairs, producing *U.S. Intelligence: An Encyclopedia* (1990), *U.S. Army: A Dictionary* (1990), *U.S. Navy: A Dictionary* (1991), and *U.S. Air Force: A Dictionary* (1991).

ELMO C. WRIGHT, JR. specializes in conflict scenarios as a military affairs analyst with the U.S. Army. Prior to 1987, he served as an intelligence officer with the U.S. Army in the United States and in West Germany. He has earned a Masters degree in Russian Studies from Georgetown University and has travelled extensively throughout the Soviet Union. During the Gulf War, Mr. Wright routinely briefed senior leaders within the U.S. Department of Defense on his analyses of Iraqi military capabilities and likely courses of action. He and his wife have three children and live in northern Virginia.

INDEX

"Your Arab allies will desert you. They will not kill other Arabs. Your alliance will crumble and you will be left lost in the desert. You don't know the desert because you have never ridden on a horse or a camel." – Iraqi Foreign Minister Tariq Aziz to U.S. Secretary of State James Baker, January 9, 1991, Geneva, Switzerland.